American
ENGLISH FILE

Christina Latham-Koenig
Clive Oxenden

OXFORD
UNIVERSITY PRESS

Paul Seligson and Clive Oxenden are the original co-authors of
English File 1 and *English File 2*

Contents

G discourse markers (1): connectors
V work
P word stress and rhythm

" I owe my success to having listened respectfully to the very best advice, and then going away and doing the exact opposite.

G.K. Chesterton, English poet and novelist "

1A What motivates you?

1 READING & SPEAKING

a Think of a person you consider to be successful. What makes you think they are successful? What, in your view, are the reasons for their success?

b Read the article and match the headings with the paragraphs. There is one heading you don't need.

A **A fierce spirit**

B **Being my own person**

C **Learning from my mistakes**

D **Needing to show them they were wrong**

E **The courage to go out and seek my fortune**

c Read the article again and write the initials (e.g., AP) of the person next to the questions below.
Who…?

1 ☐ found it hard to manage on their own
2 ☐ was motivated by the same desire until they became successful
3 ☐ thinks that a conflict helped them become stronger
4 ☐ was made fun of by a member of their family
5 ☐ is grateful for something their parents did wrong
6 ☐ asked a parent for advice
7 ☐ learned an important lesson from a parent
8 ☐ was treated in the same way at school and at work

I didn't get where I am today without...
Successful people talk about their inspiration and motivation

1 ☐ **Ann Patchett,** US novelist

2 ☐ **John Malkovich,** US actor, producer, and director

3 ☐ **Marcus Wareing,** UK chef

Revenge is a terrific motivating force for young creative people and it certainly kept me going right through to the publication of my first novel. I learned to read late, and as a result the nuns at my school in Tennessee had me marked down as being somewhere between slow and stupid. They taught me for 12 years and even after I'd caught up and gotten smarter, I was still thought of as dumb. "They'll be sorry when they discover I'm a great writer," I'd say to myself. "In retirement, the single thing they'll be most proud of will be that they had me as a student." And so it continued right through into the workplace where, in my first teaching job after leaving graduate school, the male head of the department would come to me whenever the secretarial staff were off. "Type this up for me, will you, Ann?" he'd say habitually. "One day," I would think, gritting my teeth, "One day…"

There must have been something unique or, at least, different about me as a boy, because I recall it would sometimes amuse my brother and his friends to throw cans at me. Why? Because of the clothes I wore, which they didn't like, or because I wouldn't do whatever it was that they wanted me to, or just because it was fun. But being different is fine. It was my father who encouraged in me the notion that I and I alone am responsible for my own life, for what I do and don't do, for my opinions and beliefs, and it's proved to be a great source of strength. I'm often asked if I read and take notice of critics. Which ones? Those who love the work? Who hate it? Or are indifferent? As a director, as in life, you have to know your own mind and be prepared to stick to your guns.

One of my instructors at Southport Catering College knew Anton Edelmann, the chef at the Savoy, and recommended me to him. I was very nervous about leaving my comfort zone and coming to London. I was a loner who'd never made friends because I was always working, and I was happy enough being alone and busy.

But I did come to London, and even though it was a very tough environment, I worked like a real trouper and was very quick to learn. The hardest part was being away from my family and having to deal with other people while having no management or interpersonal skills whatsoever. So I called my dad every day, to fill him in on the good and bad, and ask him how he would deal with this or that.

Glossary
dumb /dʌm/ *adj.* **OPP smart** NAmE stupid
graduate school *noun* NAmE US college for post-graduate studies

Glossary
Southport a town in northwest England
the Savoy one of London's most prestigious hotels

d Talk in small groups.

1 From reading the text, what impression do you get of the four people's personalities?

2 Which of them do you most identify with? Why?

3 What or who motivates you…?
- in your work or studies
- to improve your English
- to improve other skills, e.g., sports, music, other activities (give examples)

gritting my teeth.

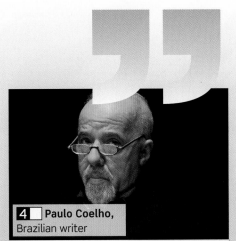

4 ☐ **Paulo Coelho,** Brazilian writer

The family is a microcosm of society. ↗ *small example*
It's where your spirit and beliefs are first tested. My mother and father wanted only the best for me and my sister, but had very rigid ideas of what that "best" should be. For me to become a lawyer or even an engineer would have satisfied them, but a writer? Never. I was a determined and rebellious kid, though, and having failed to change my mind by conventional methods, they looked for more dramatic and extreme ones. In a sense, though, I thank them for that. I wouldn't have gotten where I am without fighting to live the life I wanted for myself. I long since forgave them. We all make mistakes, parents included.

LEXIS IN CONTEXT

e Look at the highlighted phrases and guess the meaning of the ones you don't know from the context. Then match them with the definitions 1–7.

1 _Know your own mind_ to know what you want or like

2 _Stick to your guns_ **IDM** *(informal)* to refuse to change your mind about sth even when other people are trying to persuade you that you are wrong

3 _In a sense_ in one way

4 _my comfort zone_ *(colloquial)* the working or living environment in which we feel safe and unthreatened

5 ~~caught up~~ **IDM** to be determined to continue to do sth in a difficult or unpleasant situation

6 _fill sb in (on)_ **PHR V** to tell sb about what has happened

7 _I caught up_ **PHR V** (with sb) to reach the same level or standard as sb who is better or more advanced

f Choose five more words or phrases from the text that you think are useful.

g Read the information about looking up idioms in a dictionary.

> 🔍 **Looking up idioms in a dictionary**
> You can usually find the definition of an idiom under one of its "full" words (nouns, verbs, adverbs or adjectives, but NOT prepositions and articles), in a section marked, for example, **IDM**. So the definition of *stick to your guns* will probably be given under *stick* or *guns*.
> ⚠ After some very common verbs, e.g., be, get and adjectives, e.g., good, bad, the idioms are usually under the entries for the next "full" word.
> Phrasal verbs **PHR V** are always after the main verb, e.g., get back and get over would be under get.

h Now look at the following idioms with *mind*. What do you think they mean? Check with a dictionary.

speak your mind	mind your own business
cross your mind	be of two minds about sth

2 GRAMMAR discourse markers (1): connectors

a Without looking back at the text, with a partner try to remember how these sentences continue. Don't worry if you can't remember the exact words.

1 **Ann Patchett:** "I learned to read late, and **as a result**…"

2 **John Malkovich:** "It would sometimes amuse my brother and his friends to throw cans at me. Why? **Because of**…"

3 **Marcus Wareing:** "But I did come to London, and **even though**…, I worked like a real trouper and was very quick to learn."

4 **Marcus Wareing:** "So I called my dad every day, **to**…"

b Compare your answers with the text.

c Which of the **bold** connectors in **a** introduces…?

1 a result _as a result_   3 a purpose _____
2 a reason _____   4 a contrast _____

d ▶ p.138 Grammar Bank 1A. Learn more about connectors, and practice them.

e 🔊 2)) Listen to the sentences. When the speakers pause, write down how you think the sentences might continue.

f 🔊 3)) Now listen to the whole sentences. Are they similar to what you wrote?

3 🔊 4)) SONG *The Anthem* 🎵

4 SPEAKING & LISTENING

a A survey by Chiumento, a human resources consulting firm, established the ten factors that make people happy at work. With a partner, try to agree which are the two <u>most</u> important and the two <u>least</u> important factors.

What makes people happy at work?

- [ ] Being part of a successful team.
- [ ] Doing something rewarding.
- [ ] Doing varied work.
- [ ] Earning a competitive salary.
- [ ] Doing enjoyable work.
- [ ] Feeling that you are making a difference.
- [ ] Having a good boss or manager.
- [ ] Having a good work-life balance.
- [ ] Having friendly, supportive co-workers
- [ ] Having your achievements recognized.

Source: *Chiumento's Happiness at Work Index*

---

b The survey also established some other factors related to being happy at work. With your partner, discuss whether you think the following are probably true or false according to the research, and say why.

1 Statistically there are more happy people at work than unhappy people.
2 Employees of bigger companies or organizations are happier than those who work for smaller companies.
3 Men are generally happier than women with their work.
4 Full-time workers are happier than part-time workers.
5 People with higher positions in a company are happier than the people below them.
6 The longer you stay in one job, the happier you become.
7 Workers over 55 are the happiest.

c (**1 5**))) Now listen to a radio program about the survey and check your answers to **a** and **b**. Were you right?

d Look at the photos and read the short article about *innocent drinks*. Does it look like a company you would like to work for? Why (not)?

Working where the grass is always greener

In a *Sunday Times* survey, *innocent drinks* was found to be one of the companies with the happiest employees. This London-based company was set up by three college students in 1999 and started off making smoothies, a drink made with fruit juice and yogurt. It now employs over 200 people, and has added vegetable pots to its products. The company calls itself "innocent" because it only uses pure fresh ingredients. Part of its marketing strategy is to use delivery vans which are decorated to look like cows or grassy fields. The company also prides itself on being "a happy place to work" and "people-orientated," with a relaxed working environment, which includes having a grass floor in the office!

Why I like working at innocent

great people (+ free smoothies)

I DONT HAVE TO SHAVE EVERY DAY !

THE GRASS

innocent
pure fruit smoo
blackberries, ras
& boysenbe

e (1 6))) Now listen to the second part of the program where Becka Walton, who works for *innocent drinks*, is interviewed. Answer the questions.

1 In general, does she agree that there is a happy and relaxed working atmosphere at *innocent drinks*?
2 Does she mention any downsides?

f Listen again, pausing after each of Becka's answers. Answer questions 1–6 with a partner.

1 What made Becka apply for a job at the company?
2 What example does she give of how the company creates a team environment?
3 What examples does she give of the relaxed atmosphere?
4 What does she say about staff turnover?
5 Does she agree that a competitive salary is *not* an important factor in determining job satisfaction?
6 What does Becka say about the company's product?

g Now listen again with the audioscript on page 123. Is there anything you found difficult to understand? Why?

> 🔍 **Listening to English in the media**
>
> Try to listen to as much English as you can outside class in a format you can listen to repeatedly, e.g., a website, a podcast, a video clip, or a DVD. A good way of getting the most out of it is:
> - first listen and try to get used to the speaker(s) and get a general idea of what they are talking about.
> - then listen again, pausing and checking that you understand the main points.
> - listen again with an audioscript or English subtitles, if they are available, to help you figure out what you didn't understand (maybe because of the speaker's accent or speed, or use of vocabulary).

h Do Becka's answers confirm that you would / wouldn't like to work for *innocent drinks*? Why (not)?

5 VOCABULARY work

a Match the two halves of the expressions used in the interview.

1 short-term ☐ A balance
2 work-life ☐ B salary
3 work ☐ C turnover
4 staff ☐ D contracts
5 competitive ☐ E environment

b (1 7))) Listen and check. With a partner, say what you think the expressions mean.

c ▶ p.158 Vocabulary Bank *Work*.

d With a partner, explain the difference between…

a *demanding* job and a *challenging* job
wages and *salary*
a *profession* and a *career*

skills and qualifications
being *fired* and being *laid off*
getting *a raise* and getting *promoted*
good job prospects and *good opportunities for advancement*
being *out of work* and being *off work*

6 PRONUNCIATION word stress and rhythm

a Underline the stressed syllable in the **bold** words.

1 I managed to get a **challenging** and **motivating** job.
2 I don't have any **qualifications** or **experience**.
3 There's no **job security** and I could be **laid off**.
4 I've had a very **rewarding career** in publishing.
5 The job has a **competitive salary** and excellent **benefits**.
6 It's a **stimulating work environment** with good **opportunities for advancement**.
7 The **employees** don't enjoy the work, since it's very **monotonous**.
8 After she **retired**, she did **volunteer** work at her local hospital.

b (1 8))) Listen and check.

c Listen again and focus on the rhythm of the sentences. Which words are <u>not</u> stressed in the sentences? Practice saying the sentences with good stress and rhythm.

7 SPEAKING

a Think about two jobs you could talk about. Use the questions below to help you. Add any other information that you think is relevant. Use the words and phrases in **Vocabulary Bank** *Work p.158* to help you.

> **A job you would love to do**
> What do you think the advantages of the job would be?
> What makes you think you might be good at it?
> Do you know anyone who does it?
> Can you think of any drawbacks?

> **A job you would hate to do**
> What do you think the downsides of the job would be?
> Do you know anyone who does it?
> Have you ever done anything similar?
> Can you think of any positive aspects of the job?

b (1 9))) Listen to two people doing the task. What pros and cons do they mention? What two "noises" do they use to give themselves time to think?

c Work in groups of three. Take turns describing the jobs you would love to do.

d Now do the same for the jobs you would hate to do.

e Decide which of the jobs described you think is the most attractive.

8 WRITING

▶ p. 104 Writing *A job application*. Analyze an email in response to a job advertisement and write a cover letter.

G have
V personality; family
P rhythm and intonation

1B Who am I?

> I've learned that you can tell a lot about a person by the way he / she handles these three things: a rainy day, lost luggage, and tangled Christmas tree lights.
>
> *Maya Angelou,*
> *American author*

1 READING & SPEAKING

a Look at the adjectives that describe personality below. With a partner, say if you consider them to be positive or negative qualities, and why. Would you use any of them to describe yourself?

cautious conscientious curious easygoing independent logical
loyal mature quiet rebellious self-sufficient sensitive

b With a partner, read the questionnaire on page 9 and each circle the answer that best describes you. Try to guess the meaning of any unfamiliar words or expressions.

c ➤ **Communication** *Who am I? p.118*. Find out what personality type you and your partner have and read the descriptions. How accurate do you think the description of your personality is?

LEXIS IN CONTEXT

🔍 **Collocation**

Collocation is the way words combine to provide natural-sounding speech and writing, e.g., we say *a rough itinerary*, not *an approximate itinerary*. Noticing and recording words that go together will improve the accuracy and fluency of your speaking and writing.

d Complete the questions with a verb from the list in the right form. All these collocations appear in *What's your personality type?*

catch face get go with hurt keep make plan tell

1 Do you usually _____ your vacation a long time **in advance**, or at the last minute?
2 What do you do if you're reading a text in English and you _____ **stuck on** a particular word?
3 Do you always _____ **sure** that you have your cell phone with you when you leave the house?
4 When you're shopping for clothes, do you usually buy the first thing that _____ **your eye**, or do you look at a lot of things before you make a decision?
5 When you have to make a decision, do you usually _____ **your gut feeling**, or do you ask other people for advice?
6 Do you tend to _____ problems **head on**, or do you try to avoid conflict?
7 In what situations do you think it's better to _____ **a white lie** in order not to _____ people's **feelings**?
8 When you reply to a friend's email, do you usually write a lot or _____ it **short**?

e Ask and answer the questions with a partner.

f Choose five more words or phrases from the questionnaire that you think are useful for you.

2 GRAMMAR *have*

a Match sentences 1–8 with A–H.

1 He's not very sociable. ☐
2 My dad's so absentminded! ☐
3 My brother-in-law's not very ambitious. ☐
4 He's kind of a hypochondriac. ☐
5 My nephew is a little egocentric. ☐
6 He's incredibly intolerant. ☐
7 Chris is so rebellious! ☐
8 I think our boss is kind of stingy. ☐

A I think it's because he **doesn't have** any brothers or sisters.
B He often **has** lunch with us, but he never pays.
C **He's got to** make an effort to be more open-minded.
D He **has** a real tendency to argue with people in authority.
E He **has been working** at the same job for 15 years.
F He **hasn't been** to a party in years.
G He **has to** write everything down otherwise he forgets things.
H He **has** his blood pressure **checked** every week.

b With a partner, look at sentences A–H and answer the questions.

1 In which sentences is *have*
   a) a main verb b) an auxiliary verb?
2 What implications does this have for making questions and negatives?

c ➤ **p.139 Grammar Bank 1B.** Learn more about *have*, and practice it.

d With a partner, for each of the sentences below say if it's true for you or not and why.

- I can't stand having my picture taken, and I'd hate to have my portrait painted.
- I have lots of friends online (some of whom I've never met), but I only have a few close friends that I see regularly face-to-face.
- I've never bought a CD from a store. I download all my music from the Internet.
- I'm very competitive. Whenever I play a sport or game I always have to win.
- I've got to find a way to exercise more. I'm really out of shape.
- I have a few possessions that are really important to me and that I would hate to lose.
- I've been learning English for so long that it's getting difficult to motivate myself.

WHAT'S YOUR PERSONALITY TYPE?

PLANNER OR SPONTANEOUS

1 Are you...?
   a a perfectionist who hates leaving things unfinished
   b someone who hates being under pressure and tends to over-prepare
   c a little disorganized and forgetful
   d someone who puts things off until the last minute

2 Imagine you have bought a piece of furniture that requires assembly (e.g., a wardrobe or a cabinet). Which of these are you more likely to do?
   a Check that you have all the items and the tools you need before you start.
   b Carefully read the instructions and follow them to the letter.
   c Quickly read through the instructions to get the basic idea of what you have to do.
   d Start assembling it right away. Check the instructions only if you get stuck.

3 Before you go on vacation, which of these do you do?
   a Plan every detail of your vacation.
   b Put together a rough itinerary, but make sure you leave yourself plenty of free time.
   c Get an idea of what kinds of things you can do, but not make a decision until you get there.
   d Book the vacation at the last minute and plan hardly anything in advance.

HEADS OR HEARTS

7 If an argument starts when you are with friends, do you...?
   a face it head on and say what you think
   b try to find a solution yourself
   c try to keep everyone happy
   d do anything to avoid hurting people's feelings

8 Imagine you had the choice between two apartments to rent. Would you...?
   a write down what your ideal apartment would be like and then see which one was the most similar
   b make a list of the pros and cons of each one
   c just go with your gut feeling
   d consider carefully how each apartment would affect other members of your family

9 Imagine a friend of yours started going out with someone new, and they asked you for your opinion. If you really didn't like the person, would you...?
   a tell them exactly what you thought
   b be honest, but as tactful as possible
   c try to avoid answering the question directly
   d tell a "white lie"

FACTS OR IDEAS

4 ▶ **Communication** *What can you see? p.118*
   Which option best describes what you wrote down?
   a It's basically a list of what appears in the picture.
   b It tells the story of what's happening in the picture.
   c It tries to explain what the picture means.
   d It's a lot of ideas that the picture made you think of.

5 You need to give a friend directions to your house. Do you...?
   a write down a list of detailed directions
   b send a link to a website that provides directions
   c give rough directions
   d draw a simple map showing only the basic directions

6 When you go shopping at the supermarket, do you...?
   a always go down the same aisles in the same order
   b carefully check prices and compare products
   c buy whatever catches your eye
   d go around a different way each time, according to what you want to buy

EXTROVERT OR INTROVERT

10 You are out with a group of friends. Do you...?
   a say hardly anything
   b say a little less than most people
   c talk a lot
   d do nearly all the talking

11 When you meet a new group of people, do you...?
   a try to stay with people you already know
   b have to think hard about how to keep the conversation going
   c try to get to know as many people as possible
   d just try to enjoy yourself

12 If the phone rings while you are in the middle of something, do you...?
   a ignore it and continue with what you're doing
   b answer it quickly, but say you'll call back
   c have a conversation, but make sure you keep it short
   d welcome the interruption and enjoy a nice long chat

a Look at the painting *The Family of Carlos IV* by Goya and answer the questions with a partner, giving your reasons.

1 In the painting you can see the king, the queen, and their six children (three sons and three daughters). Who do you think is the eldest son and heir to the throne?

2 Now try to identify the king's sister and brother. Which ones do you think they are?

3 Who do you think the woman (5) is and why might she be looking away?

4 The queen's brother is also in the picture. Who do you think he is?

5 Who do you think is probably the most important person in the family?

6 Who do you think the man (2) in the background on the left might be?

b (1 10)) Listen to an audio guide telling you about the painting and check your answers to **a**.

c Listen again. Which of the king's children…?

A Fernando	**B** Maria Isabel	**C** Francisco	
D Carlota	**E** Maria Luisa		

1 had an arranged marriage ☐

2 eventually became a king / queen ☐ ☐

3 had a similar personality to their mother ☐

4 did not look like their father ☐

5 married someone related to the Queen ☐

d Imagine that you are going to have a portrait of your family painted. Decide who you want in it and where they are going to stand, and make a rough diagram.

e Show the diagram to your partner and explain who the people are and say something about each of them, including their personality.

4 VOCABULARY family

a Look at the family portrait again. What is the relationship between…?

10 and 7   *brother-in-law and sister-in-law*

6 and 12   _____

8 and 4   _____

13 and 9   _____

b ➤ p.159 Vocabulary Bank *Family.*

c Test your memory. Take the quiz with a partner.

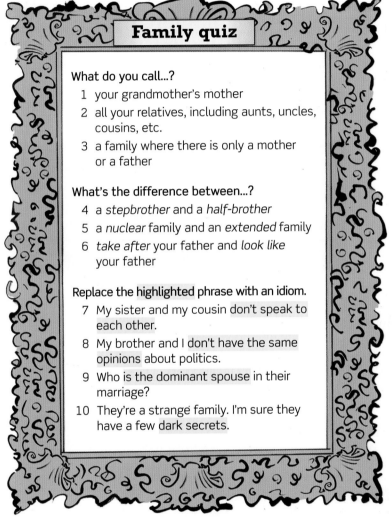

Family quiz

What do you call…?
1 your grandmother's mother
2 all your relatives, including aunts, uncles, cousins, etc.
3 a family where there is only a mother or a father

What's the difference between…?
4 a *stepbrother* and a *half-brother*
5 a *nuclear* family and an *extended* family
6 *take after* your father and *look like* your father

Replace the highlighted phrase with an idiom.
7 My sister and my cousin don't speak to each other.
8 My brother and I don't have the same opinions about politics.
9 Who is the dominant spouse in their marriage?
10 They're a strange family. I'm sure they have a few dark secrets.

d Answer the questions below with a partner. Try to use the **bold** words.

• Who do you **take after** in your family? In what way?
• Who are you **closest to** in your family?
• Is there anyone in your family you **don't get along with**?
• Are there any subjects on which you don't **see eye to eye** with other members of your family?
• Are there any people in your family who aren't **on speaking terms**?
• Are there any physical characteristics that **run in your family**?
• How often do you have **family get-togethers**? Do you enjoy them?
• Is there **a black sheep** in your family?

5 PRONUNCIATION & SPEAKING
rhythm and intonation

a Work in groups of three or four. You are going to debate some of the topics below. Each student must choose a different topic and make brief notes about what he or she thinks.

Children are left far too much on their own nowadays. It would be better if one parent didn't work and stayed at home to take care of the children after school.

Working parents should not use their own parents to look after their children. Grandparents should be allowed to relax and enjoy their retirement.

Your parents brought you up, so it's your responsibility to take care of them when they're old.

In the 21st century, friends are the new family.

It's better to be an only child than to have brothers and sisters. You get all your parents' love and attention.

The family is a trap from which it can be difficult to escape.

b (1 11)) Listen to the phrases and underline the stressed syllables. Then listen again and repeat them, copying the rhythm and intonation.

agreeing
1 I definitely agree.
2 I totally agree.
3 That's what I think, too.
4 Absolutely!

half-agreeing
5 I see your point, but…
6 I see what you mean, but…
7 I agree up to a point, but…

disagreeing
8 I completely disagree.
9 I don't agree at all.

c Have a short debate on the topics you have each chosen. The person who made the notes should give their opinion first, and then the rest of the group says what they think. Try to use language from the box in **b** to agree or disagree with the other people in your group.

1 VIDEO THE INTERVIEW Part 1

a Read the biographical information about David Torchiano. Why do you think he was interested in finding out about his family background?

> **David Torchiano** is an amateur genealogist who has spent many years researching his family tree. He was born and raised in New York City. His mother's side of the family is from Croatia and his father's side of the family is from Southern Italy. He currently works for The New York Times and has his own analytics start-up company as well as a sushi supper club.

b (1 12)》 Watch or listen to Part 1 of an interview with him. Mark sentences 1-5 below **T** (true) or **F** (false).

1 One of the reasons David started researching his family history was because he never met his grandparents on his mother's side.

2 David begins his research by talking to distant family members.

3 David believes that the Internet doesn't help the way he uses other resources.

4 David has used online message boards to overcome obstacles he has encountered.

5 David's main resource for obtaining official documents is local offices.

c Now listen again and say why the **F** sentences are false.

VIDEO Part 2

a (1 13)》 Watch or listen to part 2. What does he say about…?

1 his first time at Ellis Island
2 finding the documentation for his father's side
3 his great uncle and how he helped the rest of the family immigrate to the US
4 unexpected information he found out
5 how his parents met in New York
6 his advice for people who want to research their family trees

b Answer the questions with a partner.

1 From David's interview, what impression do you get about the process for researching family trees?
2 Do you think it's an easy process? Why (not)?
3 What hurdles might a person face?

> **Glossary**
>
> **Ellis Island** an island in upper New York Bay that served as a former US immigration station from 1892 to 1954. Ellis Island also has documentation on the millions of immigrants who passed through the station. The documentation includes passenger records that outline arrival information, passenger details, and the ship of travel.
>
> **political asylum** /pəˈlɪtɪkl əˈsaɪləm/ protection that a government gives to people who have left their own country, usually because they were in danger for political reasons.
>
> **refugee camp** /rɛfyʊˈdʒi kæmp/ a place where people who have been forced to leave their country or home live temporarily in tents or temporary buildings.
>
> **melting pot** a place or situation in which large numbers of people, ideas, etc. are mixed together.

2 LOOKING AT LANGUAGE

> 🔍 **Phrasal verbs**
> David Torchiano uses phrasal verbs that makes his interview less formal. Phrasal verbs are a combination of a verb plus a particle (preposition or adverb). The particle can change the meaning of the verb completely and the phrasal verb can have a meaning that is different from the individual words in isolation.

a 🔊 **1 14**)) Listen to some extracts from the interview and complete the phrases.

1 And the more that I went to _____ it, the more interesting the stories became to me.

2 And then I started to _____ from there using Ancestry.com or you know, different resources.

3 You know, even just going to the public library and seeing if I could _____ documents that way.

4 ...I was able to find on my dad's side when his great uncle _____ a lot of the documentation that, or the documentation when he actually _____.

5 When I _____ his documentation it was a very emotional moment.

6 And slowly but surely he was able to bring the majority of the family, who at the time was living in Southern Italy which at that time there wasn't much _____ in Southern Italy...

7 ... you know, the whole family started to _____ and my mom became very close with my would be grandmother, or her would be mother-in-law.

b Listen to the interview again with the audioscript on page 124. What do you think the phrasal verbs mean?

3 🎥 ON THE STREET

a 🔊 **1 15**)) You are going to hear four people talking about their family trees. What three questions do they answer? Who has personally done some research into their family tree? Who seems to know least about it?

1	2	3	4
Brent	Aurelia	James	Tim

b Listen again. Who...?

1 ☐ has ancestors whose lives were saved because they were ill
2 ☐ has twins in their ancestry
3 ☐ has a parent who is from a different place than their grandparents
4 ☐ has family who went to a specific place to do research
5 ☐ has family living in Canada
6 ☐ would like to know what pastimes one of their ancestors had
7 ☐ has an ancestor who was an athlete

c 🔊 **1 16**)) Listen and complete the phrases with two or three words. What do you think they mean?

> **Useful phrases**
> 1 ...due to the measles they had to _____ _____ at the last minute.
> 2 I know a _____ _____ about my family tree.
> 3 My mother and her sister have researched her family _____ _____ _____ so I know a bit from them...
> 4 I only know _____ _____ my grandparents...

4 SPEAKING

Answer the questions with a partner. Practice using phrasal verbs and where possible the useful phrases.

1 Have you ever researched your family tree? Why (not)?
2 How much do you know about your family tree?
3 Do you think it's important for people to know about their ancestry? Why (not)?
4 Can you think of any reasons why people might not want to research their family backgrounds?

G pronouns
V language terminology
P sound–spelling relationships

> If English is supposed to be the lingua franca, how come there's no word in English for lingua franca?
>
> *anonymous*

2A Whose language is it?

1 READING & SPEAKING

a Do you think these statements are probably true or false?

1 40 percent of the world's population can communicate in English reasonably well.
2 Most conversations in English today are between non-native speakers.
3 In business meetings and international conferences conducted in English, non-native speakers prefer it when there is no native speaker present.

b Read the first part of the article *Whose language?* and check your answers to **a**.

c Before you read the second part of the article, with a partner correct the mistakes in sentences 1–6 below. Do you ever make any of these mistakes? How important do you think they are?

1 "I think the movie start at 8:00."
2 "Is there restaurant in the hotel?"
3 "I think the women usually talk faster than the men."
4 "My friend gave me some very good advices."
5 "I called to my brother but his cell phone was turned off."
6 "We discussed about global warming in class yesterday."

d Now read the second part of the article and answer the questions.

1 Which of the mistakes in sentences 1–6 above are mentioned in the text?
2 Does the writer of the article think that grammatical correctness matters
   a) in written English   b) in spoken English?

Whose language?

How many people can speak English? Some experts estimate that 1.5 billion people — around one-quarter of the world's population — can communicate reasonably well in English. Never in recorded history has a language been as widely spoken as English is today. The reason why millions are learning it is simple: it is the language of international business and therefore the key to prosperity. It is not just that multinational companies such as Microsoft, Google, and Vodafone conduct their business in English; it is the language in which the Chinese speak to Brazilians and Germans to Indonesians.

David Graddol, the author of *English Next*, says it is tempting to view the story of English simply as a triumph for its native speakers in North America, Britain and Ireland, and Australasia — but that would be a mistake. Global English has entered a more complex phase, changing in ways that the English-speaking countries cannot control and might not like.

An important question one might ask is: whose English will it be in the future? Non-native speakers now outnumber native English speakers by three to one. The majority of encounters in English today take place between non-native speakers. According to David Graddol, many business meetings held in English appear to run more smoothly when there are no native English speakers present. This is because native speakers are often poor at ensuring that they are understood in international discussions. They tend to think they need to avoid longer Latin-based words, but in fact comprehension problems are more often caused by their use of colloquial English, especially idioms, metaphors, and phrasal verbs. On one occasion, at an international student conference in Amsterdam, conducted in English, the only British representative was asked to be "less English" so that the others could understand her.

Professor Barbara Seidlhofer, **Professor of English and Applied Linguistics at the University of Vienna,** records and transcribes spoken English interactions between speakers of the language around the world. She says her team has noticed that non-native speakers are varying standard English grammar in several ways. Even the most competent speakers sometimes omit the "s" in the third person singular. Many omit definite and indefinite articles where they are required in standard English, or put them in where standard English does not use them. Nouns that are not plural in native-speaker English are used as plurals by non-native speakers (e.g., "informations," "knowledges," "advices"). Other variations include "make a discussion," "discuss about something," or "phone to somebody."

Many native English speakers will insist that these are not variations, they are mistakes. "Knowledges" and "phone to somebody" are simply wrong. Many non-native speakers who teach English around the world would agree. But language changes, and so do notions of grammatical correctness.

Those who insist on standard English grammar remain in a powerful position. Academics who want their work published in international journals have to adhere to the grammatical rules followed by native English-speaking elites.

But spoken English is another matter. Why should non-native speakers bother with what native speakers regard as correct? Their main aim, after all, is to be understood by one another, and in most cases there is no native speaker present.

Professor Seidlhofer says, "I think that what we are looking at is the emergence of a new international attitude, the recognition and awareness that in many international contexts non-native speakers do not need to speak like native speakers, to compare themselves to them, and thus always feel 'less good.'"

From the Financial Times

14

LEXIS IN CONTEXT

e Look at the highlighted words in both parts of the text. They are all formal in register. Match them to their neutral equivalents below.

1 _remain_ *verb* to be (still)
2 _poor_ *adj.* bad
3 _conduct_ *verb* to do
4 _adhere to_ *verb* to follow
5 _notion_ *noun* idea
6 _omit_ *verb* to leave out
7 _required_ *verb* to need
8 _view_ *verb* to look at
9 _thus_ *adj.* so
10 _transcribes_ *verb* to write down

f Answer the questions in small groups.

1 To what extent do you agree that…?
- when non-native speakers of English talk to each other, they should not worry about making mistakes as long as they can communicate
- non-native speakers do not need to speak like native speakers, nor should they feel inferior to them
- certain grammar mistakes should be considered variants of English, not mistakes

2 How important is it to *you* to be able to…?
- speak English accurately
- write accurately in English
- pass international tests in English
- read academic texts or literature in English
- communicate with native speakers of English
- communicate with non-native speakers of English

2 GRAMMAR pronouns

a Are the **bold** pronouns right (✓) or wrong (✗)? Correct any mistakes. Which of the mistakes (if any) do you think interfere with communication?

1 Can the person who has not turned off **their** phone please do so immediately?
2 **It** used to be a movie theater near here, but **it** closed down.
3 We've known **each other** for years, since we were children.
4 I never use an electric razor when I shave **myself**. I prefer the old-fashioned kind.
5 Two men were sitting in the cafe, talking to **themselves** about the game.
6 David **himself** admitted that he should never have spoken to her like that.
7 They have a terrible relationship. They don't understand **one other** at all.
8 **One** never knows what the future holds.

b ▶ p.140 Grammar Bank 2A. Learn more about pronouns, and practice them.

3 SPEAKING

a ① 17 ﹚﹚ Look at some useful phrases for giving your opinion in English. Underline the words that you think have extra stress. Listen and check.

Emphasizing that something is your own opinion

1 I'd say that…
2 If you ask me,…
3 Personally, I think that…
4 Personally speaking,…
5 In my opinion,…
6 In my view…
7 I feel that…
8 My feeling is that…
9 As far as I'm concerned…

b Read some comments from around the world about learning or using English. Compare with a partner and say if you think the situation is the same or different in your country, and how you feel about it. Use the expressions from **a**.

"If you ask me, the one thing that would really improve the level of English here would be if they stopped dubbing all the American TV programs and movies, and had them in English with subtitles instead. But I don't think they'll ever do it. The politicians wouldn't dare."
Maite, Spain

"In my opinion, nowadays public figures should really be able to speak good English. I feel really embarrassed when I hear how some of our politicians or athletes speak."
Rie, Osaka, Japan

"Personally I think that pop groups in my country shouldn't sing in English. I mean, I know it's more universal, but not everybody in Brazil understands English. I think they should sing in Portuguese."
Marcelo, Curitiba, Brazil

"In some universities in my country, they are now teaching other subjects in English, apart from the normal English language classes. In general I think it's a really good idea — as long as the teachers' English is good, of course."
Alejandro, Santiago, Chile

"In Italian they use a lot of English words like *weekend*, *stress*, *OK*, *cool*, *know-how*, words like that. I personally hate it. I think we should use our own words for these things, not just borrow from English. And people even use some words that don't exist, like *footing*, when the English word is *jogging*."
Paola, Milan, Italy

4 LISTENING & SPEAKING

a You're going to hear Cristina from Romania and Pun from Thailand, who both live in the US, talking about their experiences of being non-native speakers of English. Before you listen, check that you understand the words in the glossary.

> **Glossary**
> **hit it out of the park** meet a goal even more than was expected. This expression comes from baseball, when the ball is hit so far that it flies outside of the ballpark or stadium.
> **slam dunk** something that is achieved easily. This expression comes from basketball, when a player jumps above the basket and "dunks" it in the hoop without opposition.

b Answer the following questions with a partner.
1 Do you find it easier to understand native or non-native speakers of English?
2 How do you feel about having your English corrected?

c (**1** **18**))) Now listen to Cristina and Pun answer the questions. What do they say? Who do you identify with most? Why?

Cristina

Pun

d Answer the following questions with a partner.
3 Do you have any funny or embarrassing stories related to misunderstanding someone?
4 Is there anything you still find difficult about English?

e (**1** **19**))) Now listen to Cristina and Pun answering the questions. Answer the following questions with a partner.
5 What anecdotes do they tell?
6 What do they still find difficult? Do you agree with them about what is difficult?

5 VOCABULARY language terminology

a Match the words with their definitions.

collocation   colloquial   an idiom   a metaphor
a phrasal verb   register   slang   a synonym

1 _____ *noun* a group of words with a different meaning from the meanings of the individual words, e.g., *to put your foot in your mouth* (= to say something inappropriate and embarrassing)

2 _____ *noun* a frequent combination of words in a language. It is often the only possible combination to express a concept, e.g., *heavy rain* (not *strong* rain)

3 _____ *noun* the style of written or spoken language that is appropriate for the situation (formal, informal, neutral), e.g., *Can you lend me five bucks?* (informal) *Should you require further assistance…* (formal)

4 _____ *noun* a verb combined with an adverb or preposition, or sometimes both, to give a new meaning, e.g., *throw away, look for, make up for*

5 _____ *noun* very informal words and expressions that are more common in spoken language, especially used by a particular group of people, e.g., teenagers. They often go in and out of fashion very quickly. They can sometimes cause offense. *I had to walk home. I didn't have enough dough* (= money) *for a taxi.*

6 _____ *adj.* (of language) words and phrases used in conversation or writing to friends but not in formal speech or writing, e.g., *kids* (= children), *you know what I mean*, etc.

7 _____ *noun* a word or expression that has the same or nearly the same meaning as another, e.g., *lately | recently*

8 _____ *noun* a word or phrase not used literally, but used to describe sb / sth in a more graphic way and to make the description more powerful, e.g., *When she heard the doorbell ring, she flew to answer it.* (= she ran fast, she didn't literally *fly*)

b Take the **Language quiz** on page 17 with a partner. All the words and expressions are from File 1.

Language quiz

1 Idioms

Can you remember what these idioms mean?

1 If you really think you're right, you should *stick to your guns*.
2 When you talk to your boss, I think you should *speak your mind*.
3 It started to rain harder, but we *gritted our teeth* and continued on.
4 My husband and I *don't see eye to eye* about our children's education.
5 I don't think there's any doubt about who *wears the pants* in their family!

2 Phrasal verbs

Replace the word or phrase in italics with a phrasal verb that means the same. Use the **bold** verb.

1 I've missed a few classes so I'll need to *get back to the same level as the other students*. **catch** _____
2 We'll have to *postpone* the meeting until next week. **put** _____
3 Your daughter doesn't *look or behave like you* at all! **take** _____
4 After her mother died, she was *taken care of until she was older* by her grandmother. **bring** _____
5 My son wants to be a pilot when he *becomes an adult*. **grow** _____

3 Synonyms and register

a Match the words or expressions 1–8 with synonyms A–H.

1 one	☐	A follow	
2 so	☐	B perks	
3 because of	☐	C but	
4 benefits	☐	D consequently	
5 omit	☐	E you	
6 however	☐	F owing to	
7 adhere to	☐	G require	
8 need	☐	H leave out	

b Which word is more formal in each pair?

4 Collocation

Circle the right word in each pair.

1 I *fully / completely* disagree with you.
2 The main disadvantage of working here is that there's no job *safety / security*.
3 I'm very *near / close* to my cousin Claudia – we tell each other everything.
4 I have some *distant / far* relatives in Turkey, but I've never met them.
5 He really *hurt / damaged* my feelings when he criticized the way I dressed.

6 PRONUNCIATION sound–spelling relationships

> 🔍 **Fine-tuning your pronunciation**
>
> According to research, when a non-native speaker is talking to another person in English, the main reason for a breakdown in communication is incorrect pronunciation — often the mispronunciation of individual sounds.
>
> Although many people think that English pronunciation has no rules, especially regarding sounds and spelling, estimates suggest that around 80 percent of words are pronounced according to a rule or pattern.

a With a partner look at the groups of words and say them aloud. Are the pink letters all pronounced the same, or is one word different? Circle the different word if there is one.

1 /h/   hurt   heir   adhere   hardly   himself
2 /oʊ/   throw   elbow   lower   power   grow
3 /aɪ/   alike   despite   river   transcribe   quite
4 /w/   whenever   why   whose   where   which
5 /dʒ/   jealous   journalist   reject   job   enjoy
6 /tʃ/   change   achieve   machine   catch   charge
7 /s/   salary   satisfying   spontaneous   synonym   sure
8 /ɔ/   awful   saw   flaw   drawback   law
9 /ɔr/   short   corner   work   ignore   reporter
10 /ər/   firm   dirty   third   T-shirt   require

b 🔊 **1 20**)) Listen and check. What's the pronunciation rule? Can you think of any more exceptions?

c Cover the phonetic spellings and definitions, and use your instinct to say the words below. Then uncover and check the pronunciation and meaning.

whirl
/wɜrl/ *verb, noun* ■ *verb* 1 to move, or make sb/sth move around quickly in a circle or in a particular direction **SYN** SPIN

jaw
/dʒɔ/ *noun* ■ *noun* 1 [C] either of the two bones at the bottom of the face that contain the teeth and move when you talk or eat

workshop
/ˈwɜrkʃɑp/ *noun* ■ *noun* 1 [U] a room or building in which things are made or repaired using tools or machinery

hierarchy
/ˈhaɪərɑrki/ *noun* ■ *noun* 1 [C, U] a system, especially in a society or organization, in which people are organized into different levels of importance from highest to lowest

G the past: narrative tenses, *used to* and *would*
V word building: abstract nouns
P word stress with suffixes

> When you finally go back to your old hometown, you find it wasn't the old home you missed but your childhood.
>
> *Sam Ewing, American writer*

2B Once upon a time

1 READING

a Read some extracts where different people recall aspects of their childhood. Choose the heading which best fits each text. There are two headings you don't need.

Washing	Fears	First love	Food	Ambitions
Sickness	School	Sundays	Toys and games	

1

My bad dreams were of two kinds, those about specters and those about insects. The latter was, beyond comparison, the worse: to this day I would rather meet a ghost than a tarantula.

C.S. Lewis British author of *The Chronicles of Narnia*

2

I was one of a group of boys who sat on the floor of our professor's office for a weekly lesson in "spoken English." One day the professor put a large sheet of white paper on the wall. The paper had a little black dot in the right-hand corner. When the professor asked, "Boys, what do you see?" we all shouted together "A black dot!" The professor stepped back and said, "So, not a single one of you saw the white sheet of paper. You only saw the black dot. This is the awful thing about human nature. People never see the goodness of things, and the broader picture. Don't go through life with that attitude."

Life teaches you lessons in surprising ways and when you least expect it. One of the most important lessons I ever learned came from a sheet of paper and a black dot. They may seem like small things, but they were enough to prompt big changes in my outlook on life.

Kofi Annan Ghanaian ex-Secretary-General of the United Nations

3

Their dream, and this went on quite far into my professional life, was that I would be the best at music school but not quite good enough for a concert career. I would then go back to Japan, live with them, teach piano and make a lot of money, because it can be very lucrative. And I'd play one recital a year where they could turn up with great pride and people would say "Mr. Uchida, aren't you lucky with your daughter?"

Mitsuko Uchida Japanese classical pianist

4

On wet days there was Mathilde. Mathilde was a large American rocking horse that had been given to my sister and brother when they were children in America. Mathilde had a splendid action — much better than that of any English rocking horse I have ever known. She sprang forward and back, up and down, and ridden at full pressure was liable to unseat you. Her springs, which needed oiling, made a terrific groaning, and added to the pleasure and danger. Splendid exercise again. No wonder I was a skinny child.

Agatha Christie British author of detective fiction

Glossary
miasma /maɪˈæzmə/ a mass of dirty, bad-smelling air (used metaphorically here) (Para 5)
bucks dollars (Para 7)
scrub board a handheld washboard, used to help in cleaning clothes (Para 7)

LEXIS IN CONTEXT

b Read the texts again carefully. Find a synonym in each paragraph for…

1 __specters__ (literary) ghosts
2 __~~~~~~~~~~~~~__ attitude toward outlook
3 __lucrative__ profitable
4 __splendid__ (old-fashioned) excellent
   __liable__ likely to
   __no wonder__ it's not surprising
   __skinny__ (informal, usually disapproving) very thin
5 __~~~~~~~~~~~~__ unhappiness miserable
6 __scolded__ (formal) tell off
7 __dissolve__ to mix with liquid

> 🔍 **Register**
>
> A good dictionary will give information about the register of a word, e.g., *formal, informal, literary, old-fashioned, taboo,* etc. When you record new vocabulary, write down this information, too.

c Choose five more words or phrases from the text which you think are useful.

5

As a child, my idea of the West was that it was a miasma of poverty and misery, like that of the homeless "Little Match Girl" in the Hans Christian Andersen story. When I was at boarding school and did not want to finish my food, the teacher would say, "Think of all the starving children in the capitalist world."

Jung Chang Chinese author of *Wild Swans*

6

My family still laughs at the story, which I remember well, of when I was five years old in Berlin, and arranged to run away with a little boy because I had been scolded. They watched me pack my clothes and go down the stairs. The little boy, six or seven, was waiting around the corner.

Anaïs Nin French author

7

My mother used to take me with her into the woods, to ponds where she would do her washing. There used to be a soap called Octagon that came in an eight-sided bar, and she used to use that to get to the dirt in the clothing. Some people who had a few bucks, they had a scrub board, but she didn't. She would beat the clothing on the rock until the dirt would sort of dissolve and float out. We would be gone most of the day on those days when she washed.

Sidney Poitier American actor

d Read the extracts again and answer the questions.

1 What was C.S. Lewis most afraid of? spider / insect
2 How do you think the lesson changed Kofi Annan's outlook on life?
3 Where did Jung Chang get her idea that the West was very poor?
4 Why was Agatha Christie's rocking horse better than an English one?
5 What did Mitsuko Uchida's parents want her to do with her life?
6 How did Anaïs Nin's parents react when she tried to run away?
7 Why didn't Sidney Poitier's mother use a scrub board to do her washing?

e With a partner cover the extracts and look at the headings. Try to remember what each writer said. Which paragraph reminds you most of your own childhood? Why?

2 GRAMMAR the past: narrative tenses, *used to,* and *would*

a Look at the paragraphs again. Which ones are about…?
1 specific incidents in the past
2 repeated or habitual actions in the past

b Look at the verbs in paragraphs 6 and 7 again. What three past tenses are used to describe the incident in paragraph 6? What verb forms are used to show that the actions were habitual or repeated in 7?

c ▶ **p.141 Grammar Bank 2B.** Learn more about narrative tenses, and practice them.

3 SPEAKING & WRITING

a (1 21)) Listen to five people starting to talk about their childhood. What are the different expressions they use to say (approximately) how old they were at the time?

b Look at the headings in exercise **1a**. With a partner, for each heading talk about things you habitually did or felt in your childhood.

> When I was little I used to be terrified of the dark, and I'd always sleep with the light on…

c Now take turns to choose a heading and talk about a specific incident from your childhood.

> I remember the time when we went on our first family vacation abroad…

d Imagine you were asked to contribute to a book of childhood recollections. Choose one of the headings and write a paragraph either about a specific incident in your childhood, or about things that happened habitually.

e ▶ **p.106 Writing** *An article*. Analyze an article about childhood and write an article for an online magazine.

4 LISTENING & SPEAKING

a (1 22)) Listen to five people talking about their earliest memory. Match the speakers to the emotion they felt at the time.

surprise ☐   sadness ☐   fear ☐   disappointment ☐   happiness ☐

b Listen again. How old was each person? What was their memory?

c Now you're going to hear about some research that has been done on first memories. Before you listen, discuss the following questions with a partner.

1 How far back in our lives can we usually remember?
   a To when we were a baby (0–2 years old)
   b To when we were a toddler (2–4 years)
   c To when we were a small child (5+)
2 Why can't we remember things before that age?
3 What kinds of a) emotions and b) events might people be more likely to remember?
4 Are our first memories mostly visual or of sounds and smells?
5 Why might some people's first memories be unreliable?

d (1 23)) Listen and check your answers with what the speaker says. Were you surprised by anything?

e (1 24)) Now listen to the story of Jean Piaget's first memory and write down what you think are the key words. Listen again and try to add more detail. Compare your words with a partner and then together retell the story.

f Talk to a partner.

Do you have any very early memories of the feelings or incidents below? Do you know approximately how old you were at the time?

feeling surprised
feeling pain
feeling shame or embarrassment
the birth of a brother or sister
a day out
managing to do something for the first time
the death of a pet
a festival or celebration
getting a wonderful or disappointing present

5 VOCABULARY & PRONUNCIATION
word building: abstract nouns; word stress with suffixes

> 🔍 **Abstract nouns**
>
> An abstract noun is one that is used to express an idea, a concept, an experience, or a quality, rather than an object. *Embarrassment* and *memory* are abstract nouns, whereas *bed* and *pants* are not. Some abstract nouns are uncountable in English, but may not be in your language, e.g., *knowledge*.

a Make abstract nouns from the words below and put them in the right columns.

adult	afraid	ashamed	believe	bored	celebrate	child	compete
dead	free	friend	happy	hate	imagine	sick	kind
lose	member	neighbor	partner	poor	relation	sad	wise

+*hood*	+*ship*	+*dom*

+*ness*	+*tion*	word changes

b (1 25)) Underline the stressed syllable in these words. Listen and check. Which ending(s) cause(s) a change in stress?

1 adult adulthood
2 celebrate celebration
3 compete competition
4 free freedom
5 happy happiness
6 relation relationship

c With a partner, guess which of the abstract nouns in **a** is missing from each quotation.

1 ❝Love, friendship and respect do not unite people as much as a common _____ for something.❞
Anton Chekhov, Russian writer

2 ❝_____ is, of all passions, that which weakens the judgement most.❞
Cardinal de Retz, French clergyman and writer

3 ❝To be without some of the things you want is an indispensable part of _____.❞
Bertrand Russell, British philosopher

4 ❝_____ is more important than knowledge.❞
Albert Einstein, physicist

5 ❝Overcoming _____ is not a gesture of charity. It is an act of justice.❞
Nelson Mandela, former president of South Africa

6 ❝There are only two emotions in a plane: _____ and terror.❞
Orson Welles, US movie director

7 ❝I enjoy convalescence. It is the part that makes _____ worthwhile.❞
George Bernard Shaw, Irish dramatist

8 ❝The enemies of _____ do not argue. They shout and they shoot.❞
William Inge, British clergyman and writer

d Say in your own words what the quotations mean. Do you agree with them?

6 (1 26)) SONG *Kid* ♫

GRAMMAR

a Complete the sentences with one word.

1 Everybody seemed to enjoy the barbecue even _____ the weather wasn't very warm.

2 Will the person who left one of _____ personal belongings at the security check please go back and collect it?

3 When I was little, my family _____ spend summers at a cottage by the sea.

4 This street looks so different from when I was a child. Didn't _____ use to be a candy store on the corner?

5 If we lived closer to _____ another, we would probably spend more time together.

6 The Chinese economy is growing, and _____ a result the standard of living in China is rising.

7 Sun-mee always seems pretty reserved to me — she never talks about _____.

8 She wore a baggy dress _____ people wouldn't notice that she had put on weight.

9 We need to _____ the heating system repaired soon, before it starts getting cold.

10 We were very delayed _____ of an accident on the highway.

b Rewrite the sentences using the **bold** word(s).

1 I broke my glasses. I need to pay someone to repair them. **HAVE**
   I broke my glasses. I need _____.

2 If you learn a few phrases, the local people will appreciate it. **ONE**
   _____ the local people will appreciate it.

3 They managed to get to the meeting on time even though the traffic was heavy. **DESPITE**
   They managed to get to the meeting on time _____.

4 It was foggy, so the flight was canceled. **DUE**
   The flight _____.

5 Jane sees Martha about twice a month. **EACH**
   Jane and Martha _____ about twice a month.

6 The children managed to wrap the present on their own. **BY**
   The children managed to wrap the present _____.

7 The last time I saw him was in 1998. **SEEN**
   I _____ 1998.

8 She wore dark glasses so that she wouldn't be recognized. **SO AS**
   She wore dark glasses _____.

9 If we buy a dishwasher, it won't be necessary to do the dishes. **HAVE**
   If we buy a dishwasher _____.

10 I can't believe the risks I used to take when I was younger. **WOULD**
   I can't believe the risks _____ when I was younger.

VOCABULARY

a Complete the idioms.

1 I know you don't want my mother to come and stay, but you'll just have to grit your _____ and put up with it.

2 Don't worry about what other people think. You need to know your own _____.

3 He's got a terrible temper. In fact it must _____ in the family, because his dad's just the same.

4 Maria definitely wears the _____ in that family. Tom lets her walk all over him.

5 I know I'm right and even if everyone in the company disagrees I'm going to stick to my _____!

6 My brothers are always getting into arguments. In fact they're not on speaking _____ at the moment.

b Circle the right word.

1 She'd like to have a *career / profession* in show business.

2 It's a *part-time / temporary* job — I only work mornings.

3 Your sisters are so *like / alike* — they could be twins!

4 My father remarried and had two girls with his second wife, so I have two *half-sisters / stepsisters*.

5 She doesn't *take after / look like* either of her parents. She's very reserved, and they're both really outgoing.

6 "Pay" is a *synonym / metaphor* for "salary," but it's more informal.

c Complete with the right preposition or adverb.

1 Who's in charge _____ the sales conference this year?

2 She's been _____ school for such a long time it will be hard to catch _____ with the others when she goes back.

3 My mother was very sick when I was a child so I was mainly brought _____ by my grandmother.

4 Can we put the meeting _____ till next week? I have too much work at the moment.

5 If you go and talk to Elena, she'll fill you _____ on how the sales campaign has gone.

6 I think we need to deal _____ this situation head _____. It's no good just hoping it will go away.

d Complete the sentences with an adjective or noun formed from the **bold** word.

1 I wish there were a few more good restaurants in our _____. **NEIGHBOR**

2 She has a terrible _____ of the dark. She has to sleep with the lights on. **AFRAID**

3 Don't let this misunderstanding get in the way of our _____. **FRIEND**

4 I'm so sorry for your _____. **LOSE**

5 _____ of speech is one of the most basic human rights. **FREE**

6 My mother always gave me good advice with her words of _____. **WISE**

CAN YOU UNDERSTAND THIS TEXT?

a Do you think being bilingual is an advantage or a disadvantage? Why?

b Read the article. Then mark the sentences **T** (true) or **F** (false).

1 There are fewer job opportunities for monolingual workers.
2 On average, people who speak more than one language earn more money.
3 Most job recruiters think it's important to be bilingual.
4 At the Willard Hotel, some positions require bilingualism.
5 Willard Hotel employees applying for management jobs have an advantage if they are bilingual.
6 Mandarin is considered the business language rather than Cantonese.
7 People who speak both English and Spanish are most likely to be hired.
8 Mainly service industries need bilingual employees.

c Read the article again. Choose five new words or phrases. Check their meaning and pronunciation and try to learn them.

CAN YOU UNDERSTAND THIS PROGRAM?

a Which of the following statements about bilingualism do you think are true?

- [ ] More than half the world's children grow up speaking two or more languages.
- [ ] Being bilingual strengthens the brain.
- [ ] Learning more than one language at a time is confusing to children.
- [ ] Children who are exposed to two languages fall behind monolingual children at school.
- [ ] For bilinguals, the brain keeps the two languages separate.
- [ ] Bilingual speakers' brains perform mental exercises all the time.
- [ ] When bilingual speakers get older, they lose their mental abilities faster than people who speak only one language.

b (**1 27**)) Now listen to a radio program about bilingualism and check your answers to **a**. Were you right?

c Do you know anyone who grew up bilingual? Does that person have any of the characteristics described in the program? Which ones?

How Being Bilingual Can Boost Your Career

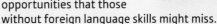

Whether you're fresh out of college or a seasoned executive, insiders agree that fluency in a second language can not only help you stand out among prospective employers, it can also open doors to opportunities that those without foreign language skills might miss.

In today's global economy, the ability to communicate in another language has become a significant advantage in the workforce. Research has found that people who speak at least one foreign language have an average annual household income that's $10,000 higher than the household income of those who only speak English. And about 17 percent of those who speak at least one foreign language earn more than $100,000 a year.

A recent survey found that nearly 9 out of 10 headhunters in Europe, Latin America, and Asia say that being at least bilingual is critical for success in today's business environment. And 66 percent of North American recruiters agreed that being bilingual will be increasingly important in the next 10 years.

"In today's global economy you really have to understand the way business is done overseas to maximize your potential. A second language equips you for that," says Alister Wellesley, managing partner of a Connecticut-based recruiting firm. "If you're doing business overseas, or with someone from overseas, you obtain a certain degree of respect if you're able to talk in their native language."

Language skills can also be key for service industries. At the Willard InterContinental Washington, a luxury hotel a few blocks from the White House, a staff of about 570 represents 42 nations, speaking 19 languages. The Willard's front-of-house employees such as the concierge speak at least two languages. Bilingualism is not an absolute requirement, but it is desirable, according to Wendi Colby, director of human resources.

Workers with skills in a second language may have an edge when it comes to climbing Willard's professional ladder. "The individual that spoke more languages would have a better chance for a managerial role, whatever the next level would be," Colby says. "They are able to deal with a wide array of clients, employees."

So which languages can give you a leg up on the job market? Insiders agree the most popular — and marketable — languages are Spanish, German, French, Italian, Russian and Japanese, with a growing emphasis on Mandarin, given China's booming economy.

"We see demand from a full range of industries," says Wellesley. "It really depends on which company you're working for and the country in which they're located."

G *get*
V phrases with *get*
P words and phrases of French origin

Don't get mad, get everything.

3A Don't get mad, get even!

1 READING & SPEAKING

a Read 10 top breakup lines from a website. Which one do you think is the best / worst way of starting a breakup conversation?

> "We need to talk."

> "It's not you; it's me."

> "When I said I was working late, I was lying."

> "Do you remember when I said that everything was all right...?"

> "You are like a brother / sister to me."

> "I think we'd be better off as friends."

> "I don't love you anymore."

> "I need some time to be on my own."

> "You're a fantastic person, but you're too good for me."

> "Can I have my keys back, please?"

b Now read three true stories about people getting revenge on a former partner. Answer the questions with a partner. Whose revenge do you think was…?

1 the most ingenious
2 the most satisfying
3 the most embarrassing for the person it was done to
4 the least justifiable
5 the most likely to have a long-lasting effect

LEXIS IN CONTEXT

c Read the stories again and choose the right word or phrase for gaps 1–12.

	a	b	c
1	a rejected	b dumped	c broke up
2	a turning	b putting	c creating
3	a praised	b blamed	c ridiculed
4	a replaced	b substituted	c revived
5	a unwillingly	b obviously	c unbearably
6	a stuck	b attached	c posted
7	a invented	b created	c made up
8	a peak	b top	c crowning
9	a get over	b get back	c get rid of
10	a find	b make	c take
11	a reciprocal	b mutual	c shared
12	a smoke	b fuel	c gasoline

50 ways to say

"Revenge may be wicked, but it's natural" according to 19th century British novelist William Makepeace Thackeray, and it remains as true today as it was then.

1 What do you do when love has run its course? How do you say "it's over"? According to the music band Train, there are "50 ways to say goodbye," and singer Paul Simon sings, "There must be 50 ways to leave your lover." Some years ago, fellow singer Phil Collins infamously [1]_____ his second wife by fax. In these more technologically advanced days, the Finnish Prime Minister recently sent a breakup message via text message. Less cowardly is the face-to-face approach ("We need to talk" / "This just isn't working" / "I love you like a friend," etc.).

When Frenchwoman Sophie Calle received an email on her cell phone, she was devastated to discover that it was a message of adieu in which her partner claimed that the breakup would "hurt me more than it will hurt you." Here is a short extract:

"Whatever happens, you must know that I will never stop loving you in my own way — the way I've loved you ever since I've known you, which will stay part of me, and never die…I wish things had turned out differently. Take care of yourself…"

With hindsight, the man almost certainly wishes that he had followed his first instinct ("It seems to me it would be better to say what I have to say to you face-to-face"), particularly as the woman he was dumping is a conceptual artist who specializes in [2]_____ private pain into art. And that is exactly what she did with her "Dear Sophie" email.

Too heartbroken to reply, she decided she would "take care of herself" by sending the man's email to 107 women (including an actress, a poet, a ballet dancer, a singer, a novelist, a psychotherapist, an etiquette consultant, an editor, a policewoman, and even a student). She asked all of them to read the email and to analyze it or interpret it according to their job while she filmed or photographed the result. The psychiatrist concluded that the man was a "twisted manipulator" while the etiquette consultant criticized his manners, and the editor [3]_____ his grammar and syntax.

"The idea came to me very quickly. At first it was therapy, then art took over. After a month, I had gotten over him. There was no suffering. The project had [4]_____ the man." The resulting exhibition *"renez soin de vous"* ("Take care of yourself") was put on at the Bibliothèque Nationale in Paris and was later a huge success at the Venice Biennale. And after becoming, [5]_____, the notorious "star" of an exhibition, it's a sure bet that when Sophie's ex-lover dumps his girlfriends in the future, he will never ever say, "Take care of yourself."

goodbye

2 Perhaps, when she embarked on a relationship with a famous composer, actress Jane Slavin was right to wonder if things were too good to be true. Jane first ⁶_____ a message on his Facebook page last July. It said, "You are one of my favorite composers."

He instantly replied, and within minutes he had added her to a list of online "friends." Later he emailed her asking for a date. "He invited me to a concert and it went on from there. It was an amazing adventure," she says. "It all seemed so magical to be with someone so hugely talented." However, three months into their relationship, he simply stopped emailing her. "It went from 30 emails a day to nothing. No phone calls, no texts, no emails. I thought he died!" So, suddenly and inexplicably rejected, Jane returned to the Internet.

"I put the words 'lovely lady' into Google and downloaded a stunning-looking photograph of a woman, and I gave her a name, Lucia. I then ⁷_____ a social networking page for her, and emailed him. The email from 'Lucia' said, 'I don't have any friends on MySpace. I'm a great fan of your music. Will you be my friend?' By the end of the first day, he had sent her more than 100 emails.

The ⁸_____ moment of her revenge came when "Lucia" agreed to a rendezvous in a little cafe in London. At the appointed time, Jane walked in and said, "Hi, how are you? I haven't heard from you for ages." He looked horrified.

"He said he was meeting a new personal assistant. I said, 'Do you mind if I sit down?' and he said, 'Yes, I do, she's going to be here any minute now.' I said, 'I'll sit down for just a second.' I opened my bag and pulled out copies of all his messages to Lucia. When he asked, 'Is she a friend of yours?' I leaned across the table and whispered to him, 'Lucia is all Jane.'"

"Lucia was my revenge," says Jane. "It helped me ⁹_____ him. I have no regrets."

3 Stephanie found an inspired way to ¹⁰_____ revenge on her _____ boyfriend, Jason. She had been seeing him for about six _____ months when they decided to make their relationship exclusive. She thought things were going well until she discovered that he was seeing someone else on the side. Soon after, a ¹¹_____ friend told Stephanie that Jason wasn't having a love affair with just one woman; there were three others!

Initially, she had no plans to get back at him. She called Jason to break up, but when she got his voice mail, she thought of a much better idea. He had given her his password, so she logged in to his voice mail and recorded a new outgoing message. She explained what a cheater he was. And then, to add ¹²_____ to the fire, she changed his password so he couldn't rerecord the message.

---

d Without looking back at the stories, try to remember what these numbers refer to.

50	107	30	more than 100
6	1	3	

e Look at some famous sayings about revenge. Which saying do you think best fits each of the three stories in **b**? Do you agree with any of them?

"Revenge is sweet."

"Revenge is a dish best served cold."

"In revenge, woman is more barbarous than man."

"An eye for an eye makes the whole world blind."

2 PRONUNCIATION words and phrases of French origin

> 🔍 **French words and phrases**
> A number of French words and phrases are used in English. They are usually said in a way that is close to their French pronunciation, and so do not necessarily follow normal English pronunciation patterns, e.g., ballet (/bæleɪ/), rendezvous (/ˈrɑndeɪvu/). These words will appear in a good English dictionary.

a Look at the sentences below, and underline a French word or expression in each one. What do you think they mean? Do you use any of them in your language?

1 I made a real faux pas when I mentioned his ex-wife.
2 When we were introduced I had a sense of déjà vu, though I knew we'd never met before.
3 For our first date, he took me to an avant-garde music concert — there was no second date.
4 She's engaged to a well-known local entrepreneur.
5 I know it's a cliché, but it really was love at first sight.
6 On our anniversary, he always buys a huge bouquet of flowers — he's so predictable!
7 I met Jane's fiancé last night. They told me they're getting married next year.

b **2** 2)) Listen and focus on how the French expressions are pronounced. Then practice saying the sentences.

3 VOCABULARY phrases with *get*

a Can you remember expressions with *get* from the texts in **1** that mean…?
  a take revenge on someone
  b recover from (a broken relationship with someone)

b ▶ p.160 Vocabulary Bank *get*

4 **2** 3)) SONG *50 Ways To Say Goodbye* ♫

5 SPEAKING & LISTENING

a Look at the back cover information from a new book. Then discuss the questions there with a partner. Why is the book called *Love by Numbers*?

b (**2** **4**)) Listen to some extracts from *Love by Numbers*, in which the author talks about the research which has been done on the topics mentioned on the back cover. According to the research what are the correct answers to the questions?

c Listen again and answer the questions below.

1 What two examples are given to show how friends can strengthen a couple's relationship?

2 What three causes of arguments in a car are mentioned? Which one is becoming less common?

3 What do psychologists say about "love being blind"?

4 What are the main advantages and disadvantages of online dating? What three pieces of advice are given about posting a profile on a dating site?

5 What percentage of people still thought about their first loves? What percentage of people already in a relationship got involved with their first love again after getting back in touch?

6 According to the Canadian study, what are the most popular ways of taking revenge?

d To what extent did the research back up your discussions in **a**? Were you surprised by any of the statistics?

Is your relationship unlikely to succeed if your friends dislike your partner?

Where is the most common place for couples to have an argument?

Do opposites really attract?

How successful is Internet dating?

Should you try to get back in touch with an ex?

Does taking revenge on an ex-partner make you feel better?

There is academic research out there that can answer these questions: Dr. Luisa Dillner, author of the column "Love by Numbers," has sifted through it to give you the facts about flirting, dating, marrying, and much more...

Popular Psychology

LEXIS IN CONTEXT

e (**2** **5**)) Listen again to some extracts and complete the expressions with two words. What do you think the expressions mean?

1 When friends tell a couple that they are a _____ _____ and how much they enjoy going out with them...

2 ... suggesting that you can _____ _____ anyone, if you get the chance to meet them.

3 Most people also _____ _____ someone as good-looking or as plain as they are.

4 After three months you can "see" again, and then you usually _____ _____ the person.

5 A study in the US of over 3,000 adults found that 15 percent knew someone in a _____-_____ relationship that started online.

6 The biggest _____-_____, apparently, is profiles with poor spelling.

7 80 percent of these people ended up _____ _____ with their lost love again.

8 Another study by Stephen Hoshimura at the University of Montana asked people what act of revenge they had _____ _____...

6 GRAMMAR *get*

a Look at some sentences from the listening, all of which contain the verb *get*. Answer the questions with a partner.

A Online dating agencies advise **getting** a picture taken that makes you look friendly, rather than seductive.

B Dr. Nancy Kalish of California State University conducted another study which **got** randomly selected American adults to agree to be interviewed about their first loves.

C Also when a couple stays together for a while, their two groups of friends start to make friends with each other, and as a result, the couple's relationship **gets** stronger.

In which sentence…?

1 ☐ does *get* mean *become*
2 ☐ does *get* mean *make* or *persuade*
3 ☐ could you replace *get* with *have* with no change in meaning

b ➤ **p.142 Grammar Bank 3A.** Learn more about *get*, and practice it.

c Read the *get* questionnaire and check (✓) ten questions you'd like to ask someone else in the class. Ask and answer in pairs.

get questionnaire

☐ Are you the kind of person who regularly gets rid of old clothes, or do you tend to keep things forever?

☐ Did you use to get into trouble a lot when you were a child?

☐ Do you consider yourself a person who usually gets their own way? Why (not)?

☐ Do you tend to keep up to date with your work or studies, or do you often get behind?

☐ Do you think young drivers get stopped by the police more than older drivers? Do you think this is fair?

☐ Have you ever gotten caught cheating on a test? Have you ever cheated on a test and gotten away with it?

☐ Do you think going on vacation together is a good way to really get to know people?

☐ Have you ever gotten the short end of the stick in a purchase or business transaction?

☐ How often and where do you usually get your hair cut?

☐ If one of your gadgets or electrical appliances stops working, do you usually try to fix it yourself first, or do you immediately call to get an expert to fix it?

☐ If you are meeting someone, do you usually get there on time, or are you often either early or late?

☐ If you were able to get just one room in your house redecorated, which would it be and why?

☐ Do you think women are better than men at getting presents for people?

☐ If you were invited to a karaoke evening, would you try to get out of going?

☐ If you were supposed to get a flight the day after there had been a serious plane crash, would you cancel it?

☐ Is there anyone in your family or group of friends who really gets on your nerves?

☐ What kinds of things do/did your parents get you to do in the house?

☐ What worries you most about getting old?

☐ Where would you go if you really wanted to get away from it all and relax?

G discourse markers (2): adverbs and adverbial expressions
V history and warfare
P stress in word families

> You come out of *Gone with the Wind* feeling that history isn't so disturbing after all. One can always make a dress out of a curtain.
>
> *Dilys Powell,*
> *British movie critic*

3B History goes to the movies

1 VOCABULARY history and warfare

a Which of the movies below do you consider to be historical films? Why (not)?

300	Che Part 1 and Part 2	The King's Speech	Gladiator	Schindler's List
Lincoln	Hotel Rwanda	Shakespeare in Love	Titanic	Les Misérables

b Read the descriptions of three famous scenes from movies. Complete each text with words from the list.

The scenes you'll never forget
— our movie critics choose their favorite moments.

1 "They will never take our freedom!"

2 "As God is my witness..."

Braveheart Mel Gibson, 1995

arrows outnumbered overthrow ~~rebel~~ troops victorious

The movie is set in 13th-century Scotland. Mel Gibson plays the Scottish [1]*rebel* William Wallace, who tries to [2] _overthrow_ the English who ruled Scotland at that time. One of the most memorable scenes is the Battle of Stirling, when Wallace's army, hopelessly [3] _outnumbered_, waits in an open field for the English to attack. The English fire thousands of [4] _arrows_ into the air, but the Scots defend themselves with shields. Then the English knights on horseback charge at full speed, but at the last moment, the Scottish [5] _troops_ raise their spears, and the English knights are thrown from their horses and killed. A fierce battle then takes place, and Wallace's army is [6] _victorious_. The scene is not a model of historical accuracy, but with its spectacular special effects and stunts, it's a lot of fun to watch. "They may take our lives, but they will never take our freedom!"

Gone with the Wind Victor Fleming, 1939

besieged Civil War looted side ~~still alive~~

Gone with the Wind is based on the best-selling book by Margaret Mitchell. It tells the story of a manipulative woman, Scarlett O'Hara (played by Vivien Leigh), and an unscrupulous man, Rhett Butler (Clark Gable), who carry on a turbulent love affair in the American South during the [1] _Civil War_. The Confederates, the [2] _side_ Scarlett's family supports, are losing, and Scarlett is living in Atlanta, which is [3] _besieged_ by the Union Army. She escapes and goes home only to find her mother dead, her father disoriented, and her family home [4] _looted_. She asks for food and is told the soldiers have taken everything. In this dramatic scene, Scarlett, starving and desperate, suddenly sees a turnip in the ground. She falls on it, pulls it from the ground and eats it. She then rises from the ground, looks around the ruined land and vows, "As God is my witness, I'll never be hungry again."

c **(2 6)))** Listen and check.

d Re-read the texts and try to memorize the information. Then in groups of three, cover the texts and take turns describing what happens in each of the scenes.

2 PRONUNCIATION stress in word families

> 🔍 **Shifting stress**
>
> It is often useful to learn words in "families," e.g. to rebel, a rebel, rebellion, etc. However, you should check whether the stressed syllable changes within the "family."

3 "I am Spartacus!"

Spartacus Stanley Kubrick, 1960

ppl who died   *mr namug*

capture casualties defeat forces rebellion weapons

o nva   to lost

This epic movie tells the story of the rise and fall of a slave in the Roman Empire. Spartacus (Kirk Douglas) is trained as a gladiator, but he rebels against his Roman owner and escapes. He forms an army of slaves and becomes their leader. Although they have fewer ¹ _Wedpons_ and are less well organized, they win several victories against the Roman ² _forces_ that are sent to put down the ³ _rebellion_. But a final, climactic battle just outside Rome results in the total ⁴ _defeat_ of the rebel army, with heavy ⁵ _casualties_ on both sides, and the ⁶ _capture_ of many of the survivors, including Spartacus. Crassus (Laurence Olivier), the Roman general, promises the captives that they will not be punished if they identify Spartacus. In this powerful scene, one by one, each surviving soldier stands and shouts out, "I am Spartacus!" Crassus finally condemns them all.

to bo find guilty.

a Complete the chart.

noun	person	adjective	verb
capture	/ captor	captive	capture
Civilization	civilion	civil / civilized	civilize
execution	execu tioner		execute
history	historian	historical / historic	
looting	looter		loot.
rebellion	rebel.	rebellious	rebel.
siege			besiege
survival.	survivor	surviving	survive
withdrawal			withdraw
victory	victor	victorious	

b **(2 7)))** Underline the stressed syllable in all the words. Listen and check. Then test a partner on the words in the chart.

3 SPEAKING & WRITING

> 🔍 **The dramatic present**
>
> In this dramatic scene, Scarlett, starving and desperate, suddenly sees a turnip in the ground. She falls on it, pulls it from the ground and eats it.
>
> We normally use the simple present ("the dramatic present") when we describe a scene from a movie, or its plot.

a Work in groups of three or four. Each think of a movie you really enjoyed that was set in a historical period or based on a real event. Make notes under the following headings to help you to talk about it.

- Where and when is the movie set?
- Who are the main characters and who are they played by?
- What is it about?
- What is the most memorable scene?
- What makes it so powerful / moving / dramatic, etc.?

b Describe the movie and the scene to others in the group, and see if they can name the title of the movie.

c Now write a paragraph describing the movie and the scene using the three texts in **1b** as models.

4 READING

a How important do you think it is for a historical film to get all the facts right? Why?

b Quickly read part of the preface of the book *History Goes to the Movies* by American author Joseph Roquemore. What kind of book is it?

  a It compares historical films to what really happened.

  b It is a guide to the best ever historical films.

  c It analyzes the effect historical films have on young people.

HISTORY GOES TO THE MOVIES

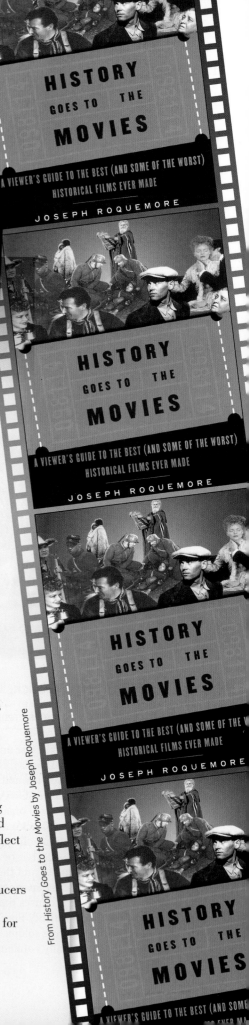

When asked in 1993 to comment on accusations that the movie *In the Name of the Father* grossly distorts contemporary British and Irish history, female lead Emma Thompson responded that she couldn't care less. Ever since the premiere in 1915 of *The Birth of a Nation*, filmmakers have rewritten history to create top-dollar entertainment. The films are very persuasive: well-made movies hold your interest continuously, riveting your attention on "what happens next," and pulling you forward with no time to reflect on individual scenes until the final credits roll. The result: you don't remember much about a movie after watching it for the first time. Very few people can recall even half the plot in reasonable sequence, and still fewer can remember facial expressions or voice intonation associated with specific dialogue sequences (including politically and morally loaded conversations). For this reason, movies have extraordinary power — unmatched by any other medium — to leave you with a strong sense of what is right and what is wrong, who is bad and who is good, even though critical details presented in the movies may be biased or false.

Well, so what? They're just movies. In fact they're not just movies. Millions of Americans are fanatical history lovers, and they pack theaters every time new movies about historical figures or events come to town. *Saving Private Ryan* and *Titanic* raked in viewers and cash for months. Many high school teachers screen movies in the classroom. Clearly countless Americans get most of their history from television and the big screen.

Some of the industry's finest historical and period films premiered during the past decades. But the 1960s also triggered a flurry of politically charged history-based movies full of factual distortions and, occasionally, outright lies. Today the trend continues on a larger scale: many movies released in the 1990s and the first decade of the 21st century reflect blatant disdain, at least as intense as Ms. Thompson's, for solid, reliable history.

History Goes to the Movies is a source of information and, it is hoped, entertainment for everyone interested in the actual history behind a wide selection of movies grouped into twelve sections — 11 covering historical periods and events and a twelfth containing biographies and period films. Each movie review includes an essay on the history covered in one or more movies, and a brief plot summary. Star ratings (five stars: don't miss it) reflect each movie's historical accuracy and — to a much lesser extent — its power to amuse.

Obviously, expecting textbook accuracy from movies would be ridiculous — and producers have delivered a remarkable number of historically faithful movies. But some of them get too much of their history wrong. *History Goes to the Movies* is a guide, however imperfect, for readers and viewers aiming to get it right.

c Now read the text again carefully and choose a, b, or c. Compare with a partner and explain why you think the answer you chose is right.

1 Emma Thompson said that ___ that the movie *In the Name of the Father* was historically inaccurate.
   a it was upsetting
   b it didn't matter
   c it was obvious

2 When people see a movie they tend to remember ___.
   a a great deal of what people said
   b what happened in chronological order
   c who the heroes and villains were

3 According to the author, what most Americans know about history comes from ___.
   a what they learned in high school
   b textbooks
   c movies they have seen at the movie theater and on TV

4 Movies made in recent years have been historically inaccurate because filmmakers ___.
   a don't check the facts
   b are not concerned about historical accuracy
   c want to make politically correct movies

5 The star system Joseph Roquemore uses refers ___.
   a equally to historical accuracy and entertainment value
   b more to entertainment value than historical accuracy
   c more to historical accuracy than entertainment value

LEXIS IN CONTEXT

d Look at the highlighted words and expressions related to the movies. With a partner say what they mean. Check any you're not sure of in a dictionary.

e Complete the sentences with a word or expression from **d**.

1 The latest James Bond movie is expected to be _____ early next summer.

2 After years as a respected theater actress, she has finally been given her chance to appear on the _____.

3 I can't stand it when people get up and leave the theater as soon as the movie ends while I'm trying to watch the _____.

4 The special effects were fantastic but the _____ was pretty implausible.

5 Many of the biggest names were there at last night's _____.

5 LISTENING & SPEAKING

a Two of the movies mentioned in *History Goes to the Movies* are *Titanic* and *Braveheart*. Have you seen either of them? How historically accurate did you think they were?

b (2 8)) Listen to a movie critic talking about them. How many stars did the author Joseph Roquemore give each movie? Does the movie critic agree?

c Listen again and take notes on what was inaccurate about the two movies. Compare your notes with a partner. How serious do you think the inaccuracies were?

> *Titanic* 1997 Director James Cameron
> Inaccuracies:
>
>
>
>
>

> *Braveheart* 1995 Director Mel Gibson
> Inaccuracies:
>
>
>
>
>

d Can you think of any movies you have seen that you think were very inaccurate? Did this detract from your enjoyment of the film?

6 GRAMMAR discourse markers (2): adverbs and adverbial expressions

a (2 9)) Listen to some extracts from what the movie critic said and complete the phrases below with one to three words. What do they tell you about what the speaker is going to say next?

1 _____, these characters and their story are fictitious...

2 _____, I think his assessment is about right.

3 William Wallace is portrayed as a kind of poor primitive tribesman living in a village. _____, he was the son of a rich landowner.

4 _____, the Scots stopped wearing woad hundreds of years earlier.

5 _____, the reason why the Scots won the battle is because the English soldiers got trapped on the narrow bridge.

b ➤ p.143 Grammar Bank 3B. Learn more about adverbs and adverbial expressions, and practice them.

c ➤ Communication *Guess the sentence* A *p.119* B *p.121.*

1 VIDEO THE INTERVIEW Part 1

a Read the biographical information about Adrian Hodges. Are there any historical dramas on TV or in the movie theaters at the moment? Have you seen any of them?

Adrian Hodges is a British television and movie screenwriter. He began his career as a journalist for *Screen International*, a magazine publication that covers movie industry news from around the world. He has over 25 television and movie credits as a writer and a producer, some of which are historical dramas. For instance, he wrote for *The Last King* which is an account of Charles II's reign on the throne and *Rome* which chronicles the lives of the Romans in the last days of the Republic.

b (2 10)) Watch or listen to Part 1 of an interview with him. Mark sentences 1-5 below **T** (true) or **F** (false).

1 Adrian believes historical dramas are popular because they're full of interesting stories that people recognize.

2 It's not always possible to tell a historical story in a way that resonates with the present.

3 According to Adrian, historical dramas are sometimes less expensive than contemporary pieces.

4 "Dressing" a movie specifically means selecting appropriate costumes for the actors.

5 Making a movie that doesn't have any anachronisms is costly and expensive.

c Now listen again and say why the **F** sentences are false.

Glossary

Caligula /kəˈlɪgyələ/ the third Roman emperor, reigning from 37 to 41 A.D.

period films /ˈpɪriəd fɪlmz/ movies that are set during the life of a particular person or in the history of a particular country.

a glaring anachronism /ˈglɛrɪŋ əˈnækrənɪzəm/ something in a book or a film that is very obviously placed in the wrong period of history

the Senate /ˈsɛnət/ a political institution in ancient Rome

toga /ˈtoʊgə/ clothing worn by the citizens of ancient Rome

VIDEO Part 2

a (2 11)) Watch or listen to part 2. Answer the questions with a partner.

What does Adrian say about…?

1 the importance of accuracy in historical drama

2 the extent to which you *can* change details when you are writing a historical drama

3 the difference between writing a drama based on ancient history and one based on recent history

4 the writer's responsibility to be truthful to history

5 the danger of a film becoming the "received version of the truth"

6 why *Spartacus* is a good example of this

7 the film *Braveheart*

b Answer the questions with a partner.

1 To what extent do you agree with what he says about the importance of accuracy in historical films?

2 Can you think of any other historical films apart from *Spartacus* where the film is the only version of the truth that people know?

Glossary

Macbeth /məkˈbɛθ/ a play by Shakespeare about a king of Scotland William the Conqueror, Charles II, Victoria English monarchs from the 11th, 17th, and 19th century

to play fast and loose with IDM (old fashioned) to treat something in a way that shows you feel no responsibility or respect for it

the received version /rɪˈsivd ˈvərʒn/ the version accepted by most people as being correct

2 LOOKING AT LANGUAGE

Idioms and idiomatic expressions

Adrian Hodges uses a lot of idioms and idiomatic expressions to make his language more expressive. Idioms and idiomatic expressions are phrases where the words together have a meaning that is different from the meanings of the individual words.

a (2 12))) Listen to some extracts from the interview and complete the phrases.

1 …but the thing about history is it's _____ with good stories, many of which people know, part, or at least vaguely know.

2 You have to make sure there are no cars, no airplanes, every shot has to _____ to make sure that there's nothing in it which, which betrays the period.

3 So unfortunately, all of that costs money and you have to have bigger crowds in many cases. *Rome* was _____.

4 … it's much easier _____ the details of what happened in Rome than it is _____ the details of what happened in the Iraq War say…

5 You can't say this is true when _____ it isn't.

6 So *Spartacus* the film, made in 1962, I think, _____, has become, I think, for nearly everybody who knows anything about Spartacus the only version of the truth.

7 There are other examples, you know, a lot of people felt that the version of William Wallace that was presented in *Braveheart* was really _____ of what history could stand…

b Listen again with the audioscript on page 127. What do you think the idioms mean?

3 🎥 ON THE STREET

a (2 13))) You are going to hear five people talking about history. What two questions do they answer? Who chooses a) the most recent b) the most distant past in answer to the first question?

1	2	3	4	5
Esther	Aurelia	Brent	James	Amy

b Listen again. Who do they admire and why?

1 _____

2 _____

3 _____

4 _____

5 _____

c (2 14))) Listen and complete the phrases with one to three words. What do you think they mean?

Useful phrases

1 I really admire Abraham Lincoln because of all the work that he did with _____ _____ _____ of American history….

2 I love his _____ and I love to be in his plays.

3 If I could have lived in another historical period I would choose the _____ _____.

4 I like jazz music a lot and that was sort of the _____ of bebop in New York.

5 I think his writing's absolutely phenomenal and very much _____ _____ _____ time.

4 SPEAKING

Answer the questions with a partner. Practice using idioms and idiomatic expressions to express how you feel about what you are saying, and where possible the useful phrases.

1 What's the best historical movie or drama you've seen? What makes it so great?

2 Which period of history do you find the most interesting? What makes it so unique?

3 If you could be any person from the past, who would you be? What would you do similarly or differently?

4 If you could change any moment or event in history what would it be? Why?

5 If you were contributing to a history book of the past twenty years, which moment would you record? What makes the moment special?

G speculation and deduction
V sounds and the human voice
P consonant clusters

"
Noise is the most impertinent
of all forms of interruption.

*Arthur Schopenhauer,
German philosopher*
"

4A Breaking the silence

1 VOCABULARY & WRITING sounds and the human voice

a How noisy is it where you work or study? What noises can you hear? Do any of the noises affect your concentration?

b Look at a list of the most annoying noises in an office (not in order). Which one do you think was voted the most irritating?

c (2 15)) Now listen to the noises, in reverse order (8 = the least annoying). Number the phrases in **b**. Which of these noises do *you* find irritating? Are there any that don't really bother you?

d Make a list of other annoying noises. Then take a class vote on which one is the most annoying.

e ➤ **p.161 Vocabulary Bank** *Sounds and the human voice.*

f (2 17)) Listen to the sounds and make a note of what they are. Then write three paragraphs based on the sounds you heard. Begin each paragraph as follows:

1 It was 12:30 at night and Mike had just fallen asleep…

2 Amanda was walking down Park Street…

3 It was a cold winter night in November…

It drives me crazy!
Office noises we just can't stand…

According to a nationwide poll, many office workers are being driven crazy by noises made by their co-workers. The problem can be particularly serious where two or three people share a small office and in companies which have "open plan" offices. Amplifon, the organization which conducted the online opinion poll, said: "People are easily annoyed by sounds in the office but very few do anything about it. Most people just suffer in silence." The most irritating noises (not in order) were:

☐ Other people's cell phone ringtones
☐ People making personal phone calls
☐ People slurping tea and coffee
☐ People typing on computer keyboards
☐ The boss's voice
☐ The crunch of people eating chips
☐ The "hold" music on the telephone
☐ The hum of the air conditioning

CRUNCH!!

CHIPS

SLUUURP!

PLEASE HOLD…

BLAH! BLAH!

CLICK CLICK

2 PRONUNCIATION
consonant clusters

> ### 🔍 Consonant Clusters
> Consonant clusters (combinations of two or three consonant sounds, e.g., *clothes*, *spring*) can be difficult to pronounce, especially if it is a combination that is not common in your language.
> Three-consonant clusters at the beginning of words always begin with s, e.g., *scream*.
> Three-consonant clusters at the end of words are often either plurals (*months*), third person singular verbs (*wants*), or regular past tenses (*asked*).

a ② 18))) Read the information box and listen to the words below. Then practice saying them.

At the beginning of a word:

two sounds:	three sounds:
click	screech
slam	scream
crash	splash
slurp	
drip	
snore	
stutter	

At the end of a word:

two sounds:	three sounds:
shouts	crunched
sniffs	mumbled
yelled	gasps
hummed	rattled

b ② 19))) Listen and repeat the sentences.

1 She **screamed** when her **fr**iend **spla**shed her in the **sw**imming pool.

2 The **br**akes **scr**eeched and then there was a **tr**eme**nd**ous **cr**ash.

3 My co-worker **sl**urps and ga**sps** for breath when he dri**nks** anything.

c Write three sentences of your own, each using two of the words from **a**. Give them to your partner to say.

3 LISTENING & SPEAKING

a When you go out for coffee or a meal, do you prefer a quiet restaurant or somewhere more lively?

b ② 20))) Listen to a radio program about noise levels in New York City's restaurants and subway system. Put a check (✓) next to the best summary of what the reporter says.

1 ☐ New Yorkers are so used to the noise levels in the city that loud noises don't bother them.

2 ☐ Some New York City restaurants and subways are so noisy that they are causing hearing damage to workers and customers.

3 ☐ New Yorkers aren't aware of the dangerous noise levels around the city because they are focused on their jobs and other priorities.

c Look at the glossary and listen to the program again. Then with a partner try to answer the questions.

> **Glossary**
> **decibel** a unit for measuring how loud a sound is
> **jackhammer** a large powerful tool, worked by air pressure, used especially for breaking up road surfaces
> **tempo** the speed of music
> **earmuffs** a pair of pads attached to a headband and worn to protect the ears from the cold or noise

1 What are the two noises in the restaurant that the reporter complains about?

2 How does the restaurant worker she interviews feel about the noise in her workplace?

3 What noise does the reporter use for comparison? Is it louder or softer than in the restaurant she visited?

4 Why is the restaurant worker getting headaches and hearing buzzing in her ears? What is the daily permissible exposure time for 95 decibels?

5 What effect does faster tempo of music have on customers? Why do restaurants think it's good for business?

6 What noise does the reporter use to compare the noise levels in the New York City subways?

7 What are some symptoms of hearing loss? Do symptoms mean permanent damage?

8 What can cause sudden hearing loss?

9 What does the commuter mean when she says, "I just want to commute in quiet sometimes, but it's a luxury"?

d Do you think restaurants and subway systems have a responsibility to protect people from hearing damage?

e Talk to a partner.

What kind of sounds or music (if any) do you think you should have…?

- in bars and restaurants
- in class at a language school
- in an office
- in an elevator
- at a hotel reception area
- at a beauty salon
- in a supermarket
- in a clothing store
- on public transportation
- in the weights room of a gym
- while you're having a massage
- at the dentist's office while you're being treated
- when a plane is taking off and landing
- when you're put on hold on the phone

4 GRAMMAR speculation and deduction

a With a partner, circle the right form. Try to say why the other one is wrong.

1 **A** That sounds like the neighbors' dog.
  B It *can't be* / *can't have been*. They went away for the weekend and they took the dog with them.

2 There's no sound coming from his room. He *probably hasn't* / *hasn't probably* woken up yet.

3 **A** Didn't you hear that bang in the middle of the night? It woke me up.
  B Yes, I did. It *must be* / *must have been* the wind.

4 Can you turn the music down? If we make too much noise, the woman upstairs *will likely* / *is likely* to call the police.

5 **A** Can I speak to Raymond, please?
  B Sorry, he's not back yet. He *must work* / *must be working* late.

b ➤ **p.144 Grammar Bank 4A.** Learn more about speculation and deduction, and practice them.

5 READING & SPEAKING

a Read the introduction to the article and look at the photos. What do you think the article is going to be about?

b Read the rest of the article. What is Susie Rea's project? What paradox of modern life does her project highlight?

c Look at the photos of people Susie sees every day in London. With a partner, speculate about…
  what they might do.
  how old they must be.
  where they might be from.
  what kind of person they might be.

Breaking the silence

Have you ever wondered who the people are you see every day on the way to work? You've never spoken to them, but you see them every single morning. You know what clothes they wear, the newspaper they read, the way they always stand at the same place at the bus stop or at the train platform. They also see you there every day. But they're still strangers…

A community is now a non-geographical concept. Friends and family are scattered widely, with communication maintained by cell phone and email. Our real-life neighborhood becomes an unknown zone. We can look at the television or the Internet to find out about what's happening thousands of miles away, day and night. But the streets outside? It can be a no-man's land that we navigate, but never really know.

Photographer Susie Rea lives in London and her latest project, entitled *Intimate Strangers*, aims to discover more about the strangers she passes every day. She says, "In London you don't talk to strangers or ask who they are and what they do. Day to day, I find myself inventing the answers; creating snapshots of lives in my head that are entirely imagined."

So what would happen if you stopped that stranger and introduced yourself? Would they shake your hand and become an acquaintance? Susie decided to find out.

Susie's starting point was seeing a man in a Panama hat every day. He was always wearing it and it intrigued her to think about who he might be. "I thought he must be a writer or a teacher wearing a hat like that." But approaching him was difficult. "It's not easy to suddenly talk to someone you recognize, but have never spoken to…it was a very weird experience."

d (2 21)) Listen to Susie talk about the people. What did you find out about them? Were you surprised by anything?

e What kind of person do you think Susie is? What do you think of her experiment? Can you imagine someone doing the same project where you live?

f Read some readers' responses to Susie Rea's experiment. Complete them with one of the phrases below. There are two phrases you don't need.

A   We exchanged a "good morning" and a smile

B   But in all this time I never actually found out what her name was

C   It is a joy to be able to walk silently among strangers.

D   It just goes to show how far a friendly gesture might go.

E   Maybe if we got to know the people who share our community

F   Maybe soon we'll be brave enough to say hello to some of our "intimate strangers."

G   My partner commutes to the city every day for work.

H   Now I really regret not speaking to her

I   Then in 1997 a hurricane hit the state

LEXIS IN CONTEXT

g Look at the highlighted words and phrases and figure out the meaning of any that you don't know. Check with your dictionary.

h Have you had any experiences similar to those of the people who wrote to the website? How well do you know *your* neighbors and people you pass every day? Would you like to get to know them better?

Add comments on this story.

For about 18 months I saw the same woman when I was on the way to work and I nicknamed her "The Iranian Lady." [1] ☐ and finding out if she really was from Iran.

Rafic, New York City

This sounds like a fascinating project! You could say the same thing about your next-door neighbors. You see the same people day in and day out, but you never find out what they're really like. [2] ☐, the world would be a safer place.

Fern, Thailand

I catch a bus to work once a week and it's always the same people. For the last six months, I've been chatting with a woman from our street, and we talk about all sorts of things, from the weather to childcare problems. [3] ☐ until last week — and that's only because she told my little girl.

Tatiana, Ecuador

I loved the article! And it definitely applies to where my parents live. My parents and I had been living on the same street for more than 10 years and had never really gotten to know our neighbors. [4] ☐ and an enormous tree blew down and crashed through our roof. The neighbors all came by and offered us food and any help we needed. But then everything went back to normal. My parents still live in the same house, and they've never spoken to the neighbors since.

Heather, Florida

I used to pass the same woman every day as I walked to work and never said hello or even acknowledged her. I decided it was ridiculous, so one morning I went up to her and said, "Hello." [5] ☐ for the next couple of weeks. But then she changed her route to work. Even though it was only a greeting and a smile, it seems some people just prefer to be left alone.

Ji-hae, South Korea

The reason why I choose to live in London is that I love the fact that I don't have to get to know my neighbors and pretend to be interested in their small talk. [6] ☐ If you want to be overly friendly with your neighbors, go and live in the north of England! London is fine as it is, thank you very much!

Carl, North London

I commute into the city every day, and I used to see the same gentleman on the station platform every morning. We would exchange nods and smiles, and eventually he came up to me and we started chatting. Then we met for dinner and got to know each other better. We are now engaged and are getting married next July. [7] ☐

Camilla, Brazil

6 WRITING

Write your own 50–70 word response to Susie's article.

G adding emphasis (1): inversion
V describing books
P words with "silent" syllables

> A room without books is like a body without a soul.
>
> *Cicero, Roman orator and philosopher*

4B Lost in translation

1 READING

a In groups of four or five, take the quiz.

First and last lines quiz

Look at some famous first and last lines from novels. Which do you think are first lines and which last lines? Write F or L.

1 ☐ All children, except one, grow up.

2 ☐ It is a truth universally acknowledged that a single man in possession of a good fortune must be in want of a wife.

3 ☐ "Oh, my girls, however long you may live, I never can wish you a greater happiness than this!"

4 ☐ James Bond...sat in the final departure lounge of Miami Airport and thought about life and death.

5 ☐ Mr. and Mrs. Dursley, of number four, Privet Drive, were proud to say that they were perfectly normal, thank you very much.

6 ☐ "Tomorrow, I'll think of some way to get him back. After all, tomorrow is another day."

7 ☐ Happy families are all alike; every unhappy family is unhappy in its own way.

8 ☐ ...tears trickled down the sides of his nose. But it was all right, everything was all right, the struggle was finished. He had won the victory over himself. He loved Big Brother.

9 ☐ Many years later, as he faced the firing squad, Colonel Aureliano Buendía was to remember that distant afternoon when his father took him to discover ice.

10 ☐ Renowned curator Jacques Saunière staggered through the vaulted archway of the museum's grand gallery.

Match the first and last lines to the novels they are from.

A ☐ *1984* by George Orwell, 1949

B ☐ *Goldfinger* by Ian Fleming, 1959

C ☐ *Gone With The Wind* by Margaret Mitchell, 1936

D ☐ *Anna Karenina* by Leo Tolstoy, 1877

E ☐ *One Hundred Years Of Solitude* by Gabriel García Márquez, 1967

F ☐ *Harry Potter and the Philosopher's Stone* by J.K. Rowling, 1997

G ☐ *Little Women* by Louisa May Alcott, 1868

H ☐ *The Da Vinci Code* by Dan Brown, 2003

I ☐ *Peter Pan* by J.M. Barrie, 1911

J ☐ *Pride and Prejudice* by Jane Austen, 1813

b Which do you think is the best first line? Does it make you want to read the book?
Which (if any) of these books have you already read? What did you think of it / them?

2 VOCABULARY & SPEAKING describing books

a Complete some readers' comments about books with an adjective from the list.

depressing entertaining fast-paced riveting haunting
slow-paced implausible intriguing moving thought-provoking

1 A wonderful book. So _____ it brought tears to my eyes!
★★★★★

2 A _____ novel that raised many interesting questions. ★★★

3 Rather _____. I really had to make an effort to finish it. ★★

4 A _____ story. I was hooked from the very first page.
★★★★★

5 A light but _____ novel, perfect for beach reading! ★★★

6 The plot was _____. It was impossible to predict how it would end. ★★★★

7 The characters were totally _____. I couldn't take any of them seriously. ★

8 A _____ story which jumps from past to present and back again at breakneck speed. ★★★★

9 A well-written novel, but so _____ it made me feel almost suicidal! ★★★

10 A _____ tale which stayed with me long after I'd finished reading it. ★★★★

b Take turns with a partner choosing an adjective from the list and saying a book or a film that you could use the adjective to describe.

c **(2 22))** Listen to a man talking to a friend about a book he couldn't put down. Write down four positive adjectives he uses to describe the book.

d Now talk to a partner about your reading preferences. Try to use a variety of adjectives to describe the books.

3 GRAMMAR adding emphasis (1): inversion

a Match the halves to make sentences from novels.

1 ☐ His voice was low, but I was able to hear what he said, though **only later** did I understand…

2 ☐ **Never** had he been so unnatural and artificial, even with an outsider or when making a formal call,…

3 ☐ **Not only** was Venus Maria an adored and controversial superstar,…

4 ☐ **Not until now** have I been ready to confess…

5 ☐ **No sooner** had one campaign come to an end…

A as he was that day.
(*Anna Karenina* by Leo Tolstoy, translated by Constance Garnett)

B what he meant.
(*Girl with a Pearl Earring* by Tracy Chevalier)

C that I am a writer.
(*Tough Guys Don't Dance* by Norman Mailer)

D she was also Lucky's best girlfriend.
(*Dangerous Kiss* by Jackie Collins)

E than the candidates began anticipating the next.
(*Imperium* by Robert Harris)

b Look at the verbs after the **bold** adverbial expressions. What is unusual about the word order? What is the effect of putting the adverbial expression at the beginning of the sentence?

c ➤ p.145 Grammar Bank 4B. Learn more about inversion, and practice it.

d Imagine you are a novelist. Complete the sentences in your own words using inversion to make them as dramatic as possible.

1 Not until the last moment…
2 Never in my life…
3 Not only…but…
4 No sooner…than I realized…

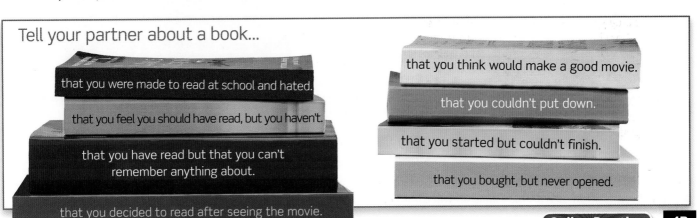

Tell your partner about a book…

that you think would make a good movie.

that you were made to read at school and hated.

that you feel you should have read, but you haven't.

that you couldn't put down.

that you have read but that you can't remember anything about.

that you started but couldn't finish.

that you bought, but never opened.

that you decided to read after seeing the movie.

4 PRONUNCIATION words with "silent" syllables

a (2 23)) You are going to hear ten sentences. For each one, write down the last word you hear.

b Read the information box below. Then cross out the vowels that are not pronounced in the words you wrote down in **a**.

> 🔍 **Silent Syllables**
>
> Some common multi-syllable words in English have vowels that are often not pronounced, e.g., the middle e in vegetable and the second o in chocolate. When this happens, the word loses an unstressed syllable. If you pronounce these vowels, you will still be understood, but leaving them out will make your speech sound more natural, and being aware of them will help you to understand these words in rapid speech.

c (2 24)) Listen and check. Practice saying the words.

5 READING

a Would you prefer to read a novel written in English in the original version or translated into your language? Why?

b You are going to read an article about translation. Before you read the article, look at the two extracts, which are different translations from the Japanese of the first lines of a novel by Haruki Murakami. Answer the questions with a partner.

  1 What details do you find out in the first translation that you don't in the second, and vice versa?
  2 What differences do you notice
    a) in tenses and vocabulary b) in the length of sentences?
  3 Which translation do you prefer? Why?

c Now read the whole article and answer the questions.

  1 What is the author's attitude toward translators?
  2 Whose translation made many readers fall in love with Murakami? Why?
  3 In what way were Constance Garnett's translations controversial?
  4 What metaphor does Kornei Chukovsky use to describe her translations? What do you think he means by it?
  5 Why do you think Andrew Bromfield chose to translate *War and Peace* in such a different way?

LEXIS IN CONTEXT

d Look at the highlighted adjectives and adverbs, and guess the meaning of the ones you don't know. Then match them to meanings 1–12.

  1 _____ *adv.* hardly
  2 _____ *adv.* deeply
  3 _____ *adv.* it could be argued
  4 _____ *adj.* enormous
  5 _____ *adj.* with little color or excitement
  6 _____ *adj.* difficult to deal with
  7 _____ *adj.* original, strange
  8 _____ *adj.* humble, low in status
  9 _____ *adj.* with short sharp sounds
  10 _____ *adv.* in an orderly way
  11 _____ *adj.* flat and even
  12 _____ *adj.* true and accurate

e Which translation of *War and Peace* do you think you would prefer to read? Why?

LOST IN TRANSLATION

THE IMPORTANCE of the lowly translator to our understanding of foreign literature shouldn't be underestimated. Like ghosts hovering over the text, these rarely mentioned linguists can profoundly alter the tone and style of a book. The difference a translator can make to the style and flow of a novel can be vast. Here are two interpretations of the opening lines of *The Wind-Up Bird Chronicle* (1997) by the Japanese novelist Haruki Murakami.

Extract 1

"When the phone rang I was in the kitchen, boiling a potful of spaghetti and whistling along with an FM broadcast of the overture to Rossini's *The Thieving Magpie*, which has to be the perfect music for cooking pasta."

Extract 2

I'm in the kitchen cooking spaghetti when the woman calls. Another moment until the spaghetti is done; there I am, whistling the prelude to Rossini's *La Gazza Ladra* along with the FM radio. Perfect spaghetti-cooking music.

The first is written by Murakami's officially sanctioned translator, Jay Rubin, and flows neatly

Jay Rubin   Haruki Murakami

and cleanly. The second, written by Alfred Birnbaum, is much more staccato, even neurotic. The former gained Murakami a wider English-speaking audience; however countless fans are besotted with Birnbaum's quirky style — to them he has become the voice of Murakami.

Constance Garnett with Tolstoy and Dostoevsky

TRANSLATING can also be a controversial business. Constance Garnett (1861–1946) was arguably the first to bring the Russian literary giants to English-speaking readers, and churned out 70 English translations of major works throughout her lifetime. She worked incredibly quickly, making mistakes and skipping awkward passages and phrases. Yet one of Garnett's greatest crimes, according to Russian critics, was that she applied Victorian sensibilities to works by the likes of Tolstoy and Dostoevsky. Kornei Chukovsky, commenting on Dostoevsky's *Notes from Underground*, wrote: "With Constance Garnett it becomes a safe, bland script: not a volcano, but a smooth lawn mowed in the English manner — which is to say a complete distortion of the original." Russian-born American poet Joseph Brodsky remarked: "The reason English-speaking readers can barely tell the difference between Tolstoy and Dostoevsky is that they aren't reading the prose of either one. They're reading Constance Garnett."

Translators continued to use Garnett's texts as a guide for decades, until the acclaimed Richard Pevear and Larissa Volokhonsky set out to finally produce faithful versions of the Russian masterworks in the 1990s. Yet in October 2007 British translator Andrew Bromfield's edition of *War and Peace* blew the debate wide open. Shortening the novel from 1,267 pages to just 886, and giving it a happy ending, his publisher Ecco boasted that the Bromfield edition was "twice as short, four times as interesting...More peace and less war."

6 LISTENING

a You are going to listen to an interview with Lara Pena, a professional translator working in Mexico. Before you listen, think of three questions you might ask her about translating.

b (2 25)) Listen to the interview. Did she answer any of the questions you or other students came up with?

c Listen again. Choose a, b, or c.

1 One of the reasons why Lara decided to become a translator was because…
   a she thought teaching English was boring.
   b she really enjoyed the postgraduate course that she took.
   c she wanted to be self-employed.

2 Most people who translate novels into English…
   a don't do any other kind of translation work.
   b prefer translating authors who are no longer alive.
   c often only ever translate one particular writer.

3 She mentions the advertising slogan for Coca-Cola™ as an example of…
   a how difficult it is to convey humor in another language.
   b how you cannot always translate something word for word.
   c how different cultures may not have the same attitude to advertising.

4 *The Sound of Music* was translated into German as…
   a "All dreaming together"
   b "Tears and dreams"
   c "My songs, my dreams"

5 Which of these is <u>not</u> mentioned as a problem when translating movie scripts?
   a Having enough room on the screen.
   b Conveying the personality of the speaker.
   c Misunderstanding the actors' words.

6 The problem with translating swear words in a movie script is that…
   a they may be more offensive in other languages.
   b they may not be translatable.
   c you can't use taboo words in some countries.

7 Which of these is mentioned as one of the drawbacks of being a freelance translator?
   a A low salary.
   b No paid vacation days.
   c Time pressure.

8 Lara's advice to would-be translators is to…
   a specialize.
   b study abroad.
   c take a translation course.

d Does being a translator appeal to <u>you</u> as a career? Why (not)?

7 WRITING

a Choose a famous novel in your own language, preferably one that has a dramatic beginning or ending. Translate either the first few sentences or the last few into English.

b Read some other students' translations and see if you can identify the novels.

c ➤ p.108 Writing *A review.* Write a review of a recent book or movie.

8 (2 26)) **SONG** *Story Of Your Life* ♫

GRAMMAR

a Right (✓) or wrong (✗)? Correct the mistakes in the highlighted phrases.

1 **Not only we saw** the sights in New York, we also managed to do some shopping as well.
2 Dave is incredibly late, isn't he? I think **he might get lost**.
3 **Only when the main character dies does her husband realize** how much he loved her.
4 **The waiter didn't probably notice** that they had left without paying.
5 **Basic,** I think she still hasn't gotten over the breakup of her marriage.
6 I think it's **unlikely that I will be given** a work permit.
7 We have interviewed all three candidates and **all of all** we think that Joe is the most suitable person for the position.
8 What a wonderful smell! **Somebody must bake** some bread.
9 **You definitely won't pass** your driving test if you drive that fast!
10 I called you yesterday. **You should have got** a message.

b Complete with the verb in parentheses in the right form.

1 She's unlikely _____ before 7:00. (arrive)
2 Not until all the guests had gone _____ able to sit down and rest. (we / be)
3 Maria is bound _____ the news — everybody was talking about it yesterday. (hear)
4 No sooner _____ married than James lost his job. (they / get)
5 Never _____ such a wonderful view. It completely took my breath away. (I / see)
6 My neighbor can't _____ very long hours. He's always home by early afternoon. (work)

c Complete the get phrases with the correct words.

1 My wife wants me to get _____ of my old motorcycle because it's taking up room in the garage.
2 Aly got _____ cheating on her final test, so her teacher failed her from the class.
3 She seems unfriendly, but once you get _____ her you'll like her.
4 I don't think Keith will ever get _____ cleaning his room on his own — his mother always cleaned it for him.
5 Juan needs to get _____ Maria. It's been three years since they've broken up.

VOCABULARY

a Complete the missing words.

1 The play was so **sl**_____-_____ that I lost interest and fell asleep in the first act.
2 Carlos is unemployed and found the documentary about the tough job market **de**_____.
3 Haruki Murakami's books are so **gr**_____ I have a hard time putting them down.
4 Annie thought there was an **in**_____ possibility that the detective in the movie was actually the criminal.
5 The story was so **ha**_____ that I could not stop thinking about it.

b Complete the verbs in the past simple.

1 Mabel **sl**_____ the door and walked off angrily.
2 "Thanks darling," she **wh**_____ softly in his ear.
3 He **wh**_____ a happy tune as he walked down the street.
4 "I'm afraid it's too late," she **si**_____. "Maybe another time."
5 The wind was so strong that the windows **ra**_____.
6 The brakes **sc**_____ and the car stopped just in time.

c Write the words for the definitions.

1 _____ (noun and verb) to make short, light, regular repeated sounds
2 _____ (noun and verb) (of liquid) to fall in small drops
3 _____ _____ (noun) polite conversation about ordinary or unimportant subjects
4 _____-_____ (adj.) something that makes you think
5 _____ (adj.) with little color, excitement, or interest
6 _____ (verb) to speak or say something in a quiet voice, in a way that is not clear
7 _____ (adj.) series of events that form the story of a novel, play, movie, etc.
8 _____ (noun and verb) to go back and forth to work or school
9 _____ (noun) an attempt by some of the people in a country to change their government, using violence
10 _____ (adj.) very great; felt or experienced very strongly

d Write synonyms for the following words or phrases.

1 to hold forcefully **c**_____
2 unlikely to be true **i**_____
3 party or faction **s**_____
4 military power **f**_____
5 deaths **c**_____
6 conquer **d**_____
7 hardly **ba**_____
8 enormous **v**_____

CAN YOU UNDERSTAND THIS TEXT?

a Read the article once. Do you think you would feel peaceful spending time in the quietest place on earth?

b Read the article again. Then mark the sentences **T** (true), **F** (false), or **DS** (doesn't say).

1 The writer used to live in New York.

2 The chamber in the Orfield Laboratories is quiet because it is out in the countryside, away from any cities.

3 Most people become distressed by absolute silence.

4 According to the writer, people need sound to reassure them that things are working properly.

5 A violinist couldn't stand being in the chamber because he was having a panic attack.

6 The only sounds the writer could hear in the chamber were from his own body.

7 Others have stayed in the chamber for longer than the writer did.

8 While he was in the chamber, the writer was frightened and anxious.

9 The writer felt peaceful and relaxed after leaving the chamber.

10 The writer still lives in the city, no longer bothered by the noise.

c Choose five new words or phrases from the text. Check their meaning and pronunciation and try to learn them.

CAN YOU UNDERSTAND THIS PROGRAM?

a Why do people take revenge? Do you think they enjoy getting even when they have the chance?

b (2 27)) Listen to an expert giving a talk about revenge. Then answer the questions in **a** again.

c Listen again and answer the questions below.

1 The speaker says she planned to take revenge on someone. Who and why?

2 What was her plan for taking revenge? Did she carry it out?

3 In the Swiss study, why did some of the participants want to get even with their partners?

4 How did the participants feel when they were taking revenge? How did the researchers know?

5 What does the study tell us about trust and revenge?

6 How does the speaker suggest avoiding situations that could cause people to take revenge?

Glossary
positive emission tomography (PET) a medical test that produces an image of your brain or of another part inside your body

---

THE QUIETEST PLACE ON EARTH

My quest started when I was in the New York subway. My children were whining, four trains came screaming into the station at once and I put my hands over my ears and cowered — the noise was deafening. In cities, the ever-present dull background roar of planes, cars, machinery and voices is a fact of life. There is no escape from it and I was beginning to be driven mad by it.

In an attempt to recapture some peace, I decided to go on a mission to find the quietest place on Earth; to discover whether absolute silence exists. The place I was most excited about visiting was the anechoic chamber at Orfield Laboratories in Minnesota. This is a small room, massively insulated with layers of concrete and steel to block out exterior sources of noise. It is the quietest place on earth — 99.9 percent sound-absorbent.

Ironically, far from being peaceful, most people find its perfect quiet upsetting. The presence of sound means things are working; it's business as usual — when sound is absent, that signals malfunction.

I had heard being in an anechoic chamber for longer than 15 minutes can cause extreme symptoms, from claustrophobia and nausea to panic attacks. A violinist tried it and hammered on the door after a few seconds, demanding to be let out because he was so disturbed by the silence.

I booked a 45-minute session — no one had managed to stay in for that long before. When the heavy door shut behind me, I was plunged into darkness (lights can make a noise). For the first few seconds, being in such a quiet place felt like nirvana, a balm for my jangled nerves. I strained to hear something and heard...nothing.

Then, after a minute or two, I became aware of the sound of my breathing, so I held my breath. The dull thump of my heartbeat became apparent — nothing I could do about that. Then I stopped obsessing about what bodily functions I could hear and began to enjoy it. I didn't feel afraid and came out only because my time was up. Everyone was impressed that I'd beaten the record, but having spent so long searching for quiet, I was comfortable with the feeling of absolute stillness. Afterwards I felt wonderfully rested and calm.

My desire for silence changed my life. I found that making space for moments of quiet in my day is the key to happiness — they give you a chance to think about what you want in life. If you can occasionally become master of your own sound environment — from turning off the TV to moving to the country, as I did — you become a lot more accepting of the noises of everyday life.

> Half our life is spent trying to find something to do with the time we have rushed through life trying to save.
>
> *Will Rogers, American humorist*

5A Are there 31 hours in a day?

1 READING & SPEAKING

a Talk to a partner.

1 Which of the following do you do? To what extent do you think doing one thing affects how well you do the other?

- Talk on a hands-free set while you are driving.
- Talk on the phone while you are doing housework or cooking.
- Check your email or chat online while you are working or studying.
- Look at a website while you are having a conversation on the phone.
- Listen to music while you are studying or working.
- Listen to music while you are exercising.
- Send a text while talking to a friend.

2 Are there any other activities you do simultaneously?

3 Have you ever made a mistake or had an accident because you were multitasking?

4 Do you think multitasking helps you to use your time better?

b Work in pairs, **A** and **B**. You are going to read different articles about new research into multitasking. Read your texts and be ready to tell your partner about the following:

- what the research has shown
- what kind of multitasking people do
  a) during the day b) in the evening
- Mark Vickery and his wife's experience
- what he thinks the pros and cons are

- a typical teenager's attitude toward multitasking
- what the research has shown about multitasking
- what things we can do successfully simultaneously
- what happens when we try to do two or more related tasks simultaneously
- problems that arise from multitasking while we are driving

c Now tell each other the main points of the articles you read.

A

Multitasking = 31/7

1 The latest research suggests that typical middle-class city dwellers now have so many time-saving gadgets that they can fit into 24 hours the same quantity of tasks that a decade ago would have taken 31 hours to complete.

2 For many people, the frenzy starts over breakfast, reading emails on a hand-held BlackBerry® while making toast. It carries on in the car where a driver with a Bluetooth® earpiece holds a conference call while keeping an ear on the radio and checking the GPS.

3 Work is then a blizzard of emails, phone calls, and meetings, often happening simultaneously. However, according to OTX, an American consumer research organization, the most intense period of multitasking appears to be in the evening. "People will be pressing the television remote control while using a wireless laptop computer balanced on their knee, emailing and texting friends on a smartphone, and holding a conversation with friends or family members," said Patrick Moriarty, one of the authors of the report. "They may be far more mentally engaged than they are in the office."

4 According to the study, while television remains the main focus of attention in the evening, nearly half the respondents were also using computers and phones to catch up with friends, update their Facebook™ or other social networks, or download and listen to music.

5 Mark Vickery, 35, agreed that for him and his wife Susan, a doctor, the evening was the peak of multitasking. "Both of us are out of the house during the day," said Vickery, a marketing manager. "When we come back in the evening we tend to use a lot of technology on the go. We'll be using online banking, Facebook™, email, and programming the TV shows we want to watch later.

6 On the one hand it's good — you get more done. On the other hand, when I left college seven years ago, life was much simpler. There was more talking face-to-face and more time spent over dinner"

> **Glossary**
>
> **BlackBerry®** hand-held device that makes available email, phone, web browsing, etc.
>
> **Bluetooth®** technology that makes it possible for various devices and peripherals to communicate with each other and with the Internet without the need for cables
>
> **GPS** a navigation system that receives information via satellite

From The Times

B

The great myth of multitasking

1 You open the door to your teenage daughter's room. "What are you doing?" you ask.

"Nothing much," she answers. "Uploading pictures, doing my homework, helping Jade with hers online…"

"All at the same time?"

"Sure, it's easy."

2 While your daughter may be convinced that she can do all these things at the same time, a number of recently published neuroscience research papers argue that this is not in fact the case. Apparently what is really happening is that our brains juggle these tasks, rapidly switching from one to the other and choosing a sequence in which to do them.

3 This may seem counterintuitive. Multitasking is a perfectly natural everyday occurrence. We can cook dinner while engrossed in a show on TV or we can talk to a friend while walking down the street without bumping into anybody or getting run over. However, research suggests that there is an enormous difference between how the brain can deal with what are referred to as "highly practiced tasks," such as stirring or walking, and how it responds when, for example, you think about adding another ingredient or you decide to change the direction you are walking. In this case, our brains require us to concentrate on the activity at hand.

4 The problem, it seems, occurs when human beings try to carry out two or more tasks that are in some way related. We can see the effect of this if we look at what happens when people use cell phones while driving (even if they are hands-free). Most people feel they are capable of driving and having a conversation at the same time. This is fine until they need to process language while driving, for example on a road sign. Then the language channel of the brain gets clogged and the brain can no longer cope. A similar thing occurs if the conversation changes to something visual, for example your friend describing what his new apartment looks like. In this case, as you try to imagine what he is describing, the visual channel of the brain is overloaded and you can no longer concentrate on the road.

5 David E. Meyer, director of the Brain, Cognition, and Action laboratory at the University of Michigan, who is considered to be one of the world's experts in this field, believes that human beings "will never, ever be able to overcome the inherent limitations in the brain for processing information during multitasking. It just can't be done, any more than the best of all humans will ever be able to run a one-minute mile."

LEXIS IN CONTEXT

d Work with the same partner. Find words which mean:

A 1 _____ *noun* a small tool or device that does something useful (Para 1)

2 _____ *noun* a state of great activity (Para 2)

3 _____ *noun* a snowstorm; a large quantity of things that may seem to be attacking you (Para 3)

4 _____ **PHR V** to find out what people have been doing; to get the latest news (Para 4)

5 _____ *noun* the top of a mountain, the point when sb / sth is best, highest, or strongest (Para 5)

B 6 _____ *verb* to throw a set of three or more objects in the air and catch and throw them again quickly, one at a time; to try to deal with two or more activities at the same time (Para 2)

7 _____ *adj.* so interested in sth that you give it all your attention (Para 3)

8 _____ *verb* to deal successfully with sth difficult (Para 4)

9 _____ *verb* to block (Para 4)

10 _____ *verb* to succeed in dealing with a problem that has been preventing you from achieving sth (Para 5)

> 🔍 **Metaphors**
>
> When you look up a word in the dictionary, the first meaning(s) listed will normally be the literal meaning(s), and metaphorical meanings will be listed later. However, if you know the literal meaning of a word or phrase you can often guess the metaphorical meaning in a text, e.g., if you know the literal meaning of blizzard you can easily understand the metaphor a blizzard of emails.

e After reading the two articles, do you think that multitasking saves you time, or are you probably wasting time by doing things less effectively? Give examples from your own experience.

2 GRAMMAR distancing

a Look at the highlighted phrases in the two articles. What do they have in common?

b ➤ p.146 Grammar Bank 5A. Read the rules and do the exercises.

c You are a journalist. Your editor has asked you to write a paragraph about one of the news stories with the headlines below. However, she has asked you to be careful what you say, as the facts haven't been confirmed yet. Choose one story and write a paragraph of approximately 100 words.

EATING SUGAR HELPS YOU STUDY BETTER!

Actor's wife seeks divorce

POLITICIAN LINKED TO CHARITY SCANDAL

Is jungle plant the key to eternal youth?

3 PRONUNCIATION & LISTENING
linking

a Read the information about a radio call-in show. Who or what are the "Time Bandits"?

The Time Bandits

They creep up on us when we least expect it and steal one of the things we value most — our time. They are the time bandits — the people (and situations) that waste our precious minutes and make our lives even more rushed.

> **How can we stop the time bandits?**
> Call our expert, Richard Anderson, and tell us about your "time bandits" and find out how to deal with them.

b (**3 2**)) Before you listen to the whole program, listen and complete some extracts.
1 I think that's a common problem _____ of us.
2 _____ don't complain aloud…
3 _____, there's this friend of mine and…
4 _____ on time.
5 It's just _____ time.
6 It's been _____ to you…

c Read the information about linking. Then look back at the extracts. Which words are linked? Why? Now practice saying the sentences and phrases trying to link the words.

> **🔍 Linking**
> When people speak quickly, they usually link words together, i.e., the sound at the end of one word is linked to the sound at the beginning of the next. Being aware of linking will help you understand rapid speech better, and make your own English sound more natural. Some of the rules for linking words are:
> 1. A consonant sound at the end of a word is linked to a vowel sound at the beginning of the next, e.g., I met him a long time ago.
> 2. When a word ending in -r or -re (e.g., are) is followed by a word beginning with a vowel sound, an /r/ sound is added to link the words together, e.g., We're early.
> 3. hen a word ending with a consonant sound is followed by a word beginning with the same consonant sound, one long consonant sound is made, e.g., I need some more time.

d (**3 3**)) Now listen to five callers to the radio show. Write a sentence to summarize their problem.

Caller 1 _She wastes a lot of time talking to a friend on the phone._
Advice ☐

Caller 2 _____
Advice ☐

Caller 3 _____
Advice ☐

Caller 4 _____
Advice ☐

Caller 5 _____
Advice ☐

e With a partner, imagine you are the expert. Discuss and decide what advice you might give the five callers.

f (**3 4**)) Now listen to the expert's advice (A–E), and match the advice with the problems.

g (**3 5**)) Listen to the whole program and check your answers to **f**. Was any of the expert's advice similar to yours? What differences were there?

h Do you have any "time bandits"? What do you do about them? Are there any ideas in the advice the expert gave that you might use?

4 VOCABULARY expressions with *time*

a Can you remember the missing words in these sentences?

1 …I should say **w**_____ **of** my **time**, waiting for people.
2 I have kids and I work full time, so as you can imagine I don't have much **sp**_____ **time**.
3 My friend swears it **s**_____ her **a lot of time**.
4 Tell them you're a little **s**_____ **on time** today.
5 Well, I'm afraid **time's u**_____ for now, but thank you all for your calls.

b **3 6**)) Listen to the extracts and check. What do the expressions mean?

c ➤ p.162 **Vocabulary Bank** *time*.

5 SPEAKING

Work with a partner and answer the questions in the *Time questionnaire*.

Time questionnaire

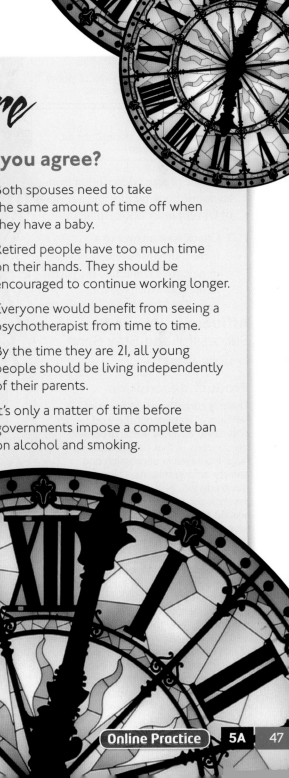

About you

🕐 On a typical weekday morning, are you usually pressed for time?

🕐 Do you have any electronic gadgets that you think really save you time?

🕐 What do you usually do to kill time while you're waiting at an airport or at a station?

🕐 When you go shopping, do you like to buy things as quickly as possible or do you prefer to take your time?

🕐 Is there anything or anybody who is taking up a lot of your time at the moment?

🕐 Are you usually on time when you meet friends? Does it bother you when other people aren't on time?

🕐 Do you like to get to the airport or station with time to spare or at the last minute?

🕐 When you were younger, did your parents give you a hard time if you came home late?

🕐 When you take a test, do you tend to have time left at the end or do you usually run out of time?

Do you agree?

🕐 Both spouses need to take the same amount of time off when they have a baby.

🕐 Retired people have too much time on their hands. They should be encouraged to continue working longer.

🕐 Everyone would benefit from seeing a psychotherapist from time to time.

🕐 By the time they are 21, all young people should be living independently of their parents.

🕐 It's only a matter of time before governments impose a complete ban on alcohol and smoking.

G unreal uses of past tenses
V money
P *ea* and *ear*

"
You can be young without money,
but you can't be old without it.

5B Do you have *Affluenza?*

1 READING & SPEAKING

a Look at the lesson title. "Affluenza" is an invented word, made by putting two words together, *affluent* and *influenza*. Look at the dictionary definitions, and decide what you think it means.

---
affluent
/ˈæfluənt/ *adj.* ▪ having a lot of money and a good standard of living

---
influenza
/ˌɪnfluˈɛnzə/ *noun* ▪ (formal) the flu, an infectious illness

---

b Read the product description from an online book retailer and a review of Oliver James' book *Affluenza*.

1 Check your answer to **a**.
2 Is the journalist's review positive or negative? Underline the parts of the text which tell you.

Affluenza: How to Be Successful and Stay Sane
by <u>Oliver James</u>

- -

Product description

There is currently an epidemic of "affluenza" throughout the world — an obsessive, envious, keeping-up-with-the-Joneses — that has resulted in huge increases in depression and anxiety among millions. Over a nine-month period, best-selling author and psychologist Oliver James traveled around the world to try and find out why. He discovered how, despite very different cultures and levels of wealth, "affluenza" is spreading. Cities he visited include Sydney, Singapore, Moscow, Copenhagen, New York, and Shanghai, and in each place he interviewed several groups of people in the hope of finding out not only why this is happening, but also how one can increase the strength of one's emotional immune system. He asks: why do so many more people want what they don't have and want to be someone they're not, despite being richer and freer from traditional constraints?

REVIEW

The sick society
Affluenza by Oliver James

In his earlier book *Britain on the Couch*, Oliver James asserted that "advanced capitalism makes money out of misery and dissatisfaction, as if it were encouraging us to fill up our emotional emptiness with material goods." In this book, he explores the idea further, and it's terrific. A lot of readers, wanting to put their finger on why the affluent world they live in makes them so uneasy, will want to cheer. Here he is saying, loud and clear, that capitalism is bad for your mental health. And then he tells us why this is the case, and what we can do about it.

"My focus," explains James, "is on why we are so messed up, not with giving a false promise of the possibility of happiness." So why are we so messed up? It's because of what James calls "selfish capitalism," or, more catchily, *Affluenza*, a virus-like condition that spreads through affluent countries. In these countries, notably English-speaking ones, people define themselves by how much money they make. They are also ruled by superficial values — how attractive they look, how famous they are, how much they are able to show off.

It's a wonderfully clear and cogent thesis. *Affluenza*, as defined by Oliver James, is clearly recognizable as our way of life. It spreads because it feeds off itself; when you try to make yourself feel better by buying a car, or building muscles in the gym, or spraying on a fake tan, or getting a facelift, you actually make yourself feel worse, which makes you want to buy more things.

The author's antidote for *Affluenza* is simple: look inward, not outward. Don't be a sheep. Try to be "beautiful" rather than "attractive." Embrace the family. Don't see life as a competition. Don't watch too much TV. Simple, perhaps. But will it be enough?

From The Guardian

c Read both texts again and answer the questions with a partner.

1 How did Oliver James do his research for this book?
2 What did he want to find out?
3 According to Oliver James, why do we feel the need to buy material goods?
4 What four things do sufferers of "affluenza" value most?
5 Explain what the reviewer means by "it feeds off itself."
6 What do you think the advice "be beautiful rather than attractive" means?

d Would you like to read this book? Why (not)?

e Complete the questionnaire below from the book *Affluenza*.

HAVE YOU CONTRACTED THE "AFFLUENZA" VIRUS?

Put a check (✓) or put an (X) next to the following statements:

- ☐ I would like to be a wealthy person.
- ☐ I would like to have my name known by many people.
- ☐ I would like to successfully hide the signs of aging.
- ☐ I would like to be admired by many people.
- ☐ I would like to have people comment often about how attractive I look.
- ☐ I like to keep up with the latest hair and fashion trends.
- ☐ I often compare what I own with what others own.
- ☐ Possessions can be just as important as people.
- ☐ Shopping or thinking about what to buy greatly preoccupies me.
- ☐ I'm less concerned with what work I do than with what I get paid for it.
- ☐ I admire people who own expensive homes, cars, and clothes.
- ☐ My life would be better if I owned certain things I don't have now.
- ☐ The things I will own will say a lot about how well I've done in life.
- ☐ I want a lot of luxury in life.

f ➤ **Communication** *Do you have "affluenza"? p.119.* According to your answers, are you suffering from "affluenza"? Do you think the questionnaire is fair?

g Talk to a partner. Do you agree with the author of *Affluenza* that…?

- in our society people are defined by how much money they earn
- nowadays people are ruled by superficial values
- people today have an unhealthy interest in the lives of celebrities
- people buy things to make themselves feel happier
- being affluent makes people unhappy

2 VOCABULARY money

a Can you remember words from the text which mean…?
1 rich: **a**_____, **w**_____
2 to have something that belongs to you: **o**_____
3 (the enjoyment of) special and expensive things, e.g., food, clothes, surroundings: **l**_____

b ➤ **p.163 Vocabulary Bank** *Money.*

c Choose the right word from each pair according to meaning, collocation, or register.
1 Mom, can you lend me some money? I'm *broke | penniless*.
2 I'm trying to get a *loan | mortgage* from the bank to buy a car.
3 We're going to have to be a little careful this month if we don't want to end up in the *red | black*.
4 The company has been *in | on* debt for the last six months and may go out of business.
5 One of my cousins is absolutely *affluent | loaded* — she inherited a fortune from her parents.
6 When you're abroad, you get a better *currency | exchange rate* if you take money out at an ATM.
7 We like living here because we have a much better *cost | standard* of living.
8 I need to get a better job. We can't *make | get* ends meet.

d Take turns telling your partner about a person you know who…

is pretty tight-fisted.	buys and sells shares of stock.
lives beyond their means.	charges high fees for what they do.
has more money than sense.	has difficulty making ends meet.
was given a grant to study abroad.	has spent a fortune on cosmetic surgery.

3 PRONUNCIATION *ea* and *ear*

a Say the sentences below. Do the pink letters make the same or different sounds in each sentence?

1 My great-grandfather was very wealthy, but incredibly cheap.
2 I just had a really good idea!
3 Even though I left home early, I nearly missed the flight.
4 I heard that he doesn't earn much.

b (3 7)) Listen and check.

c Put the words from the list in the right columns.

appear   bear   beat   break   cheer   creak   deal   death   earring
earth   fear   hear   heart   jealous   learn   neatly   pear   please
pleasure   scream   spread   steak   unhealthy   wear

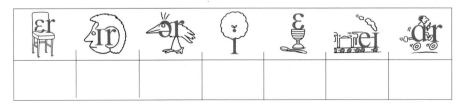

d (3 8)) Listen and check. What are the most common pronunciations of *ea* and *ear*?

> ⚠ When you come across a new word with *ea* or *ear*, you should check the pronunciation in a dictionary.

4 READING

a Do you know of any couples in which you think one spouse married for money? Are / Were the marriages successful, as far as you know?

b You are going to read one of a series of articles from *The Times* called *Family Secrets*, which are unsigned and use fictitious names, and in which readers of the newspaper confess a secret. Read the article once. What is your initial reaction to what the woman says?

I wish I had married for money, not love

WHEN BILL AND I GOT MARRIED, his relaxed attitude toward money amused me. He's a teacher and enjoys his job. I work in medical sales: more stressful, but it pays well. I have, however, become secretly, overwhelmingly, envious of my friends,
5 who can rely on their husbands as the breadwinners.

Our first home was a tiny apartment in a lovely area, which was fine even when our first daughter was born. Our second daughter's arrival two years later put a strain on space and finances, so we had to move — and I had to learn to bite my tongue so as not to seem ungrateful.
10 It was then that I noticed that my best friend Carol's standard of living was better than ours: her husband is a chief surgeon, and their first home was a five-bedroom house. We bought a three-bedroom house on a nice street, but I couldn't help comparing it with friends' houses. I've had promotions, but Bill has no plans to apply for
15 anything above classroom teacher, his current position; I think he should go for an assistant principal position.

Bill is a great dad, and with the girls now reaching their teens, I appreciate how well he gets along with them and puts so much effort into their homework and hobbies. But although I'd never admit this
20 to friends, I believe that there's more to life than being good parents. Carol is having a fantastic party for her 40th birthday, as well as a week in Paris with her husband and a weekend in New York with their 14-year-old daughter. I pretended to be thrilled, but was green with envy. I know many people can't take a vacation at all, but we mix
25 with people who have no mortgages, work part-time or not at all, can afford private education and have three or four vacations a year.

I feel resentful, especially since it's the men who bring in the money; and even if Bill were the school principal, he wouldn't come close. When I go out with my girlfriends I hear Susan whine about
30 John's business trips, and I have to stop myself from shouting that his $350,000 salary must make up for some of his absences. Or Trisha: she inherited a house from her parents, which means that although her husband is on a normal salary, she doesn't have to work, and spends her time at the gym. Bill tells our girls that they can achieve anything and I
35 agree, but when they start dating, I'll try to guide them (behind his back) toward men who can give them the kind of life I've never had.

Feminism's fine, but there's a lot to be said for having your bills paid.

Glossary
principal /ˈprɪnsəpl/ the director of a school
chief surgeon /tʃif ˈsɜrdʒən/ a surgeon of the highest rank in a hospital

c Read the text again and then discuss the following with a partner:

1 how and why the woman's opinion of her husband's attitude to money changed over the years.

2 what is it about her friends that makes her feel so envious.

3 how she plans to "guide" her own daughters.

LEXIS IN CONTEXT

d With a partner, say in your own words what the woman means by these idioms and phrases.

1 rely on their husbands as the breadwinners (l.5)
2 put a strain on space and finances (l.8)
3 **IDM** to bite my tongue (l.9)
4 **PHR V** go for an assistant principal position (l.16)
5 reaching their teens (l.17)
6 **IDM** green with envy (l.23)
7 he wouldn't come close (l.28)
8 whine about (l.29)
9 **PHR V** make up for some of his absences (l.31)
10 **IDM** behind his back (l.35)
11 there's a lot to be said for (l.37)

e Which of these sentences best sums up your reaction to the woman's confession?

"She's refreshingly honest!"

"I'd hate to be married to her. I pity her poor husband (and her daughters)."

"It's depressing that a woman can think like this in the 21st century."

"She's only saying what a lot of women think but don't dare say."

"It's a little over the top, but she has a point."

"She's unbelievably materialistic."

5 ⟨3·9⟩⟩ **SONG** *Material Girl* ♫

6 GRAMMAR

unreal uses of past tenses

a Look at the highlighted verbs in these sentences. Which ones are really about the past? What time do the others refer to?

1 When Bill and I got married, his attitude toward money amused me.

2 If Bill got promoted, our standard of living would go up.

3 I wish we were better off.

4 I was so jealous when I heard about Carol's weekend in New York.

5 I think it's time we thought about moving to a bigger house.

6 I'd rather my daughters married a man with money.

7 I wish I'd married my first boyfriend!

8 If I'd married Sean, I would have a much better standard of living.

b ➤ p.147 Grammar Bank 5B. Learn more about unreal uses of past tenses, and practice them.

c Make questions to ask a partner.

Do you ever wish...?

- you could meet a wealthy significant other
- you had been born in another decade or century
- you could have a year off to travel
- you could learn a new skill
- you had a boring but high-paying job or a stimulating but low-paying job
- you had chosen to study different subjects at school / college
- you had more free time for your hobbies
- you lived in another town or city
- you had bitten your tongue and not said something
- you were self-employed or you worked for someone else

7 LISTENING

a You are going to listen to a lecture given by Michael Norton, Assistant Professor in the Marketing unit at Harvard Business School, who has recently been researching the relationship between money and happiness. Before you listen, what do you think his conclusion will be? Choose from a–c.

Having more money than they had before…

a never makes people happier, regardless of what they do with it.

b can make people happier if they spend some of it on other people.

c always makes people happier even if the amount of extra money is small.

b (3 10)》 Read the glossary. Then listen to the first part of the lecture. Did you predict correctly?

c Listen again and answer the questions.

1 What is the paradox that puzzled Norton?

2 What did he and his colleagues think the reason for this was?

3 What did the research show?

> **Glossary**
>
> **the University of British Columbia** one of the top Canadian universities
>
> **domain** /doʊˈmeɪn/ area, field
>
> **field study** research or study that is done in the real world rather than in a library or laboratory
>
> **Boston** a university city on the east coast of the US
>
> **profit-sharing bonus** an extra payment made to workers when the company has made a profit

d (3 11)》 Now listen to the rest of the lecture and choose the correct answer.

1 The research into prosocial spending done with employees in Boston showed that the important factor was…

a the size of the bonus they received.

(b) the percentage of the bonus that they spent on others.

c the total amount of money that they spent on others.

2 The second study showed that _____ will affect your happiness.

(a) even spending a small amount on others

b only spending a large amount on others

c only regularly spending money on others

3 Previous research showed that people become happier when they…

a get at least a ten percent raise in their salary.

b are rich and then become extremely rich.

(c) have very little money and then become reasonably well off.

4 Norton and his researchers also wanted to test whether knowing in advance about prosocial spending _____ the effect on people's happiness.

a would minimize

(b) would eliminate

c would increase

5 The research showed that this knowledge _____ the positive effect of prosocial spending.

(a) did not reduce

b greatly reduced

c slightly reduced

e Are you convinced by the results of Norton's research? Why (not)?

1 ◼◼ VIDEO THE INTERVIEW Part 1

a Read the biographical information about Sarita Gupta. Who exactly does Women's World Banking try to help, and how?

Sarita Gupta is an executive with more than 25 years' experience in promoting awareness and raising funds for international non-profit organizations. She's worked for different initiatives that tackle poverty around the world. From 2007 to 2010, she was the Vice President of Development and Communications at Women's World Banking. The mission of the Women's World Banking is to strengthen and expand its global network of microfinance institutions and banks to help support low-income women access financial services and information. The organization believes that with the right tools, women can overcome poverty by building assets and protection in times of economic stress.

b ③12))) Watch or listen to Part 1 of an interview with her. Mark sentences 1-5 below **T** (true) or **F** (false).

1 The idea behind Women's World Banking originated in 1975 at a United Nations meeting in Mexico.

2 The members at the meeting decided to focus on a number of issues such as education and domestic violence.

3 Muhammad Yunus is credited for pioneering the concept of microfinance.

4 One of Dr. Yunus's innovations was creating a system where the poor would pay back their loans in lump sums.

5 The incentive system encourages the poor to borrow small amounts that they can successfully pay back.

c Now listen again and say why the **F** sentences are false.

Glossary

microfinance /'maɪkroʊfaɪnæns/ *noun* the provision of financial services to low-income clients, to help poor people out of poverty

Muhammad Yunus Bangladeshi developer of the microcredit movement, and winner of the 2006 Nobel Peace prize

collateral /kə'lætərəl/ *noun* property or sth valuable that you promise to give to sb if you cannot pay back money that you borrow

peer /pɪr/ *noun* a person who has the same social status as you

◼◼ VIDEO Part 2

a ③13))) Watch or listen to part 2. Make notes for each case study about:

The country the woman lived in
The situation she was in
The business she set up

b Answer the questions with a partner.

1 Sarita mentions how the several decades of "the Western World" giving massive aid to developing nations was not working. Why do you think it wasn't effective?

2 To what extent do you think microfinance would be useful in your country?

3 What obstacles might local people face with the Dr. Yunus's innovations?

Glossary

the DR the Dominican Republic

cantina /kæn'tinə/ noun Spanish for a cafeteria or kitchen

embroider /ɪm'brɔɪdər/ *verb* to decorate cloth with a pattern of stitches usually using colored thread

middleman /'mɪdlmæn/ *noun* a person or a company that buys goods from the company that makes them and sells them to somebody else

2 LOOKING AT LANGUAGE

> 🔍 **Restating information**
> Sarita Gupta often restates information in a slightly different way to make her point clear. This can useful for clarifying complicated technical information and making it comprehensible.

a ▶ **3 14**)) Listen to some extracts from the interview and complete the phrases.

1 So if we could only discuss one issue, sort of ___focus on 1 issue___, put all our energies behind it, what would that be…

2 "What is it that ___the poor lack___? What is it that they need?"

3 And the third was really an incentive system, that the poor _____, they only borrowed what they could use in their business and then pay back…

4 …and what she did was to start out, _____ from her kitchen, making excess food and selling it to the factory workers…

5 …and this is going to ensure income in her old age, because at some point she's going to be too old to work in the kitchen and to be, you know, standing on her feet behind the cantina counter and she's looking at these rental rooms that she has been able to put on as her, _____.

6 …and what she really wanted to do was to amass enough income so that she would cut out the middle man, because she basically _____, because she was handing it over to a middle man.

3 📹 VIDEO ON THE STREET

a **3 15**)) You are going to hear five people talking about money. What three questions do they answer? Do the majority of speakers consider themselves good or bad with money?

1	2	3	4	5
Andrew	James	Nazia	Jerry	Katie

b Listen again. Who…?

1 ☐ gives both arguments for women being better managers of money than men
2 ☐ gives a specific example of how men and women spend money in different ways
3 ☐ is still financially dependent on their parents
4 ☐ confesses to being extravagant on one thing
5 ☐ has met people from genders who were both good and bad with money

c **3 16**)) Listen and complete the phrases with one to three words. What do you think they mean?

> **Useful phrases**
> 1 I've been kind of on a _____ of buying T-shirts.
> 2 I just found out recently that I have a really _____ _____ _____, one of the highest you can get.
> 3 …they spend most of the time shopping and _____ _____ with friends.
> 4 I try to make sure my savings get a _____ _____ of interest.
> 5 I never _____ _____ of cash.

4 SPEAKING

Answer the questions with a partner. Practice restating information to clarify how you feel about what you are saying, and where possible the useful phrases.

1 Do you think women are better at managing money than men? Why (not)?
2 Would having more money would make you happier? Why (not)?
3 What characteristics do people need to be good at managing money?
4 Do you think it's a good idea to give money to good causes / charities?
5 Are limits to the things money can buy?

G verb + object + infinitive or gerund
V compound adjectives
P intonation in polite requests

> A kleptomaniac is a person who helps himself because he can't help himself.
>
> *Henry Morgan,*
> *American humorist*

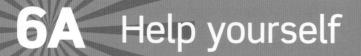

6A Help yourself

1 READING & SPEAKING

a What do you understand by the term "self-help book"? Can you think of any which have been best sellers in your country?

b Look at the front cover of a recent self-help book, and read the description from the back cover below. Answer the questions with a partner.

1 Who is this book written for and how would it help the reader?
2 Can you guess the answers to the two questions at the beginning?
3 Does this description make you want to read the book? Why or why not?

YES!

50 secrets from the science of persuasion

Small changes can make a big difference in your powers of persuasion.

- What one word can you start using today to increase your persuasiveness by more than fifty percent?
- Why can asking for less often result in more?

Every day we face the challenge of persuading others to do what we want. But what makes people say yes to our requests? Persuasion is not only an art, it is also a science, and researchers who study it have uncovered a series of hidden rules for moving people in your direction. Based on more than sixty years of research into the psychology of persuasion, *Yes!* reveals fifty simple but remarkably effective strategies that will make you much more persuasive at work and in your personal life, too.

Co-written by the world's most quoted expert on influence, Professor Robert Cialdini, *Yes!* presents dozens of surprising discoveries from the science of persuasion in short, enjoyable, and insightful chapters that you can apply immediately to become a more effective persuader.

Often counterintuitive, the findings presented in *Yes!* will steer you away from common pitfalls while empowering you with little known but proven wisdom.

Whether you are in advertising, marketing, management, or sales, or just curious about how to be more influential in everyday life, *Yes!* shows how making small, scientifically proven changes to your approach can have a dramatic effect on your persuasive powers.

---

c Work in pairs **A** and **B**. Each read a different extract from the book to find the following information.
What is the technique suggested?
What experiment(s) were done to prove that it worked?

d Tell your partner in your own words about the technique and the research.

A single word will help your persuasion.

Let's think about waiting in line. Whether you're at a bank, a supermarket, or an amusement park, waiting in line is probably not your idea of fun. Under what circumstances would you be willing to let another person cut in front of you? Is it possible that just a single word from a requester could drastically increase the likelihood that you'd say, "Yes, go ahead?"

Yes, and the word is *because*. Behavioral scientist Ellen Langer and her colleagues decided to put the persuasive power of this word to the test. In one study, she arranged for a stranger to approach someone waiting to use a photocopier and ask, "Excuse me. I just have five pages. May I use the machine?" In this situation, 60 percent of the people agreed to allow the stranger to go ahead of them. However, when the stranger followed the request with a reason ("because I'm in a rush") almost everyone (94 percent of the people) complied. Then Langer repeated the experiment. This time the stranger also used the word *because*, but followed it with a completely meaningless reason ("because I have to make copies"). Even with this meaningless reason, 93 percent agreed to let the stranger go first.

This study demonstrates the unique motivational influence of the word *because*.

Of course like most things, the power of *because* has its limits. In the previous study the request was small — five copies. Langer repeated the experiment, but told the person to ask to make 20 copies. This time, when the stranger did <u>not</u> use the word *because*, only 24 percent agreed, and when the meaningless reason was added, this produced no increase in compliance at all. However, when the request was made with a good reason, 50 percent of the people asked agreed.

These findings serve as a reminder to always be sure to accompany your request with a rationale, even when you think the reasons might be pretty clear. Too often we mistakenly assume that other people understand the reasons behind our requests. Rather than telling your children to "come to the table for dinner now" or "go to bed immediately," a more effective strategy would be to provide a reason why you are asking them to take that action — and not just "because I said so."

e Discuss with a partner:
- What did you think of the two strategies? Do you think they would work on you?
- Do you think they would help you in situations where you need to persuade someone to do something?

B
Asking for a little can go a long way.

Throughout this book we've attempted to provide evidence to support our claims that we can successfully and ethically move people to say yes. But in certain situations and environments it's also important to understand why people say no to reasonable requests, such as a request to donate to a legitimate charity.

Along with several colleagues, one of us set out to do just that. We thought that, when asked to make a donation, even those who would like to support the charity in some way say no, because they can't afford to donate very much, and they assume that the small amount that they can afford wouldn't do much to help the cause. Based on this reasoning, we thought that one way to urge people to donate in such a situation would be to inform them that even an extremely small sum would be helpful.

To test this hypothesis our research assistants went door to door to request donations for the American Cancer Society. After introducing themselves, they asked the residents, "Would you be willing to help by giving a donation?" For half the residents the request ended there. For the other half, however, the research assistant added "Even a penny will help."

When we analyzed the results we found that, consistent with our hypothesis, people in the "even a penny will help" half of the sample were almost twice as likely to donate to the cause. And the amount the individuals gave was also found to be more or less the same in both halves, so the people in the "even a penny" half did not donate less.

The study suggests that if you want somebody to do something for you, simply pointing out that even a little assistance on their part would be acceptable is likely to be an effective strategy. Applications in the workplace might be: to a co-worker regarding a joint project, "Just an hour of your time would really help;" to a co-worker whose handwriting is illegible, "Just a little more clarity would help." The chances are that this little step in the right direction won't prove so little after all.

From *Yes! 50 secrets from the science of persuasion* by Noah J. Goldstein, Steve J. Martin, and Robert B. Cialdini

2 GRAMMAR
verb + object + infinitive or gerund

a Right (✓) or wrong (✗)? With a partner, correct any mistakes in the highlighted phrases.

1 The man with *Spare Change News* was trying to persuade people to buy his newspaper.
2 When I was a child I was often made do the dishes.
3 I want that you finish these exercises in five minutes.
4 I'll meet you there at 7:00 — and please don't keep me waiting!
5 Do you think you could let me have the reports before the end of the week?
6 I don't mind you not finish everything, but at least eat your vegetables!
7 I suggest you taking the 7:30 train — it'll be less stressful than trying to catch the earlier one.
8 He convinced Elisa to join us for dinner.
9 My father recommended that we should go to the museum before lunch, when it's less crowded.
10 The job involves me to travel abroad at least twice a month.

b ➤ p.148 Grammar Bank 6A. Learn more about verb + object + infinitive or gerund, and practice it.

3 PRONUNCIATION
intonation in polite requests

a **3 17**)) Listen and write down six requests.
1 _____? It's a little stuffy in here.
2 To Penn Station. _____?
3 _____? I need someone to help me with this report.
4 If you're going to the cafeteria, _____?
5 _____, and not this one?
6 _____? My car's in the shop.

b **3 18**)) Now listen to the same requests said twice. Which of the two do you think sounds the most polite? Why? How does the other one sound?
1 a b   2 a b   3 a b
4 a b   5 a b   6 a b

c **3 19**)) Listen to the polite requests again and repeat, copying the intonation.

d Think of something you would really like someone to do for you, e.g., give you a ride home, take care of a pet for the weekend, lend you some money, go somewhere with you, etc. Ask other students, and see if you can find three people who are prepared to help you. Try to be as persuasive as possible. Remember the advice you read in the extract from *Yes!* and use polite intonation.

4 LISTENING & SPEAKING

a Look at the covers of four more self-help books. Which of the four, if any, might you be tempted to buy? Which one would you definitely not buy?

b Now read an extract from each book. Was it more or less what you expected from the cover? Why (not)?

A **The Bluffer's Guide to** (Psychology)

Whenever there is an obvious flaw in your argument that is apparent to everyone around you, don't be fazed. Instead, say with great self-assurance that this is not a flaw at all but the operation of another important psychological process of which you were already fully aware. In fact, you have been researching it. Here is where your powers of imagination come into play. Make up a phrase to label it, which will always begin with "The" and end with "Effect." The middle is up to you, and the more obscure and ponderous, the better. "The Indirect McCollough Effect" is a real example, and "The Coaxial Reverse Bunion Effect" isn't. But no one will know the difference.

B **Neris and India's Idiot-Proof Diet** *How we lost ten stone*

We can be massively depressed or microscopically annoyed by something completely trivial, but if we associate food with comfort, we'll eat. We both ate when our children weren't feeling well, and we both ate when the plumber had failed to turn up. We ate because it was raining. We ate because we'd had a tiny argument with our husbands. We ate because we'd stubbed our toe, or because somebody was in the hospital. The gravity or otherwise of the situation had nothing to do with it. We ate because, for whatever reason, we felt sad.

C **THE RULES FOR MARRIAGE** Time-tested Secrets for Making Your Marriage Work ELLEN FEIN AND SHERRIE SCHNEIDER

We believe once you get engaged a wedding date should be set — no endless engagements. When a man proposes, it should be with a ring and a wedding date within one year, not longer, unless you are young (under twenty-five years old) in which case a two-year engagement is fine. If your fiancé is stalling on a wedding date, you may have to give him back the ring and move on.

D **I CAN MAKE YOU RICH** FOREWORD BY RICHARD BRANSON PAUL McKENNA INCLUDES FREE HYPNOSIS CD

1 Imagine that it's five years from today, and your life is filled with the most wonderful things imaginable. Your life is truly rich in every way! Write a paragraph or two about what has happened in each of the following areas:
   Health Career / Finances Relationships Spirituality Lifestyle

2 Go back to each paragraph you've written and circle, underline, or highlight each key goal or milestone that emerged.

3 Now, for each of the major goals or milestones, ask yourself "What do I want this for? What will having this give me?" Your answers should be just a few words long — things like "a feeling of joy," "a sense of achievement," "freedom," or "making a contribution."

c (3 20)) Now listen to a radio program in which people discuss these self-help books. How many of the books did they find helpful?

d Listen again and match the books (A–D) to the statements.

1 It is packaged with supplementary material. ☐
2 It was not the first book of this kind that the reviewer had read. ☐
3 It will help the reviewer socially. ☐
4 The reviewer may try out things recommended by the book. ☐
5 The reviewer chose it because of a recent event in their personal life. ☐
6 The reviewer intends to read more about the subject. ☐
7 The book is very one-sided. ☐
8 The book promises to help you by changing the way you think. ☐

BOOKSHOP

"No, I *won't* show you where the self-help books are."

www.CartoonStock.com

LEXIS IN CONTEXT

e **(3 21))** Look at some extracts from the listening which all include modifiers. Listen and complete the phrases with between two and four words. What do they mean?

1 Well, I have _____ friends who are into psychology...

2 ...I see myself as _____ expert on diet books.

3 According to this book, making a marriage work is _____ the wife.

4 The husband doesn't have to _____.

5 The wife just has to try to be exactly what her husband wants her to be, and then everything will be _____.

f Does what the speakers said change your mind about reading one of the books?

g Look at a list of some typical self-help topics. Have you used any books, DVDs, magazines, or websites related to any of these areas? Did you find them helpful?

childcare

health, nutrition, and diets

fitness

personality and relationships

men and women

astrology

business, money, and economics

DIY and home improvements

food and cooking

improving your appearance

improving memory

study tips

www.CartoonStock.com

5 (3 22)) **SONG** *Never Say Never* ♫

6 VOCABULARY compound adjectives

> 🔍 **Compound adjectives**
>
> A compound adjective is an adjective made up of two parts. It is usually written with a hyphen before a noun, e.g., *a self-help book, a bad-tempered person, a well-off person, a one-sided article.*
>
> The second word in compound adjectives is often a past participle.

a Combine words from each circle to make ten compound adjectives to complete questions 1–10.

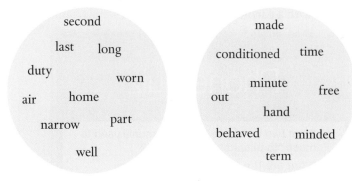

1 Have you ever bought a _____ car or motorcycle? Did you have any problems with it?

2 Do you think it's possible for people to maintain a _____ relationship if they are living in different towns or countries?

3 Do you usually do a lot of _____ reviewing the night before a test?

4 Do you sometimes buy things in the _____ shop when you travel by plane? What kinds of things do you buy?

5 Do you have any old clothes that you still like wearing even though they are a little _____?

6 Do you prefer _____ food to restaurant meals? Why (not)?

7 In the summer do you spend much time in _____ buildings or cars? Do you consider it a necessity or a luxury?

8 Would you like to have a _____ job, i.e., only work a few hours a day? Why (not)?

9 Do you think as people get older they tend to get more _____ and intolerant?

10 Do you think children should be asked to leave restaurants if they are not reasonably _____?

b Ask and answer the questions with a partner.

c Now combine words to make ten more compound adjectives. Write three questions to ask a partner using some of the adjectives.

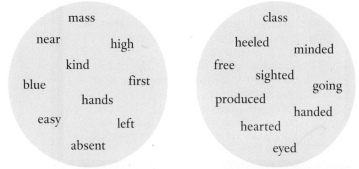

G conditional sentences
V phone language; adjectives + prepositions
P sounds and spelling: /ʃ/, /tʃ/, /ʒ/, /dʒ/

> Every form of addiction is bad, no matter whether the narcotic be alcohol, morphine, or idealism.
>
> *Carl Jung, Swiss psychologist*

6B Can't live without it

1 VOCABULARY & LISTENING

a How good is your "phone vocabulary"? Take the quiz with a partner.

Phone quiz

1 What two verbs are most commonly used to mean "to telephone" somebody?

2 What are the missing verbs in these phrases?
a Can you _____ me a **call** this afternoon?
b I need to _____ a few **calls** now. I'll get back to you later.

3 What's the missing word in these phrasal verbs?
a Sorry, I have to **hang** _____ now. I'm in a hurry.
b I'm going to have to _____ my phone **off** now — my flight's boarding.
c We were suddenly **cut** _____ in the middle of a conversation.
d I never have to **write** _____ phone numbers because I use an app to transfer and store contacts.
e I'm **running** _____ **of** minutes on my cell phone plan, so I don't know how long we can keep on talking.
f I tried calling her office all day but I couldn't **get** _____. The lines were busy.
g Sorry, I can't hear you very well. Could you _____ **up** a little?
h If you hold, I'll _____ you **through** to the accounts department.

4 Complete the missing words.
a I need to **c**_____ my phone — the battery's very low.
b Do you want my cell phone number or my **l**_____?
c I've been calling Tom on his cell phone, but it's **b**_____ all the time.
d I know he's been trying to call me all day because I have three **m**_____ calls from him.
e If you don't know the number, call **d**_____ assistance.
f You have reached the **v**_____ **m**_____ for 555-4890. Please leave a message when you hear the tone.
g There are usually **p**_____ **p**_____ in public places such as airports and stations for people who don't have or can't use a cell phone for some reason.

b How would not having a cell phone or smartphone affect your life? Read the article. What is the writer's experiment? What do you think he means by "cold turkey"?

Has our cell phone use gone a little too far?

Could you survive one whole week without your cell/smartphone? That's right, no iPhone®, no Blackberry®, no Android™? Believe it or not, I tried this. Yes I am still alive.

I know what some of you may be wondering: why in the world would anyone want to be without a cell phone for an entire week? After all, in the span of only a few years, smartphones have become part of us. We can hardly live without them. According to a recent study, about a third of smartphone users check their phones before getting out of bed in the morning. 40 percent of us use them in the bathroom. And 64 percent of us have texted while driving. We use them as cameras, appointment books, alarm clocks, and to make the odd phone call (although increasingly less frequently).

I can't help wondering if we've gone a little too far.

One day I came home from work around 6:00 p.m. and sat down to dinner with my wife and two kids (five-year-old twins. Yes, twins are cute, thank you). I started noticing that during dinner both my wife and I were checking our phones fairly regularly.

The more I thought about it the more I was, frankly, disappointed in myself. I get home from work at 6:00 and my kids go to sleep at 7:30. That's an hour and a half. Can I really not try and focus my attention on my family for 90 minutes without being distracted?

Now I suppose I could have tried to gradually decrease my cell phone use at home, but that would have been too easy. Instead, I wondered if I could go a whole week with absolutely no cell phone. Cold turkey.

We were going away for a family vacation for a week and I thought that this provided the right opportunity. So we left for the airport with both cell phones back at home. I really hoped they would be OK by themselves.

By Richard Rabkin

One-Week
NO CELL PHONE
Challenge

c (3 23)) Listen to Richard describing his week without a cell phone. Look at the sentences below and put a check (✓) next to the things that happened.

- ☐ He started to miss his cell phone at the airport.
- ☐ It felt as if his leg was vibrating even without a cell phone in his pocket.
- ☐ He couldn't find his wife when they got separated at the mall.
- ☐ He and his wife couldn't locate their car at the mall without a phone.
- ☐ They tried to search for a restaurant they'd heard about.
- ☐ They didn't know how to find the restaurant they wanted and went home instead.

d Listen again for more detail about what happened during the week. Compare with a partner and retell the events that Richard describes.

e (3 24)) Now listen to what Richard says about the advantages of the no cell phone challenge. What two incidents does he describe? What decisions did he and his wife make after returning home?

f If you had done the same experiment as the writer, do you think you would have come to the same conclusion?

> **Glossary**
> **Play-Doh®** a soft clay-like material that children use for making models or shapes

2 PRONUNCIATION sounds and spelling:
/ʃ/, /tʃ/, /ʒ/, /dʒ/

a Look at the words below from **Vocabulary & Listening**. Decide what sounds the pink letters make, and write the words in the right column.

addiction   anxious   arrangement   attachment   century
conclusion   condition   crucial   decision   engaged   future
journalist   message   obsession   occasion   officially
pleasure   pressure   surgery   switched   technician

/ʃ/	/tʃ/	/ʒ/	/dʒ/
addiction anxious condition crucial pressure technician	attachment century future switched	concision decision occasion pleasure	arrangement engaged journalist message surgery

b (3 25)) Listen and check. Practice saying the words.

c Now practice saying these sentences.
1 Addictions and obsessions can make you anxious.
2 We need to make some crucial decisions in the near future.
3 It's a pleasure to attend this social occasion.
4 The journalist sent a message to make arrangements.

3 GRAMMAR conditional sentences

a Match the halves of the conditional sentences.

1 If I'd had my phone with me,
2 If my phone wasn't so new,
3 If I didn't have a landline,
4 If my phone numbers weren't all in my phone,
5 If I hadn't called you,

- ☐ A you wouldn't have known what to do.
- ☐ B I wouldn't be able to have broadband.
- ☐ C I'd have texted you to say where I was.
- ☐ D I might actually remember some of them.
- ☐ E I wouldn't have bothered to get it repaired.

b Which sentences refer to present or future situations and which ones refer to the past? What is different about sentence 2?

c ▶ p.149 Grammar Bank 6B. Learn more about conditional sentences, and practice them.

d In groups of three or four, discuss the questions.
- What gadgets do you use that you wouldn't be able to live without?
- Supposing the Internet hadn't been invented, to what extent would it affect the way you work / study / use your free time?
- If you could go back in time, is there anything you would change about your career / studies?
- Would you be prepared to go and work or study in another country even if you didn't speak the language at all?
- What language would you have chosen to study if you hadn't had to learn English?

4 READING

a Other than cell phones, what other gadgets or activities do you think people are addicted to or obsessed with in the 21st century?

b Read the article once. What exactly are "behavioral addictions"? In what way are they different from what most people think of as addictions? How can they be treated?

Are we hooked on addiction?

The word "addict" for most people conjures up images of substance abuse. But today there is a new breed of addicts...

Dr. MARK COLLINS is the head of the addictions unit at an expensive clinic. "Over the last 18 months we have noticed a big rise in the number of behavioral addictions, so-called to distinguish them from substance dependencies," he says. "People look down on people addicted to substances but then go and spend five hours in an Internet chat room," says Collins. Behavioral addictions include compulsive attachments to plastic surgery, the Internet, cell phones, and even tanning beds.

It seems that in our fast-paced, high-pressure modern life, we are increasingly turning to comfort behavior, activities that temporarily make us feel happier, less stressed and lonely. And experts warn that these are the very things that can lead us into dependency no matter how harmless they may seem at first. And while behavioral addictions may sound less serious than being hooked on alcohol or drugs, according to experts, their potential for destroying lives may actually be very similar. They can lead to obsession, debt, and the breakdown of relationships.

Internet addiction

Caroline Harrison, 37, a full-time mother of three, admits to compulsively using the Internet. "I was surfing, looking for something about my youngest child's skin problem when I found this amazing parenting website with lively message boards," she says. "Soon I found I couldn't go a day without logging on. I started spending all evening "chatting" with my new online friends instead of spending time with my husband. It never crossed my mind that it could be addictive. But now I feel edgy and tense if I can't access my computer. It's as if I can't help myself. The people there seem more real and supportive than my own family and friends. I often feel depressed and lonely in real life because my husband works long hours, so being on the site makes me feel good. Well, temporarily good."

Tanning obsession

Even more worrying is the behavior of 14-year-old Tracey Barlow, who is now seeking treatment for her addiction to tanning. The teenager has been visiting tanning salons three times a week, and at one stage was having tanning sessions five days a week. Her skin is already prematurely aged, and she has been warned that she risks getting skin cancer, but despite being warned about the risks she says she feels overwhelmingly anxious if she perceives her tan to be fading. "It's like a sickness with her," says her despairing mother. "She hates being pale."

Shopaholic

For 26-year-old sales manager Emily Lane, it was her love of shopping that got dangerously out of hand. Her compulsive spending on designer clothes, shoes, and handbags left her over $40,000 in debt and destroyed her relationship with her boyfriend, James. She admits that many of the items she bought remain unused, but that she found it impossible to stop spending. "Coming home with armfuls of bags gave me an enormous high, and I needed to keep on buying more clothes, shoes, and accessories to keep getting it. I would shop during my lunch hour, after work, and on weekends, but I couldn't see that I had a problem until James broke up with me over it."

Dr. ROBERT LEFEVER, of the Promis Recovery Center, who has himself overcome an addiction to work, explains, "Deep down sufferers are usually depressed. In that state you can get hooked on anything that changes the way you feel, and even if you try to stop the behavior, you will find it extremely hard, at least without becoming bad-tempered or anxious."

Dr. Lefever believes that compulsive behavior often manifests itself in clusters. There is, for example, the "eating disorder cluster," which also includes shopping and spending, work, cosmetic surgery, and exercise, and the "relationship cluster" which includes compulsive helping of others, and addiction to love and being in love. "If you are addicted to one thing in the cluster, you are at risk of becoming addicted to the others," he says.

Whatever your age, Lefever believes that if you have a serious compulsive problem that is interfering with your life, then the most effective treatment is a stay in a clinic, or therapy with a psychologist who understands addiction. "Addiction is treatable," he says. "And I see this every day, in myself and in other people."

From the *Daily Mail*

c Read the article again. Then choose a, b, or c from the options below.

1 According to experts, behavioral addictions ___.
   a are not as serious as being addicted to substances
   b are more serious than being addicted to substances
   c can be just as serious as being addicted to substances ✓

2 Caroline Harrison says that she feels the need ___.
   a to do something about her addiction
   b to chat online every day ✓
   c to spend more time with her husband

3 Tracey Barlow ___.
   a is slightly less addicted than she used to be ✓
   b can no longer afford to pay for so many tanning sessions
   c has developed an illness as a result of her addiction

4 Emily Lane thinks that ___.
   a if she hadn't been a shopaholic, her boyfriend wouldn't have left her ✓
   b her boyfriend should have helped her overcome her addiction
   c the money she owed caused the break-up with her boyfriend

5 Dr. Lefever thinks that ___.
   a if you are addicted to coffee, you might also become addicted to shopping
   b if you have an eating disorder, you will probably become addicted to shopping
   c if you are addicted to going to the gym, you may also become addicted to having cosmetic surgery ✓

LEXIS IN CONTEXT

d Look at the highlighted words and phrases related to addictions. With a partner, decide what you think they mean.

e Do you think the addictions referred to in the article are a problem in your country?

5 VOCABULARY adjectives + prepositions

a Complete the prepositions column with one from the list.

for of on to with

                                                                prepositions

1 A lot of people are **obsessed** ☐ celebrities and their lifestyles. ___
2 Some young people are becoming **addicted** ☐ social networking websites. ___
3 People are usually very kind and **helpful** ☐ foreign tourists. ___
4 Most young people are **dependent** ☐ their parents until their mid-twenties. ___
5 People are totally **fed up** ☐ the number of commercials on TV. ___
6 Older people aren't as **open** ☐ new ideas and fashions as younger people are. ___
7 People are **sick** ☐ being bombarded with depressing news by the media. ___
8 Our country is **famous** worldwide ☐ its cuisine. ___
9 A lot of people are **hooked** ☐ Latin-American soap operas. ___
10 As a nation we are very **proud** ☐ our technological achievements. ___
11 Many people who are **fond** ☐ animals adopt pets from animal shelters. ___

b Cover the prepositions column and say the sentence with the correct preposition.

c With a partner, say to what extent the sentences are true for your country, and give examples.

6 LISTENING & SPEAKING

a **3 26**)) Listen to five people talking about obsessions. What are they or the people they mention obsessed with or addicted to?

b Listen again and answer with the number(s) of the speaker. Who…?
   ☐ A says that their obsession started as a result of a family incident
   ☐ B doesn't really think that they are obsessive
   ☐ C thinks that the obsession makes the person unpleasant to be around
   ☐ D says that the obsession started because of a family member
   ☐ E doesn't think that the obsession serves any purpose

c Talk in small groups. Try to think of someone for as many categories as possible.

Do you know anyone who is

"addicted" to…?	obsessed with…?
• a machine or gadget	• organizing / cleaning
• a particular TV series	• their appearance
• work	• keeping in shape
• shopping	• healthy eating
• anything else	• anything else

How long has it been going on?
Does it interfere with his / her life?
Does it affect the people around him / her?
Does he / she talk about it?
How serious do you think it is?
Do you think he / she should do something about it?

7 WRITING

➤ **p.110 Writing** *Discursive essay (1): a balanced argument.*
Analyze a model essay and write a discursive essay.

GRAMMAR

a Choose the best answer, a, b, or c.

1 _____ by the founder of the company at the press event that he has sold the company.
   a It is said   b It has been announced   c It is understood

2 _____ new research, eating a lot of salt may not have long-term health effects.
   a Apparently   b According to   c Considering

3 I'd _____ you didn't step in the house with your dirty shoes.
   a prefer that   b prefer it   c wish

4 I really wish we _____ that sofa — it gets dirty much too easily.
   a haven't bought   b hadn't bought   c don't buy

5 _____ had she heard such horrible insults.
   a Never   b Hardly   c No sooner

6 If only she _____ talking on the phone at work!
   a shouldn't keep   b wouldn't keep   c doesn't keep

7 I'd like _____ at about 6:00, if that's possible.
   a that they come   b them coming   c them to come

8 If we hadn't had to work late tonight, _____ the game right now.
   a I'd be watching   b I'd have watched   c I'll watch

9 I dislike people _____ in front of me in a line even if they give me a reason.
   a cut   b to cut   c cutting

10 I'll pay for the classes _____ you promise not to miss any.
   a supposing   b unless   c providing

b Put the verb in parentheses in the right form.

1 My parents always encouraged me ___to learn___ foreign languages. (learn)

2 If I hadn't read the book before I saw the movie, I think I ___would have enjoyed___ the movie more. (enjoy)

3 My new job involves me ___traveling___ to North America two or three times a year. (travel)

4 They are incredibly generous people and they wouldn't let me ___pay___ for anything. (pay)

5 Daniel can stay the night as long as he ___doesn't mind___ sleeping on the sofa. (not mind)

6 Supposing our team drew our last game, who _____ the league in that case? (win)

7 Marcus might have hurt his head badly if he _____ a helmet when he fell off his bike. (not wear)

8 We would like you _____ our annual conference this year. (attend)

9 ___If___ you ___had told___ me earlier that you were coming, I would have taken the day off. (tell)

10 The children are staying indoors today. I don't want to risk them _____ a cold just before our vacation. (catch)

11 If my husband hadn't inherited a lot of money, we definitely _____ in a house like this now. (not live)

12 It's impossible to imagine how beautiful the Taj Mahal is unless you _____ it with your own eyes. (see)

VOCABULARY

a Complete the missing words.

1 We thought we were going to be late, but we arrived with plenty of time to s_____.

2 I just got out of a relationship and lost my job. I just can't c_____ with it all.

3 Addictions may seem h_____, but they can have serious health and financial risks.

4 She wasn't answering her cell phone so I left a message on her v_____ m_____.

5 My father-in-law is rather intolerant and narrow-m_____.

6 We can call directory a_____ and get the number of the restaurant.

7 I'm getting a little near-s_____. I think I need glasses.

8 Jane gets all her vintage clothes from a second-h_____ store.

9 You'd better throw those jeans away. They're completely w_____ out.

10 Lara spent her paycheck on a handbag and she's completely b_____.

11 The s_____ of living is higher in New York City than it is in Phuket.

b Complete the phrasal verbs.

1 I was on the phone with my sister when we suddenly got **cut** _____ and her line went dead.

2 I tried to call Bill at the office, but I couldn't _____ **through**. All the lines were busy.

3 You'll have to **speak** _____ a little. My grandmother is very deaf.

4 I'm only the receptionist. Please hold and I'll _____ you **through** to Mr. Richardson.

5 I've **run** _____ **of** minutes on my cell phone.

6 Gina got so angry with me on the phone last night that she **hung** _____ on me.

c Complete with a preposition.

1 I'm so proud _____ you. I never thought you would pass.

2 Luke is nearly 30, but he's still dependent _____ his parents.

3 I'm completely fed up _____ my job. I dread going to work every morning.

4 My sister is totally hooked _____ that new reality show on TV.

5 We're going to drive to Mexico City, since my wife isn't very fond _____ flying.

CAN YOU UNDERSTAND THIS TEXT?

a   Read the article once. Do you wear a wristwatch? Would you like to have a watch like the ones described in the text?

b   Read the article again. Then mark the sentences **T** (true) or **F** (false).

1   Wearing a wristwatch became less common when cell phones and smartphones started gaining popularity.

2   Older people wear wristwatches more than younger people.

3   Watches were first made in the 1880s.

4   The first watches were worn on the wrist.

5   Most people wore wristwatches for most of the 20th century.

6   Newer smart watches do much more than tell the time.

7   You can take a video with the new smart watches.

8   You still need a phone to talk; no wristwatch allows users to do that yet.

9   The writer thinks newer wristwatches have some advantages over smart phones.

10   The writer believes that smart wristwatches are too expensive for most people to afford.

c   Choose five new words or phrases from the text. Check their meaning and pronunciation and try to learn them.

CAN YOU UNDERSTAND THIS INTERVIEW?

a   Where do you see or hear advertisements to buy products? Which ones persuade you to buy something?

b   **3 27)))** Listen to Sam Pocker, author of the book *Retail Anarchy*, talking about products that are sold to consumers. Then put a check (✓) next to the things he says.

☐ When the economy is bad, people go shopping less.

☐ Even when they have less money to spend, people want to buy things they don't need.

☐ Companies are not so interested in making quality products anymore.

☐ People are often unaware of marketing tactics that get them to spend their money.

☐ He admires successful ideas like Freeze-and-Eat Fruit Tubes and Lobster Fest.

☐ Some discount airlines offer a good value.

☐ Companies need to focus more on marketing their products effectively.

c   Can you think of any silly or useless products that are marketed successfully? Why do people want to buy them?

The wristwatch will rise again

Conventional wisdom says people don't wear wristwatches anymore — especially young people. The story goes that because we now have cell phones, we no longer need to put anything on our wrists. But wristwatches have been coming in and out of fashion for centuries — a trend driven by technology. And now, technology is bringing the wristwatch back to an arm near you.

Why people think the wristwatch is dead

High school and college students don't wear wristwatches anymore, at least not the kind that merely tell the time. In fact, young people don't even recognize the pointing-to-the-wrist gesture as having anything to do with time, as sign language for "what time is it?" Because young people grew up with cell phones as timepieces rather than wristwatches, they don't associate the wrist with the time.

But all these naked wrists are part of a back-and-forth cycle rather than a one-way trend leading to the end of the wristwatch.

The watch wars

The watch was arguably the world's first mobile consumer gadget when it arrived in the 16th century. The first watches were worn around the neck or attached to clothing, because they were too large for pockets — or wrists. In the 1880s the first wristwatches were used by the German navy, and from then until the present day the use of wristwatches by sailors and soldiers has been constant.

The wristwatch formed a standard part of the wardrobes of both men and women from the 1930s until around 2000. But then, cell phones — and later smartphones — became universal, and wristwatches began losing ground.

Why the wristwatch will rise again

Using a cell phone to tell the time isn't ideal. For example, you can't check the time during a movie without annoying others. And although you can use a smart phone to measure your speed and distance while jogging, you have to leave it behind when swimming.

Now, just in time (pun intended!), here come smart wristwatches. In the era of being connected, watches are no longer limited to just telling the time. All kinds of stuff is being crammed into new smart wristwatches. There are now cell phone wristwatches, HD video camera wristwatches, and watches with a constant Bluetooth® connection to your smartphone. In fact, some smart watches can sync with most of your electronic devices. And all of these wristwatches are becoming more and more mainstream as they get better and cheaper.

Wearing a big-brand device on your wrist is the Next Big Thing in consumer electronics. And why not? The wrist is a great place to put a gadget.

G permission, obligation, and necessity
V word formation: prefixes
P intonation in exclamations

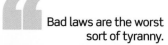

Bad laws are the worst
sort of tyranny.

*Edmund Burke, Irish writer
and philosopher*

7A Who's in control?

1 READING & SPEAKING

a Read the encyclopedia entry for the expression "nanny state." With a partner, summarize in one sentence what the expression means.

Nanny state

In general, this expression is used in reference to policies where the state is characterized as being excessive in its desire to protect ("nanny"), govern, or control particular aspects of society or groups of people. Policies such as mandatory helmet laws, high taxes on junk food, bans on large sodas and sugary drinks, gun control, political correctness, and censorship, are often criticized as "nanny state" actions. Such actions result from the belief that the state (or, more often, one of its local authorities) has a duty to protect citizens from their own harmful behavior, and assumes that the state knows best what constitutes harmful behavior.

b Now look at the title of the article below. What do you think it will be about?

c Read the article and mark the sentences below **T** (true), **F** (false), or **DS** (doesn't say).

1 The use of trans-fats is limited in New York restaurants.
2 When you're crossing the street in Fort Lee, New Jersey, it's illegal to talk on a cell phone.
3 Kids in Tennessee are not allowed to wear jeans.
4 Children's toys are banned in fast-food meals in San Francisco.
5 In Kansas, noise from tires is restricted.
6 In Hilton Head, South Carolina, you are not allowed to keep trash in your car.
7 You are not permitted to swear when you are in a car in Rockville, Maryland.
8 The US government limits the amount of salt and sugar in packaged foods.

Is the Nanny State out of Control?

Want to buy a greasy donut in New York, wear your jeans low in Tennessee, use foul language in Maryland, or keep trash in your car in South Carolina? You'd better think twice, because some of these things might be against the law. Local politicians in
5 different parts of the United States have been proposing laws described as enhancing the "Nanny State," leaving many to wonder whether the government is going too far and interfering too much with individual choice.

Former New York Mayor Michael Bloomberg stood out for his
10 attempts to control the diets of New Yorkers. As mayor, he called for fast-food restaurants to include calorie information on menu boards and banned the use of trans-fats by all the restaurants in New York City. But the control isn't limited to food.

We've all come across pedestrians carelessly crossing the street
15 without looking at the oncoming traffic because they are too busy texting on their phones. In Fort Lee, New Jersey, these pedestrians will have to wait to text because they will be fined $85 for the offense of texting while crossing the street.

In the state of Tennessee, children will have to think twice before
20 putting on their pants. Under the saggy-pants law, any children found exposing their underwear or body parts in an "inappropriate manner" will be fined $250 or up to 160 hours of community service.

Children in San Francisco, California, must travel to other cities if they want a free toy with their Happy Meal, thanks to the local government's ban on free toys in children's fast-food meals.
25 Did you know it's unlawful for drivers to screech their tires in Kansas? And in Hilton Head, South Carolina, it is illegal to keep garbage in your car. A violation is considered a public nuisance and is subject to a fine of up to $500 and/or jail time of up to 30 days.

Even if your car is free of trash, you'd better keep your language clean,
30 or you may have to answer to the law in Rockville, Maryland. It doesn't matter where you are in Rockville, if someone else hears you swearing, whether you're on the street, sidewalk, or in your home, you'll have to keep your voice down if using expletives.

Not to be outdone, the US government is also thinking of ways
35 to regulate people's food choices. The Food and Drug Administration has been looking into ways to crack down on food advertisements as well as limits on salt and sugar in food items sold in supermarkets and restaurants.

Clearly the Nanny State has gotten out of control. People don't need
40 more government workers enforcing absurd regulations. Yet there's a larger issue at stake. We must ask ourselves: Do we really want the government taking charge of public behavior, even "for our own good"? Is this really fitting for a country of free citizens?

Glossary

expletive a swear word, i.e., a rude word used when someone is angry

trans-fat also trans-fatty acid, an unhealthy kind of fat which encourages the development of cholesterol

LEXIS IN CONTEXT

d Look at the following phrasal verbs and prepositional verbs in context. With a partner say what you think they mean.

stand out (1.9)

call for (1.10)

come across (1.14)

answer to (1.30)

keep (your voice) down (1.33)

look into (1.36)

e Read the article again. Underline phrases and sentences that show the writer's attitude toward the laws in some parts of the US. What is the writer's point of view? Do you agree with the writer's opinion?

f Which of the laws mentioned in the article would you like to see passed in the area where you live? Why? Are there laws or regulations where you live which you consider to be "nanny state"?

> We've all come across pedestrians carelessly crossing the street without looking at oncoming traffic...

2 GRAMMAR permission, obligation, and necessity

a Look at the pairs of sentences. With a partner, say if they are the same or different in meaning. In which pair of sentences is there a difference in register?

1 **It is not permitted to** take food or drinks into the library.
 You're not allowed to take food or drinks into the library.

2 **You'd better** turn your cell phone off.
 You should turn your cell phone off.

3 **We're supposed to** speak English all the time in class.
 We have to speak English all the time in class.

4 **You don't have to** wear a suit — the party's going to be casual.
 You don't need to wear a suit — the party's going to be casual.

5 **I should have** bought my mother a present.
 I had to buy my mother a present.

b ▶ p.150 Grammar Bank 7A. Learn more about permission, obligation, and necessity, and practice them.

3 SPEAKING

a Talk in small groups. Imagine the following laws have been proposed for the area where you live. Would you be in favor of them or do you think they are too "nanny state"? Try to use the **bold** expressions in your answers.

On the road

⊘ Bicyclists **should have to** pass a test to get a bicycling license before they are allowed on the road.

⊘ Car drivers **should not be allowed to** eat or drink while driving.

⊘ **It should be against the law for** pedestrians to cross the street while wearing headphones.

At home

⊘ **It should be compulsory for** people to turn off all electrical appliances at night in order to save energy.

⊘ **It should be illegal to** leave children under 12 alone in the house.

⊘ **It should be against the law for** parents to give fast food to obese children.

Public health

⊘ Smoking on the street **should be banned**.

⊘ Restaurants **should not be allowed to** serve more than one large sugary drink per person.

⊘ People who abuse their health **should be made to** pay higher health insurance premiums.

Society

⊘ **It should be against the law not to** vote in elections.

⊘ All advertising aimed at children under the age of 12 **should be banned**.

⊘ Couples **should be required to** attend three months of marriage counseling before they are allowed to get divorced.

Education

⊘ Teachers **should not be allowed to** use red pens to correct exercises as this is psychologically harmful to students.

⊘ Schoolchildren **should not be given** grades on tests, only general comments, so that they can't compare themselves with other children.

⊘ Competitive sports **should be banned** in the school system, so that children's self-esteem is not affected by losing.

b In your groups, agree on a new law or regulation that you would like to see introduced for two of the categories. Then try to convince other groups to vote in favor of passing your law.

4 VOCABULARY word formation: prefixes

> ...passing a law preventing students from exposing underwear in an "**in**decent manner."
> And in Hilton Head, South Carolina, it is **ill**egal to store trash in your car.

a Look at the two highlighted words from *Is the Nanny State Out of Control?* which both have prefixes. What do the prefixes add to the meaning of the base word?

b Look at some more highlighted words with prefixes from previous lessons and with a partner say what the prefix means.

1 Non-native speakers now **out**number native English speakers by three to one.

2 I think this movie is very **over**rated. Personally, I thought it was pretty mediocre.

3 **Re**awakening a romance can be an incendiary experience.

4 The character of Captain Smith was **mis**represented in the movie *Titanic*.

5 The importance of the lowly translator to our understanding of foreign literature should not be **under**estimated.

6 When people spend that money **pro**socially on others (giving gifts to friends, donating to charities) they are happier than when they spend it on themselves.

7 Her skin is already **pre**maturely aged.

8 The US dollar has been **de**valued so much that foreign vacations can be very expensive.

c Add a prefix from **a** or **b** above to the **bold** word and make any other necessary changes to complete the sentences.

1 I completely _____ Alan. I thought he lacked resolve, but I see I was wrong. **judge**

2 This paragraph in your essay is totally unclear. You're going to have to _____ it. **write**

3 I resent how my boss criticizes my ideas and _____ my work. **value**

4 My wife and I have a _____ signal for when we want to leave a dinner or a party. **arrange**

5 I can't read my doctor's handwriting. It's completely _____ . **legible**

6 Having to take care of my sister's five dogs is terribly _____ . **convenient**

7 The team seems kind of _____ since the coach was fired. **motivate**

8 I'd hardly studied at all for the test, so I felt very _____ . **prepare**

9 We're not going back to that restaurant — they _____ us last time we went. **charge**

10 The hotel has an _____ swimming pool that's open from June to September. **door**

5 LISTENING & SPEAKING

a Divide into teams. Try to agree on answers to the questions below, which come from a quiz book based on a popular TV show.

b ➤ **Communication** *QI quiz.* **A** *p.119* **B** *p.121.*

QI Quiz

1 What was Tutankhamun's curse?

2 What do chameleons do, and why?

3 What man-made structures can be seen from the moon?

4 What do kilts and whisky have in common?

5 Which metal is the best conductor?

6 Which African mammal kills more humans than any other?

From *The Book of General Ignorance*

c **(3 28))** Listen to someone talking about the TV quiz show and books that the questions below came from. Answer the questions with a partner.

1 Why did they call the show *QI*?
2 What is the basic principle behind the show and its books?
3 What examples does he give from the books?
4 Why is it so popular?
5 What are the two reasons Lloyd and Mitchinson give for why children often do badly in school?

7 What would probably have killed you in an 18th-century sea battle?

8 What did the American Thomas Edison invent that English speakers use every day?

9 How does television damage your health?

10 Why is a marathon 26.219 miles long?

d **(3 29))** Now listen to the speaker explaining how the *QI* principles could change education. Check (✓) the seven suggestions mentioned.

• Children should not start school before they are seven years old.
• Learning should never feel like hard work.
• Children should be able to choose their own curriculum.
• The same importance should be given to arts as to science and mathematics.
• Children shouldn't be expected to learn to read until they actually want to.
• Children shouldn't be forced to go to school every day if they don't want to.
• There should be no evaluation or assessment of children by teachers.
• Children should make their own classroom rules and should be responsible for enforcing them.
• Children should teach each other skills that they have mastered, e.g., how to ride a bike or play a musical instrument.
• Children should learn theories through practical activities.
• Children should spend at least half their time outdoors, interacting with nature.
• There should be no official graduation age.

e What do you think of Lloyd and Mitchinson's suggestions? Do you think any of the other suggestions in **d** would improve learning in schools?

6 PRONUNCIATION intonation in exclamations

a **(3 30))** Listen to the dialogues, and complete the exclamations.

A Did you know that in California schools they're not allowed to say "mom" and "dad" anymore in case they offend someone from a single-parent family?
B _____!

A Did you know that America was named for the Italian explorer Amerigo Vespucci?
B _____! I always wondered where the name came from.

b Listen again and focus on the intonation in the exclamations. Answer the questions with a partner.

1 Does the intonation on the adjectives in the exclamations go _____?
  a up   c up and down
  b down   d down and up
2 What consonant sound is added between *How* and the adjective? Why?

c Practice saying some more common exclamations with *What* and *How*.

What a great idea!   What an amazing coincidence!   What a terrible experience!   How annoying!   How embarrassing!   How weird!
---

d ➤ **Communication** *What a ridiculous idea!* **A** p.119 **B** p.122. Respond to what your partner says with an exclamation.

7 WRITING

➤ **p. 112 Writing** *A report.* Analyze a model report and write a report.

G verbs of the senses
V place and movement
P extra stress on important words

"There are painters who transform the sun into a yellow spot, but there are others who, with the help of their art and their intelligence, transform a yellow spot into the sun.

*Pablo Picasso,
Spanish painter*"

7B Just any old bed?

1 LISTENING & SPEAKING

a Look at the photos. Four of the objects are famous and expensive works of art. The other four are ordinary objects. With a partner, decide which are the works of art.

b ➤ **Communication** *Four works of art p.120.* Did you guess right? What do you think the artists were trying to communicate?

c (4 2)) Listen to an art expert talking about two of the works of art and answer the questions.

1 What are…?
  a installations
  b modern sculptures
2 What basic similarity is there between installations and other more traditional forms of art?
3 Why might artists today choose to create an installation rather than a painting?
4 Why are some people skeptical when they see an installation?
5 What special skills did Damien Hirst need to create *Away from the Flock*?
6 What does it communicate?
7 How is Tracey Emin's *My Bed* different from her real bed?
8 What does it communicate?
9 Why might it communicate more than a traditional self-portrait?

d Listen again and check your answers.

e Talk in small groups.

1 Does what the expert said change the way you see the two works of art? What did you agree / disagree with?
2 Would you pay to go and see any of the four works of art? Why (not)?
3 Have you seen any installation art? What did you think of it?
4 If you were going to make an installation to represent your life, what objects would you include?
5 Do you have a favorite…?
  • portrait
  • landscape painting   • self-portrait
  • still-life   • abstract painting
  Do you have any other favorite works of art?

2 GRAMMAR verbs of the senses

a (4 3)) Complete three sentences from the listening with the right form of one of the following verbs. Listen again and check.

look as if   look at (x2)   look like   see

1 When people _____ some installations, they think "Well, I could do that." They don't _____ that there's any expertise involved at all.
2 And then of course, he had to arrange it in a particular way, put the animal in a particular pose, so that it _____ it's alive, although of course we all know that it isn't.
3 I mean the bed is something that you _____ and you think "Yeah, that _____ my bed in the morning."

b Answer the questions with a partner.

1 What's the grammatical difference between *look as if* and *look like*, and the difference in meaning between *look at* and *see*?

2 Other than *sight*, what are the other four senses?

3 What verbs do you associate with them?

c ▶ **p.151 Grammar Bank 7B.** Learn more about verbs of the senses, and practice them.

d Ask and answer the questions with a partner.

• Are there any paintings or images that you like or dislike looking at because of how they make you feel?

• If you were offered plastic surgery to make you look like a celebrity, which celebrity would you choose, and why?

• What makes a voice sound attractive / unattractive to you?

• Are there any sounds or kinds of music that you don't like hearing because they make you feel uncomfortable?

• Do you think people tend to dislike foods more because of their smell, their taste, or their texture?

• What kinds of perfume or cologne do you really like or dislike on yourself or on other people? Why?

• Would you be prepared to touch these creatures in a zoo? Why (not)?
  a snake   a tarantula   a lion   a lizard   a rat   a parrot

• Are there certain materials you never wear or love to wear because of the way they feel?

3 PRONUNCIATION extra stress on important words

a (4 4)》 Read and listen to the poem and answer the questions.

1 Where does the conversation take place?

2 Who are "they"?

3 What does the speaker do, and why?

4 What do you think the poet is trying to communicate?

b Listen to the poem again. Why do you think some of the words are in *italics*? In pairs, practice reading it aloud.

c (4 5)》 Read the information box below. Then listen to the sentence *I wanted to buy a condo in Boston* pronounced in five different ways. Listen again and match each version to the continuations below.

> 🔍 **Extra stress on important words**
>
> Sometimes we give extra emphasis to a word in a sentence to convey meaning. These may even be words which are not usually stressed, e.g. articles or pronouns.
> This is not just *any* cold fried egg on *any* chipped plate. (= they are special)
> I don't want *this* bag. (= I want another one)
> Excuse me. I ordered a *chicken* sandwich. (= not the one you've brought me)

A ☐ ____, but my wife didn't.

B ☐ ____, but my wife wanted a house.

C ☐ ____, but we couldn't afford one.

D ☐ ____, not in San Francisco.

E ☐ ____, not rent one.

d (4 6)》 Listen and check. Then practice saying the five complete sentences, stressing a different word each time.

e ▶ **Communication** *Stressing the right word.* **A** *p.120* **B** *p.122.*

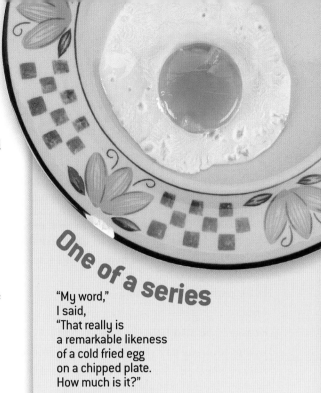

One of a series

"My word,"
I said,
"That really is
a remarkable likeness
of a cold fried egg
on a chipped plate.
How much is it?"

"Actually,"
they said
"It *is* a cold fried egg
on a chipped plate.
It is one of a series
created
by Laura Carambo.
£150,000."

And I said
"?????"

And they said
"This is not just
any cold fried egg
on *any* chipped plate.
It is *this* cold fried egg
on *this* chipped plate.

Carambo's work celebrates
the *thisness* of things.

She shows us how *this* and the *other*
move in a perpetual dance,
mediating between
and uniting
the amphimetropic opposites
of our Janus-faced universe."

Well
I could see that it all made sense
And between you and me,
I've looked at the reviews
and the auction catalogs,
and I reckon
I got a real bargain.
Come and look.

by Michael Swan

> **Glossary**
> **amphimetropic** an invented word
> **£150,000** = 150,000 pounds. The pound is the unit of currency of the UK.

4 READING

Read and listen to the story and answer the questions, section by section.

In a Season of Calm Weather

BY RAY BRADBURY

GEORGE AND ALICE SMITH detrained at Biarritz one summer noon and in an hour had run through their hotel onto the beach into the ocean and back out to bake upon the sand. To see George Smith sprawled burning there, you'd think him only
5 a tourist flown to Europe and soon to be transported home. But here was a man who loved art more than life itself.

"George?" His wife loomed over him. "I know what you've been thinking. I can read your lips."

He lay perfectly still, waiting.

10 "And?"

"Picasso," she said.

He winced. Some day she would learn to pronounce that name.

"Please," she said. "Relax. I know you heard the rumor this morning, but you should see your eyes — your tic is back.
15 All right, Picasso's here, down the coast a few miles away, visiting friends in some small fishing town. But you must forget it or our vacation's ruined."

"I wish I'd never heard the rumor," he said honestly.

"If only," she said, "you liked other painters."

20 Others? Yes, there were others. He could breakfast most congenially on Caravaggio still-lifes of autumn pears and midnight plums. For lunch: those fire-squirting, thick-wormed Van Gogh sunflowers. But the great feast? The paintings he saved his palate for? Who else but the creator of *Girl Before*
25 *a Mirror* and *Guernica*?

---

4 7))

1 What do you find out about the characters George and Alice Smith from this first section?

2 Guess what these verbs might mean from the context: *detrained* (1.1), *sprawled* (1.4), *loomed* (1.7), and *winced* (1.12).

"I keep thinking," he said aloud, "if we saved our money..."

"We'll never have five thousand dollars."

"I know," he said quietly. "But it's nice thinking we might bring it off some day. Wouldn't it be great to just step up to
30 him, and say 'Pablo, here's five thousand! Give us the sea, the sand, that sky, or any old thing you want, we'll be happy...'"

After a moment, his wife touched his arm.

"I think you'd better go in the water now," she said.

"Yes," he said. "I'd better do just that."

35 During the afternoon George Smith came out and went into the ocean with the vast spilling motions of now warm, now cool people who at last, with the sun's decline, their bodies all lobster colors, trudged for their wedding-cake hotels.

The beach lay deserted for endless mile on mile save for two
40 people. One was George Smith, towel over shoulder. Far along the shore another shorter, square-cut man walked alone in the tranquil weather. He was deeper tanned, his close-shaven

head dyed almost mahogany by the sun, and his eyes were clear and bright as water in his face. So the shoreline stage
45 was set, and in a few minutes the two men would meet.

---

4 8))

3 What is George's dream?

4 What do you understand by the metaphors...? "their bodies all lobster colors" "their wedding-cake hotels" "the shoreline stage was set"

5 What impression do you get of what the other man on the beach looks like?

The stranger stood alone. Glancing about, he saw his aloneness, saw the waters of the lovely bay, saw the sun sliding down the late colors of the day, and then half-turning spied a small wooden object on the sand. It was no more than the
50 slender stick from a lime ice-cream delicacy long since melted away. Smiling he picked the stick up. With another glance around to re-insure his solitude, the man stooped again and holding the stick gently with light sweeps of his hand began to do the one thing in all the world he knew best how to do.

55 He began to draw incredible figures along the sand. He sketched one figure and then moved over and still looking down, completely focused on his work now, drew a second and a third figure, and after that a fourth and a fifth and a sixth.

George Smith, printing the shoreline with his feet, gazed here,
60 gazed there, and then saw the man ahead. George Smith, drawing nearer, saw that the man, deeply tanned, was bending down. Nearer yet, and it was obvious what the man was up to. George Smith chuckled. Of course, of course... along on the beach this man — how old? Sixty-five? Seventy? — was
65 scribbling and doodling away. How the sand flew! How the wild portraits flung themselves out there on the shore! How...

George Smith took one more step and stopped, very still.

The stranger was drawing and drawing and did not seem to sense that anyone stood immediately behind him and the
70 world of his drawings in the sand.

---

4 9))

6 What does the stranger start doing, and how does George react?

7 Look at the two groups of three words. What's the connection between the three?
a *glance* (1.46) *spied* (1.48) *gazed* (1.60)
b *sketched* (1.56) *scribbling* (1.64) *doodling* (1.65)

George Smith looked down at the sand. And, after a long while, looking, he began to tremble.

For there on the flat shore were pictures of Grecian lions and Mediterranean goats and maidens and children dancing. And
75 the sand, in the dying light, was the color of copper on which was now slashed a message that any man in any time might read and savor down the years.

The artist stopped.

George Smith drew back and stood away.

80 The artist glanced up, surprised to find someone so near. Then he simply stood there, looking from George Smith to his own creations flung like idle footprints down the way. He smiled at last and shrugged as if to say, "Look what I've done; see what a child? You will forgive me, won't you? One day or another we are all fools...
85 you, too, perhaps? So allow an old fool this, eh? Good! Good!"

But George Smith could only look at the little man with the sun-dark skin and the clear sharp eyes, and say the man's name once, in a whisper, to himself.

They stood thus for perhaps another five seconds, George
90 Smith staring at the sand-frieze, and the artist watching George Smith with amused curiosity.

George Smith opened his mouth, closed it, put out his hand, took it back. He stepped towards the pictures, stepped away. Then he moved along the line of figures, like a man viewing a
95 precious series of marbles cast up from some ancient ruin on the shore. His eyes did not blink, his hand wanted to touch but did not dare to touch. He wanted to run but did not run.

4 10 》)

8 What is the artist's attitude to George, and George's to the artist?

9 Look at these verbs in the text: *tremble* (1.72), *slash* (1.76), *draw back* (1.79), *shrug* (1.83), *stare* (1.90), *blink* (1.96). What kind of actions do you think they are?

10 Why might George have "wanted to run"?

He looked suddenly at the hotel. Run, yes! Run! What? Grab a shovel, dig, excavate, save a chunk of this all too crumbling
100 sand? Find a repairman, race him back here with plaster-of-Paris to cast a mould of some small fragile part of these? No, no. Silly, silly. Or...? His eyes flicked to his hotel window. The camera! Run, get it, get back, and hurry along the shore, clicking, changing film, clicking until...

105 George Smith whirled to face the sun. It burned faintly on his face, his eyes were two small fires from it. The sun was half underwater and, as he watched, it sank the rest of the way in a matter of seconds.

The artist had drawn nearer and now was gazing into George
110 Smith's face with great friendliness as if he were guessing every thought. Now he was nodding his head in a little bow. Now the ice-cream stick had fallen casually from his fingers. Now he was saying good night, good night. Now he was gone, walking back down the beach towards the south.

115 George Smith stood looking after him. After a full minute, he did the only thing he could possibly do. He started at the beginning of the fantastic frieze and he walked slowly along the shore. And when he came to the end of the animals and men he turned around and started back in the other direction, just
120 staring down as if he had lost something and did not quite know where to find it. He kept on doing this until there was no more light in the sky, or on the sand to see by.

4 11 》)

11 What is George's dilemma? What options does he consider? What does he decide to do in the end? Why?

12 Look at these verbs in the text: *grab* (1.98), *flick* (1.102), *whirl* (1.105), *nod* (1.111). What kind of movements do you think they are?

He sat down at the supper table.

"You're late," said his wife. "I just had to come down alone.
125 I'm ravenous."

"That's all right," he said.

"Anything interesting happen on your walk?" she asked.

"No," he said.

"You look funny; George, you didn't swim out too far, did you,
130 and almost drown? I can tell by your face. You did swim out too far, didn't you?"

"Yes," he said.

"Well," she said, watching him closely. "Don't ever do that again. Now — what'll you have?"

135 He picked up the menu and started to read it and stopped suddenly.

"What's wrong?" asked his wife.

He turned his head and shut his eyes for a moment.

140 "Listen."

She listened.

"I don't hear anything," she said.

"Don't you?"

"No. What is it?"

145 "Just the tide," he said, after a while, sitting there, his eyes still shut. "Just the tide, coming in."

4 12 》)

13 Why do you think George didn't tell his wife about his experience?

14 How do you think he is feeling as he listens to the tide come in?

5 VOCABULARY place and movement

a Look at six sentences from the story. Without looking back at the story, complete the sentences with a word from the list. Then check with the story.

> along   away   back (x3)   into   onto
> around   ~~through~~   towards (x2)   upon

1 George and Alice...in an hour had run *through* their hotel _____ the beach _____ the ocean and _____ out to bake _____ the sand (1.2).

2 He stepped _____ the picture, stepped _____. Then he moved _____ the line of figures, like a man viewing a precious series of marbles... (1.93).

3 Now he was saying good night, good night. Now he was gone, walking _____ down the beach _____ the south (1.113).

4 And when he came to the end of the animals and men he turned _____ and started _____ in the other direction (1.118).

b ▶ p.164 Vocabulary Bank *Place and movement.*

6 **4 13 》) SONG** *All The Rowboats* ♫

1 🎥 VIDEO THE INTERVIEW Part 1

a Read the biographical information about Patricia Melvin. Why do you think she chose to study in Paris and Amsterdam?

Patricia Melvin is an American *plein air* painter from New York City. She paints cityscapes, landscapes, portraits, still-life, and people. She is primarily self-taught, but she has studied in Paris and Amsterdam, where she began her plein air painting career. Over the past twenty-five years she's had solo and group exhibitions around the world and features in various publications. She has a permanent collection in the Cahoon Museum of American Art in Massachusetts.

b 🔊 (4 14)) Watch or listen to Part 1 of an interview with her. Mark sentences 1-5 below **T** (true) or **F** (false).

1 Patricia believes New York is a special place because no matter how long people have lived there, they feel ownership of the place.
2 Patricia doesn't paint while she is on location, but from memory and sketches.
3 Patricia believes that a painting is a work-in-progress that can take years to complete.
4 Patricia likes to paint in the city because of all the distractions.
5 Patricia prefers to use photos when painting people.

c Now listen again and say why the **F** sentences are false.

Glossary

plein air a French term that means "open air" and is used to describe the act of painting outdoors.

in situ /ɪn ˈsaɪtu/ *noun* (from Latin) in the original or correct place

sketch / skɛtʃ/ *noun* a simple picture that is drawn quickly and doesn't have many details

pose / poʊz/ *noun* a particular position in which sb stands, sits etc. especially in order to be painted

canvas /ˈkænvəs/ *noun* a piece of strong, heavy material used for painting on

the Hudson /hʌdsən/ one of the rivers that flows through New York

🎥 VIDEO Part 2

a 🔊 (4 15)) Watch or listen to part 2. Answer the questions with a partner.

What does she say about…?
1 the Hudson River; her parents
2 sunrise
3 the advantages of painting during the spring
4 the places where she'd like to paint
5 what an artist has to sacrifice and why

b Answer the questions with a partner.

1 Patricia mentions that being an artist requires a lot of sacrifice. To what extent do you think it's true?
2 If you were an artist, what would you choose to paint and why?

2 LOOKING AT LANGUAGE

> 🔍 **Expressing time**
> Patricia Melvin uses several poetic phrases to express time. Using phrases to clarify time provides context for events and emphasizes important moments.

a (4 16)》 Listen to some extracts from the interview and complete the phrases.

1 I was born here and raised nearby and so I have memories of New York City _____ and to me it was always a magical place.

2 Things like that happen _____ of a painting and they can be just perfect.

3 …so if I started painting _____, it's hard to finish it later in a different season or later on in the same season.

4 I've worked on some paintings _____ and sometimes I'll come back to a painting _____ when the season and the different light is right for that painting.

5 I love painting portraits, but it's very rare to find someone who will sit for a few hours, _____, and I don't like to do portraits from photos.

6 …and also my mother painted some, so I, _____, she painted, so, there were a lot of influences on me.

7 It requires _____, it requires being free to suddenly change your plans at a moment's notice

3 🎥 VIDEO ON THE STREET

a (4 17)》 You are going to hear four people talking about art. What three questions do they answer? Which speaker(s) go to art galleries most / least often?

1	2	3	4
Ezra	Jackie	Aurelia	Amy

b Listen again. Match the speakers to the statements.

1 ☐ They liked seeing an artist's work through his lifetime.

2 ☐ Their favorite artist is a famous photographer.

3 ☐ They don't have any paintings in the home.

4 ☐ They have a photograph of a famous landmark.

5 ☐ They studied a subject in which they had to go to art galleries.

6 ☐ They would probably go to art galleries more often if they lived in a big city.

c (4 18)》 Listen and complete the phrases with one to three words. What do you think they mean?

> **Useful phrases**
> 1 …it actually takes you through like a _____ of his life and all the paintings that he painted throughout the different ages of his life.
> 2 I majored in Fine Arts in college so I did a lot of _____ of the Chelsea galleries over there.
> 3 I'd say in general in regards to a _____ _____ _____, I really love photography and printmaking.
> 4 You can see the _____ _____ through the triangle and it creates a beautiful setting…
> 5 It's a painting that my best friend did for our family because she's an _____ _____ _____.

4 SPEAKING

Answer the questions with a partner. Practice using phrases to clarify time and where possible the useful phrases.

1 Who is your favorite artist? What do you appreciate about the artist?

2 What do you believe is the greatest source of inspiration for artists (e.g., environment, people, other artists, etc.)? Why do you think it's so important?

3 Do you think that certain types of art are more valuable than others? Why (not)?

4 Do you go to museums or art galleries? How often do you go?

5 Do you think artwork should be kept in museums or art galleries instead of people's homes? Why (not)?

G gerunds and infinitives
V health and medicine; similes
P word stress

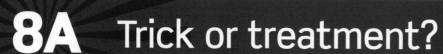

"" The art of medicine consists in amusing the patient while nature cures the disease.

Voltaire, French author and philosopher ""

8A Trick or treatment?

1 SPEAKING & LISTENING

a How much medical vocabulary do you know? Take the quiz with a partner.

> # Medical Quiz
>
> **1** When might you get...?
> a a bruise
> b a blister
> c a rash
>
> **2** Why might you be given...?
> a a cast
> b a bandage
> c antibiotics
> d stitches
> e an X-ray
> f an ultrasound
>
> **3** When might you need to see...?
> a a primary care physician
> b a specialist
> c a surgeon
>
> **4** What are the symptoms of...?
> a a cold
> b the flu
> c food poisoning
> d a heart attack
> e asthma
>
> **5** What might happen to you if you...?
> a had to stand for a long time in a hot, crowded room
> b drank too much coffee
> c were stung on your hand by a wasp
> d turned on a light with wet hands

b Look at some commonly-held beliefs related to health and medicine below. With a partner, discuss each one and decide if you think it is true or a myth.

c (4 19)) Now listen to a doctor talking about these beliefs. Were you right?

d Listen again. Why is each belief true or a myth? Take notes and then compare with a partner.

LEXIS IN CONTEXT

e (4 20)) Complete the extracts from the listening with the missing word. Listen and check.

1 If you're **w**_____ your weight, what matters is *what* you eat, not *when* you eat it.

2 Colds, we know, are caused by **v**_____, which you catch from an infected person…

3 But recent research has found that being exposed to cold temperatures does, in fact, lower our body's **d**_____.

4 As a matter of fact there is a medical condition called "night-eating **s**_____," which affects two percent of the population.

5 Reading in the dark or in dim light can cause a temporary **s**_____ on the eyes, but it quickly goes away once you return to bright light.

6 …our body heat, and certain chemicals in our **s**_____.

f Did any of this information surprise you? Will it affect the way you behave? Are there any other strongly-held beliefs about health and medicine in your country which you think are probably myths?

Never shower in a thunderstorm.
Surprising facts and misleading myths about our health and the world we live in...

Truth or myth?

1 Avoid eating late at night if you don't want to gain weight.

2 If you stay out in the cold and wind, you are more likely to catch a cold.

3 Never take a shower during a thunderstorm — you might get electrocuted.

4 Reading in dim light will ruin your eyesight.

5 Some people attract mosquitoes more than others.

6 Bottled water is safer than tap water.

2 VOCABULARY similes

a Read the information about similes. Then complete sentences 1–10 with a word from the list.

> 🔍 **Similes**
>
> A simile is a fixed informal / colloquial expression of comparison using *as* or *like*. Similes add emphasis to an adjective, adverb, or verb, e.g., *I think Jane's underweight for her age — she's **as light as a feather**. (=very light).

bat dream dog
flash gold horse log
mule post sheet

1 My husband's **as stubborn as a** _____. He refuses to go to the doctor about his bad back.

2 She's **as white as a** _____. I think she's going to faint.

3 He's as **sick as a** _____. He should go to the hospital and see a doctor.

4 He's **as deaf as a** _____. You'll have to speak up a little.

5 She **sleeps like a** _____. I don't think she's ever had problems with insomnia.

6 Your mother's **as blind as a** _____. I think she should get her eyes tested.

7 She's been **as good as** _____. She took all her medicine without making any fuss.

8 My new medication **works like a** _____. I feel a hundred times better.

9 When I pressed the button the nurse came **as quick as a** _____, and immediately changed my IV bag, which was running out.

10 My son **eats like a** _____. I sometimes think he has worms.

b Try to think of three people or things you could describe with these similes. Compare with a partner.

3 GRAMMAR gerunds and infinitives

a (4 21)) Listen and write the verbs or phrases in the right box.

+ *to* + infinitive

+ gerund

+ base form

b Use your instinct. Cross out the wrong form. Check (✓) if both are possible.

1 I regret *not going | not having gone* to the doctor earlier.

2 I hate *telling | being told* that I've gained weight.

3 I would like *to have brought | to bring* you some flowers, but I didn't have time.

4 I was unwise *not to take | not to have taken* all the antibiotics.

5 Is there anywhere *to park | park* near the hospital?

6 I have enough tablets *to last | for lasting* until the end of the month.

7 It's no use *worrying | to worry* until you know what's wrong with you.

8 She was the first woman *to become | becoming* a professor of cardiac surgery.

c ➤ p.152 Grammar Bank 8A. Learn more about gerunds and infinitives, and practice them.

d ➤ Communication *Guess the sentence.*
A p.120 B p.122.

4 VOCABULARY & PRONUNCIATION

health and medicine; word stress

a Look at some words which describe types of alternative medicine. Do you know what any of them are, and what they're used for?

☐ homeopathy   ☐ chiropractic
☐ osteopathy   ☐ reflexology
☐ aromatherapy   ☐ hypnotherapy
☐ herbal medicine   ☐ acupuncture

b **4 22))** Now listen to eight definitions and match them with the words.

c **4 23))** Listen and check. Then underline the main stressed syllable.

d **4 24))** Listen and underline the main stressed syllable in the following words. In which word families does the stress change?

---

an acupuncturist   a chiropractor   a homeopath   homeopathic medicine

hypnosis   a hypnotherapist   an osteopath   a reflexologist

---

5 LISTENING & SPEAKING

a What forms of alternative medicine are popular in your country? Why do you think some people are skeptical about them?

b **4 25))** Listen to four people talking about their experiences with alternative medicine. Complete the chart.

	What did they use?	What for?	Was it successful?
Speaker A			
Speaker B			
Speaker C			
Speaker D			

c Listen again. Write the number of the speaker.

Who...?

1 took more than the recommended dose ☐
2 had a physical side effect ☐
3 felt slightly better immediately after the treatment ☐
4 had been unwell for some time before trying alternative medicine ☐
5 has been using alternative medicine for a very long time ☐
6 thought that the dose they had to take was very high ☐
7 tried alternative medicine because of a previous bad experience ☐
8 never gave their children conventional medicine ☐

d Have *you* ever used any alternative medicine, or do you know anyone who has? Was your / their experience positive or negative?

6 READING & SPEAKING

a Read a review from *The Sunday Times* about a new book on alternative medicine and answer the questions with a partner.

1 Do the authors of the book believe that alternative medicine is a trick or a valid form of treatment?
2 Do they think there are any exceptions?
3 Does the reviewer agree?

Trick or treatment?
Alternative Medicine on Trial

"For 2,400 years," wrote the historian of medicine, David Wootton, "patients believed doctors were doing them good; for 2,300 years they were wrong." Only in the past 100 years have treatments in mainstream
5 medicine been consistently subject to clinical trial, to discover what works and what doesn't. Much medicine, though, still stands defiantly outside this mainstream. Can these alternative therapies really claim to be medically effective judged by today's
10 standards, or are they no better than the blood-letting and snake oil of darker centuries?

Simon Singh, a science writer, and Edzard Ernst, a doctor, have set out to reveal the truth about "the potions, lotions, pills, needles, pummeling, and
15 energizing that lie beyond the realms of conventional medicine." Their conclusions are damning. "Most forms of alternative medicine," say the authors, "for most conditions remain either unproven or are demonstrably ineffective, and several alternative
20 therapies put patients at risk of harm."

One by one, they go through the most influential alternative therapies (acupuncture, homeopathy, chiropractic, and herbal medicines) and subject them to scientific scrutiny. In each case, they
25 ask what the evidence is for saying that a given therapy "works." Acupuncture, homeopathy, and chiropractic all come out badly. Singh and Ernst build a compelling case that these therapies are at worst positively dangerous — chiropractic neck
30 manipulation can result in injury or death — and at best, are more or less useless. For example, tests done in Germany have shown that "real" acupuncture works no better in easing migraines than sham acupuncture, a random application of
35 wrongly positioned needles, working as a placebo.

Singh and Ernst do not deny that placebos are powerful things. This being so, does it matter if homeopathy really "works" in scientific terms? If it makes me feel better to rub arnica cream into a
40 bruise, what harm is done? The authors argue that it does matter, for three reasons.

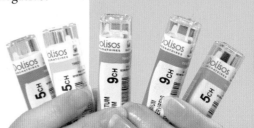

First, if, as the evidence indicates, homeopathy is merely a placebo, then the price tag is a rip-off. A second problem lies in the ethics of the doctor-
45 patient relationship. In order to make the placebo effect work, doctors would have to suppress their knowledge that homeopathy was bogus. "In fact, the best way to exploit the placebo effect is to lie excessively to make the pill seem extra-
50 special, by using statements such as 'this remedy has been imported from Timbuktu,' etc." Third, and most worrying, by putting his or her faith in homeopathy, a patient may fail to seek out more effective conventional treatment. In the case of a
55 minor bruise, this doesn't matter. It's altogether more serious when it comes to asthma or even cancer.

Does this mean that all alternative therapies are to be dismissed? In the case of herbal medicines, Singh and Ernst admit that some are effective, but even here
60 they argue that, once an alternative treatment passes proper tests, it is accepted into the mainstream and ceases to be alternative. Two examples they give are fish oils for preventing heart disease, as well as osteopathy (a gentler alternative to chiropractic).
65 They would like to see all alternative medicines jump through the same expensive hoops as mainstream drugs. Until they have passed such tests, they should come with cautions ("Warning: this product is a placebo"), though of course any such warning would
70 work against the placebo effect.

The authors admit that, in the 19th century, patients were sometimes better off with homeopathy (i.e., no treatment at all) than with the mainstream practices of "bloodletting, vomiting, sweating, and blistering,
75 which generally stressed an already weakened body," but point out that today's medicine is, of course, infinitely more effective in the treatment of disease. However, in my opinion, mainstream medicine is hopelessly primitive when it comes to preventing
80 disease. The "evidence-based" medicine that Singh and Ernst are so fond of does not look so great when we consider the profiteering of big pharmaceutical companies, which would rather sell us drugs to manage our diseases than help us stay well.
85 Alternative medicine flourishes in the space that conventional medicine, which, focusing on cure rather than prevention, neglects. Is it any wonder that some people — against all the evidence — prefer the warm lies of the alternative practitioners
90 to the cold drugs of the men in white coats?

From *The Sunday Times*

b Read the article again and choose the right answers.

1 "Mainstream medicine" (1.4) refers to…
   a medicine that is considered normal and used by most doctors.
   b all kinds of medicine, including alternative medicine.
   c medicine that has been given to patients for thousands of years.

2 "Damning" (1.16) means…
   a rather unclear.   b extremely negative.   c ambiguous.

3 In paragraph 3, the German tests are cited to show that…
   a acupuncture is the least effective of the three therapies mentioned.
   b any benefits from acupuncture are due to the placebo effect.
   c some alternative therapies can be dangerous.

4 What most concerns the authors about alternative medicine is that…
   a seriously sick patients may choose to use it and not get effective mainstream treatment.
   b it is ridiculously expensive considering that it does no real good.
   c doctors would have to be dishonest in order for the placebo effect to work.

5 Fish oils are given as an example of a medicine that…
   a doesn't really work.
   b has not passed proper tests.
   c should no longer be considered alternative.

6 The reviewer believes that some people use alternative medicine because…
   a the practitioners pay more attention to them than mainstream doctors.
   b it is cheaper than having to pay the high prices charged by big pharmaceutical companies.
   c they believe all the evidence about alternative medicine.

LEXIS IN CONTEXT

c Find the opposite of the **bold** word or expression in the text.

1 **alternative medicine**   *conventional* or _____ medicine
2 a **proven** theory   an _____ theory
3 **effective** treatment   _____ treatment
4 a **useful** remedy   a _____ remedy
5 **real** acupuncture   _____ (or *bogus*) acupuncture
6 **a bargain**   a _____

d Do you agree with the following points made in the article?

• Alternative medicine only works because of the placebo effect.
• Mainstream medicine is far more effective in treating serious diseases.
• Some alternative medicine can actually be harmful.
• All alternative medicines should be tested in the same way that conventional medicines are.
• Drug companies have no interest in preventing or eradicating diseases, only in controlling them.
• Alternative medicine does more than mainstream medicine to prevent illness.

Glossary
bloodletting medical treatment used in the past in which some of a patient's blood was removed
pummel to keep hitting hard with your hand or fist
placebo a substance that has no physical effects, given to patients who do not need medicine but think that they do, or when testing new drugs

G expressing future plans and arrangements
V travel and tourism
P homophones

> I have found out there ain't no surer way
> to find out whether you like people or
> hate them than to travel with them.
>
> *Mark Twain,*
> *American writer*

8B A moving experience

1 READING & SPEAKING

a The guidebook series *The Rough Guide* has published a book called *25 Wonders of the World*.
Think of five places, sights, or monuments that you would put in it. Compare your list with a partner.

b Read the article once. Why is it called "My 25,000 Wonders of the World"?

My 25,000 Wonders of the World

The buses at the Uluru Sunset Viewing Area were parked
three deep. Guides were putting up tables and setting out
beverages and snacks. Ten minutes to go. Are we ready? Five minutes,
folks. Got your cameras? OK, here it comes...

5   Whether an American backpacker or a wealthy traveler, Danish,
British, or French, we all saw that sunset over Uluru, or Ayers Rock,
in what seems to be the prescribed tourist manner: mouth full of corn
chips, glass full of Château Somewhere, and a loved one posing in a
photo's foreground, as the all-time No 1 Australian icon behind us
10   glowed briefly red.

Back on the bus, our guide declared our sunset to be "pretty good,"
although not the best she'd witnessed in her six years. Behind me,
Adam, a student from Manchester, reinserted his iPod earphones:
"Well, that's enough of that rock." Indeed. Shattered from getting up
15   at five in order to see Uluru at dawn, I felt empty and bored. What
was the point? What made this rock the definitive sunset rock event?
Why had we come here? Well, I suppose my sons would remember it
always. Except they'd missed the magical moment while they checked
out a rival tour group's snack table, which had better chips.

20   So now I've visited four of the "25 Wonders of the World," as decreed
by Rough Guides. And I think this will be the last. While in my heart I
can see myself wandering enchanted through China's Forbidden City,
in my head I know I would be standing grumpily at the back of a group
listening to some Imperial Palace Tour Guide. At the Grand Canyon I
25   would be getting angry with tourists watching it through their cameras —
eyes are not good enough, since they lack a recording facility.

As we become richer and consumer goods are more widely
affordable, and satisfy us only briefly before becoming obsolete,
we turn to travel to provide us with "experiences." These will endure,
30   set us apart from stay-at-home people and, maybe, fill our lives with
happiness and meaning. Books with helpful titles like *1,000 Places
to See Before You Die* are best sellers. I bet many backpacks on the

> **And yet viewing the main sight of any destination
> is rarely the highlight of a trip. Mostly it sits there on
> your itinerary like a duty visit to a dull relative.**

Machu Picchu Inca Trail are filled with copies, with little checkmarks
penciled in the margins after each must-see sight has been visited.
35   Travel is now the biggest industry on the planet, bigger than
armaments or pharmaceuticals. And yet viewing the main sight of
any destination is rarely the highlight of a trip. Mostly it sits there
on your itinerary like a duty visit to a dull relative. The guilt of not
visiting the Sistine Chapel, because we preferred to stay in a bar
40   drinking limoncello, almost spoiled a weekend in Rome.

In Queensland, the Great Barrier Reef reproached us. How could
we travel 15,000 miles without seeing it? How would we explain back
home that we were too lazy, and preferred to stay playing a ball game
in our hotel pool? In the end we went to the reef and it was fine. But
45   it won't rank highly in the things I'll never forget about Australia. Like
the fact that the money is made of waterproof plastic: how gloriously
Australian is that? Even after a day's surfing, the $50 bill you left in
your surfing shorts is still OK to buy you a drink! And the news story
that during a recent tsunami warning, the surfers at Bondi Beach
50   refused to leave the sea: what, and miss the ride of their lives? Or the
stern warning at the carry-on luggage X-ray machine at Alice Springs
airport: "No jokes must be made while being processed by this facility" —
to forestall, no doubt, disrespectful Aussie comments: "You won't find
the bomb, mate. It's in my suitcase."

55   The more I travel, the clearer it seems that the truth of a place is
in the tiny details of everyday life, not in its most glorious statues
or scenery. Put down your camera, throw away your list, the real
wonders of the world number infinitely more than 25.

From The Times by Janice Turner

c Read the article again. Then answer the questions with a partner.

1 What do you think the author means by "the prescribed tourist manner" in l.7? Does she think it's a good thing?

2 What were her main emotions after seeing the sunset?

3 Why does she think that Uluru is probably the last "wonder of the world" she will see?

4 What kind of tourists is she criticizing when she says "eyes are not good enough…" in l.26?

5 What does she say that a lot of backpackers carry with them nowadays? Why?

6 What does she compare visiting the main tourist sights to? Why?

7 What does she mean by "the Great Barrier Reef reproached us"?

8 What three aspects of Australia did she find really memorable? Why?

d Talk to a partner.

1 Have you ever…?
- been to see a famous sight and thought it was overrated
- been to see a famous sight that lived up to your expectations
- felt guilty about not seeing a sight when you were on vacation somewhere
- been disappointed at not being able to see a famous sight

2 Think of the last place you visited as a tourist. Can you think of a "tiny detail of everyday life" that made the place or the moment special?

3 What "real wonders of the world" would you recommend to people visiting your country / town?

2 VOCABULARY & SPEAKING
travel and tourism

a Find words from the text in 1 that mean…

1 _____ a person who travels cheaply carrying their equipment and clothes in a bag they carry on their back.

2 _____ an interesting place in a town or city often visited by tourists.

3 _____ the place where you are going.

4 _____ a plan of a trip including the route and the places that you visit.

5 _____ the natural features of an area, e.g., mountains, valleys, rivers, or forests.

b ➤ **p.165 Vocabulary Bank** *Travel and tourism.*

c Complete the questionnaire with a partner. Which alternative would you choose in each case, and why? Try to use the expressions below.

> 🔍 **Expressing preferences**
>
> I'd prefer to… I (definitely) wouldn't…
> I'd (much) rather… (than…) Given the choice, I'd…
> I'd go with option b, because… If it were up to me, I'd…

What kind of a traveler are you?

1 **You are in Naples, Italy, for work, and you have one free day. You can…**
   a go on a day trip to Pompeii, which is about an hour away.
   b spend the day shopping, walking, and getting to know the city.
   c stay in your hotel, go to the pool, and have a great meal.

2 **Your family is planning a vacation. Which would you try to persuade them to choose?**
   a Going on a safari in Botswana, with accommodations in tents.
   b Renting a villa on a lively but very touristy Greek island.
   c A package tour to Brazil, with several day trips to the main sights included.

3 **You and three friends want to go away for a short vacation together. The possibilities are…**
   a a three-day getaway in a foreign city, staying at a cheap hotel.
   b three days in a luxury spa hotel in your country.
   c a week camping somewhere off the beaten track with beautiful scenery.

4 **You have to go on a business trip from San Francisco to Tokyo that involves a long-distance flight. There are two possible itineraries:**
   a an economy-class flight that leaves very early in the morning, with a 24-hour layover in Hawaii.
   (Flying time: San Francisco–Hawaii 5 hours; Hawaii — Tokyo 8 hours)
   b a business-class flight that leaves at midday, but with no layover. (Flying time: 11 hours)

5 **You and a friend really want to visit Vietnam, which you have heard is very beautiful. You can…**
   a book a package tour through a travel agent, including guided tours of famous sights.
   b go backpacking, booking your flight beforehand, but finding accommodations as you go.
   c buy a good guidebook and arrange the trip yourself, booking hotels and transportation on the Internet.

6 **You are booking a flight with a budget airline to a major city, where you are going to spend the weekend with some friends. Besides the flight, would you also…?**
   a take out insurance
   b pay extra to offset your carbon footprint
   c pay extra to check a suitcase

d Look at your partner's answers again. What kind of traveler do you think he / she is?

3 PRONUNCIATION homophones

> 🔍 **Homophones**
>
> "We visited the **site** of the Battle of Gettysburg."
> "I didn't have time to see many of the tourist **sights** in New York."
> *site* and *sight* are homophones. They are words that are spelled differently and have different meanings, but are pronounced exactly the same.

a With a partner, think of homophones for the **bold** words:

1 We're going to have to **wait** for two hours before the flight to check in. /weɪt/
   What's the maximum _____ for carry-on luggage on this flight?

2 We're **bored**! We don't want to visit any more museums! /bɔrd/
   The passengers are waiting to _____ the plane.

3 We spent spring **break** in Cancún. /breɪk/
   The airport bus had to _____ suddenly when a truck pulled out in front of us.

4 It's not **fair**! Jane's family's going to Thailand and we're just going to New Jersey. /fɛr/
   How much is the air _____ to Australia?

5 Where's the **piece** of paper with our flight details? /pis/
   We want to go somewhere off the beaten track for some _____ and quiet.

6 I slept in a tent on an old army **cot**. /kɑt/
   We just barely _____ the train — it left seconds after we got on it.

7 I was walking my poodle on the beach when I was told that dogs aren't **allowed** there. /əˈlaʊd/
   My grandfather had forgotten his glasses, so he asked me to read the menu _____ to him.

8 I can take you to the beach on my motorcycle, but you'll have to hold on to my **waist** really tight. /weɪst/
   Don't bother going to see the battlefield. It's a _____ of time. It's just an empty meadow.

9 We're staying at a beautiful hotel for our honeymoon — we've booked the bridal **suite**. /swit/
   I don't really like the local desserts, they're too _____ for me.

10 We walked along the **pier**, watching the fishing boats returning with their catch. /pɪr/
    Searching for elephants, the safari guide continued to _____ into the distance.

11 If you're taking out travel insurance, make sure you give them the **serial** numbers of your gadgets. /ˈsɪriəl/
    There wasn't much choice for breakfast — just toast and _____.

b Test a partner. **A** say one of the homophones, **B** say what the two spellings and meanings are. Then swap roles.

4 GRAMMAR
expressing future plans and arrangements

a How do you usually get to the place where you work or study? How long does it take you? Do you know any people who travel for more than an hour each way every day?

b Read an article about "extreme commuting." What are the pros and cons for Maj-Britt Hagsted?

> ## "Extreme commuting" — would *you* do it?
>
>
>
> **J**ob recruiters say that it is getting more and more difficult today to convince candidates to relocate. Instead people are increasingly open to "extreme commuting" as an alternative to relocation. Extreme commuting is the term used to describe a daily commute by car or train that takes more than 90 minutes each way, or commuting to work each week by airplane. Family ties are the leading reason for resistance to relocating, according to half the recruiters surveyed, while lifestyle preferences (25 percent) and housing market costs (10 percent) are also contributing factors.
>
> Maj-Britt Hagsted works in publishing in New York City. She commutes every day to get from her home in Westport, Connecticut to her office in Manhattan, and then back again. "Commuting usually eats up about four hours of my day. The morning commute involves getting up at the crack of dawn. Going home is a little more tiring because I have to contend with rush-hour traffic. If I leave the office by 6:00 p.m. I'll usually struggle through my front door by around 8:00 p.m. Then I'll have half an hour to run, an hour to eat, watch TV, and spend time with my family before I go to bed.
>
> I do it because living in Westport allows me to escape the city. Also, it's a great place to raise a family. As for me, I enjoy my job so I feel it's worth the commute. The long commute does have its advantages, too. It gives me some precious 'me time' when I can read books or interesting articles on my iPad."

c (5 2)) Listen to Maj-Britt on a typical morning and answer the questions.

1 What time does she leave home?
2 What four different ways does she travel?
3 What time does she get to work?

d (5 3)) Now listen and complete some of Maj-Britt's sentences. What do they have in common?

1 I _____ for work in twenty minutes.
2 I'm _____ get on the commuter bus to the train station.
3 My train _____ at 7:15.
4 It's _____ arrive at Westport train station in about 30 minutes, depending on the traffic.
5 I need to be on time today — I _____ a client at 8:45.

e ➤ p.153 Grammar Bank 8B. Learn more about expressing future plans and arrangements, and practice it.

5 LISTENING & SPEAKING

A journey to remember

G-LAZL

Famous people recount travel experiences they remember and sometimes would rather forget...

a (5 4)» You are going to listen to a radio program, *A journey to remember*, in which an orchestra conductor describes a trip he took by air taxi. Listen to part 1 and answer the questions.

1 Where was he going to / from, and why?
2 Why did he choose to use an air taxi?
3 What problem did he find when he got to the airport?
4 What problem did he notice when he got on the plane?
5 If you had been in that situation, what would you have done?

b (5 5)» Listen to part 2 and take notes about the problems that arose during the flight.

c (5 6)» Listen to part 3 and answer the questions.

1 What happened next? Did he make it in time for his rehearsal?
2 After that experience, would you have made the return trip with the same company?
3 What did he do? What happened on the way back?

LEXIS IN CONTEXT

d Look at the highlighted expressions. What do you think they mean? Can you remember how the sentences continued?

1 ...when I arrived at the airport, my heart sank because...
2 ...I was still hoping to make it in time for...
3 ...then to my horror I realized that...
4 By this point the co-pilot himself had realized that...
5 but presumably because of the pressure or the cold — I don't know what...
6 To my relief we landed...
7 Then on the way back the pilots were...
8 ...nothing was going particularly wrong, but I noticed that...

e If you were asked to speak on the program *A journey to remember*, what travel experience would you talk about? (It could be an exotic trip when you were traveling somewhere, or just something unexpected that happened on your way to work or school.) Work in groups of three or four and tell each other about your experience.

6 WRITING

➤ **p.114 Writing** *Discursive essay (2): taking sides.* Write an essay that supports your argument.

7 (5 7)» SONG *Over The Rainbow* ♫

GRAMMAR

a Put the verb in parentheses in the right form.

1 Do you think I should _____ to Mario? (apologize)
2 Rick hates _____ that he doesn't dance very well. (admit)
3 I would love _____ the exhibition, but it finished the day before we arrived. (see)
4 Alex seems _____ a lot recently. Do you think he's studying enough? (go out)
5 Isn't there anywhere _____ here? (sit down)
6 You'd better _____ to the doctor about that cough. (go)
7 There's no point _____ him. He always has his cell phone turned off while he's driving. (call)
8 It's important for celebrities _____ at all the right parties. (see)
9 You're not supposed _____ your cell phone at work, but everyone does. (use)
10 Let's go get a coffee. The meeting isn't due _____ for ten minutes. (begin)

b Circle the right phrases. Check (✓) if both are possible.

1 *I'm supposed to take | I have to take* the medicine every day.
2 *I can hear | I am hearing* voices in the apartment next door. I thought the neighbors were away.
3 It looks *as if | as though* there's going to be a storm tonight.
4 *You should have listened | You should listen* to my advice, but it's too late now.
5 I'll *be | have been* working in the office this afternoon, so you can call me there.
6 *You look | You seem* a little down today. Is everything OK?
7 This coffee *tastes like | tastes of* tea. It's undrinkable!
8 You'd better get on the train now. It *is to | is about* to leave.
9 I'll *have a white suit on | be wearing a white suit*, so you'll easily recognize me at the airport.
10 It smells *as if | like if* someone has burned the toast.

VOCABULARY

a Circle the right word.

1 We drove *under | below* the bridge and into the center of town.
2 It was a very exhausting *travel | trip* to Buenos Aires.
3 I was so tired I slept like a *bat | log* last night.
4 I've been walking all day and my new shoes have given me a *blister | bruise* on my toe.
5 The actor *scribbled | sketched* his autograph on the piece of paper.
6 My husband is as stubborn as a *horse | mule*.
7 Why don't we go for a walk *along | through* the riverbank?
8 I only *glanced | gazed* at the woman, but I would say she was Spanish or Italian.
9 He never hears the doorbell. He's as deaf as a *wall | post*.
10 It's a very quiet place completely off the beaten *road | track*.

b Write words for the definitions.

1 _____-_____ *noun* a painting or drawing that you do of yourself
2 _____ *verb* to open and shut your eyes quickly
3 _____ *noun* a piece of modern sculpture made using objects, sound, etc.
4 _____ *noun* a Chinese method of treating pain and disease using needles
5 _____ *verb* to shake because you are nervous, frightened, excited, etc.
6 _____ *noun* a kind of treatment that uses hypnosis to treat physical or emotional problems
7 _____ *verb* to draw lines or shapes, especially when you are bored or thinking about something else
8 _____ *noun* the natural features of an area, e.g., mountains, valleys, rivers, or forests

c Complete the sentences using the **bold** word and a prefix.

1 The man didn't speak clearly, and I totally _____ what he said. **UNDERSTAND**
2 I get very _____ when I feel that I'm not making any progress. **MOTIVATE**
3 Even though the Scottish soldiers were completely _____ by the English, they won the battle. **NUMBER**
4 The movie isn't as good as everyone says it is. I think it is very _____. **RATE**
5 Look, I think they have _____ us. The check should be 80 dollars, not 60. **CHARGE**
6 When I am traveling, I usually use _____ phone cards to make calls. **PAY**
7 The meeting has been postponed and will be _____ for a later date. **SCHEDULE**
8 I think trying to make people happier by imposing all kinds of new laws on them is _____. **LOGICAL**

CAN YOU UNDERSTAND THIS TEXT?

a Read the article. Then mark the sentences **T** (true) or **F** (false).

1 After Amber Young contacted an online health service, a doctor visited her home in Minnesota.
2 eMedicine is limited to emergencies.
3 When Kris Taylor was in the hospital, his doctor was in a different city.
4 Kris Taylor couldn't see his doctor, but his doctor could see him.
5 Specialists in Boston helped with Gibson's knee surgery in the South Pole using telecommunication.
6 eMedicine has been expanding rapidly since the 1970s.
7 Most patients are satisfied with the lower costs and convenience of eMedicine.

b Choose five new words or phrases from the text. Check their meaning and pronunciation and try to learn them.

CAN YOU UNDERSTAND THIS PROGRAM?

a ⑤⑧)) You are going to hear a radio program with two different opinions about whether or not to climb Uluru. Listen and choose the correct answers.

1 Tour operator Robert Cowan is **for/against** climbing Uluru. His company's owners and tour guides **have/ haven't** climbed the rock.
2 Journalist Dominic Hughes is **for/against** climbing Uluru. He **believes/doesn't believe** in the sacred stories of the Anangu people.

b Listen to the program again. Then mark the sentences **T** (true) or **F** (false). If the sentence is false, explain why.
1 More and more people have been climbing Uluru recently.
2 The Aboriginal people ask tourists *not* to climb.
3 According to Cowan, the tour operator, it's mostly wealthy tourists who want to climb.
4 Cowan's tour company does not allow their passengers to climb Uluru.
5 If the climb is prohibited, Cowan's tour company will make more money.
6 Hughes, the journalist, thought his friend had good reasons to say no to climbing.
7 Hughes believes you can respect others' beliefs without following them.
8 In the end, Hughes convinced his friend to climb Uluru.

c After listening to the arguments on both sides, would you climb Uluru?

eMedicine is here

Tired of feeling "like the walking dead," Amber Young sat on her bed near tears one recent Friday night in Woodbury, Minnesota.

Then she logged onto an Internet site run by an online health care company and "met" with a doctor hundreds of miles away in Texas. After talking with the physician via instant messaging and then by telephone, Young was diagnosed with an upper respiratory illness and prescribed antibiotics that her husband picked up at a local pharmacy.

"I was as suspicious as anyone about getting treated over the computer," said Young, 34. "But I could not have been happier with the service."

Experts say Internet- and telephone-based medical services are transforming health care, giving consumers access to inexpensive, round-the-clock care for routine problems — often without having to leave home or work. Yet "eMedicine" isn't limited to non-emergency problems. When Arizona resident Kris Taylor, 32, was admitted to a nearby hospital's intensive-care unit (ICU), he was diagnosed with a potentially life-threatening diabetic reaction.

In the "eICU," Taylor was treated by a doctor in a different city, via a two-way camera in the patient's room. From far away, the doctor evaluated Taylor's condition and regularly communicated with him and his nurses. Taylor received medications to treat his diabetes and was out of the hospital's ICU within 48 hours. As a patient, Taylor was satisfied that the doctor, located miles away, checked him several times during the day and night.

Another, more extreme, case of eMedicine took place when doctors in Boston helped a physician at a South Pole station surgically repair the damaged knee of a meteorologist spending the winter in Antarctica. Using a "telemedicine" connection, two specialists in Boston, an orthopedic surgeon and an anesthesiologist, helped South Pole physician Dr. Timothy Pollard repair a damaged tendon in the left knee of Dar Gibson, a meteorologist who had injured his knee in a fall.

The field of eMedicine developed in the 1970s as a way to deliver health care to patients in remote areas, though its growth was slow. That has changed in recent years thanks to the development of high-speed communications networks and the push to lower health costs.

Nonetheless, some doctors and patients resist eMedicine, despite overwhelmingly positive reviews from consumers who have actually used it — those patients often say it is more convenient and less costly than traditional health care.

G ellipsis and substitution
V the natural world
P weak and strong pronunciation of auxiliary verbs and *to*

9A Pets and pests

"I loathe people who keep dogs. They are cowards who haven't got the guts to bite people themselves.

August Strindberg, Swedish dramatist"

1 READING

a Look at the photos of animals. What kinds of people do you think would choose them as pets?

b Read an article about pets and their owners. Which of the owners do you think has most in common with their pet(s)?

Pets and owners "become more alike over time"

Pets and their owners are just like married couples and become more alike over time, according to recent research. In a recent study, 2,500 pet owners were asked to complete an online questionnaire about their personalities and those of their pets. The study showed that many dog lovers, cat owners, and even reptile owners shared many of the same traits such as happiness, intelligence, and sense of humor as their pets.

The dog owner

Paul Keevil, a photographer and artist, believes he and his pet dog Crosby are growing more grumpy together as they get older. Mr. Keevil bred Crosby, a rare Dandie Dinmont terrier, and has kept him as a pet for the past eight years. Not only does he think they look alike, he says they have increasingly developed the same personality over the years. "I'm becoming a little more bad-tempered as I get older," Mr. Keevil said, "and so is he. We like our own space, and we are not as tolerant as we used to be. I certainly enjoy my food as much as he does, although I'm a little fussier. Other than that, I think I am a little bit more intelligent." He added "I think it's possible that pets and owners do grow alike as they get older. It may also be that there is something subliminal when it comes to us choosing our pets. If someone is happy and cheerful, then they tend to choose a dog that is always wagging its tail."

The fish owner

Sarah Ogilvie believes she is far more serene since acquiring a similarly relaxed goldfish called Garfield. A marketing consultant who works in a stressful environment, Ms. Ogilvie says she looks forward to coming home from work to see him swimming lazily in his tank. "I just sit in my armchair and watch him swirl around," she said. "It's better than watching TV by far. I'm sure he recognizes me — he always comes up to the glass when I walk toward him, but maybe that's because I feed him. He's more friendly than a lot of those aquarium fish you see in big offices. He's quite a character. Am I happier because of Garfield? I think I probably am. They say that being near water is calming in itself, so maybe that has something to do with it."

The cat owner

Laila El Baradei said that she and her cat shared one behavior trait: they both enjoy harassing her husband. The 30-year-old London lawyer has owned Philphil (Arabic for Papa) for four years. "She bites my husband's toes and attacks him on my behalf, constantly harassing him when he's trying to do something," Mrs. El Baradei said. "In that sense she is like me — and shares my sense of humor. We both like to snuggle up at night. I get very cold, and warm myself up, and Philphil sleeps on the radiator." While Mrs. El Baradei admitted to numerous similarities, she hoped there were differences. "While she is smart, I'd like to think I am more intelligent than my cat."

The reptile owner

Graham Martin, who keeps lizards, said their personalities change to become more like his. "I've had bearded dragons calmly sitting and watching TV when I do. If you have lots of energy, they pick up on that, and if you are afraid, they are too. They tend to reflect whoever has brought them up. If they've had a stressed owner, then they can be very stressed, they can behave like complete lunatics. But generally, because I'm calm, they tend to calm themselves down."

The bird owner

Friends tell Juliet Eberle that she is eccentric, just like her five birds. "It's not so much me who thinks that, but I think some of my friends do," she conceded, "and if enough people say it, then it might be true." Ms. Eberle said that she had undoubtedly picked up some of her birds' traits. "The way I talk sometimes and bob my head has become more parrot-like," she admitted. Her parrots include a huge Mealy Amazon called Molly, two Eclectus parrots, and a pair of African greys. They all have individual traits she sees in herself. "Molly loves people," said Ms. Eberle. "At times she's kind of a show-off, like me. And the greys have a great sense of humor."

From *The Daily Telegraph*

c Now read the article again and find answers to the questions below. Answer with D (the dog owner), F (the fish owner), C (the cat owner), R (the reptile owner), or B (the bird owner).

Who…?

1 finds that their pet creates a different atmosphere from the atmosphere at work ☐
2 enjoys the same pastimes as their pet ☐
3 thinks that having a pet has changed them ☐
4 says that other people think that they and their pet have similar personalities ☐
5 thinks that people unconsciously buy pets that are like them ☐
6 thinks that pets' personalities change according to the owners they have had ☐
7 thinks that they and their pet have developed in the same way simultaneously ☐
8 thinks that their pets are changing to become more like them ☐
9 thinks that they now have gestures they have picked up from their pets ☐
10 sleeps in the same way as their pet ☐

LEXIS IN CONTEXT

d Find the following words in the text related to personality.

Introduction
1 _____ (adj.) similar to sb / sth
2 _____ (noun) a particular quality in your personality

The dog owner
3 _____ (adj.) bad-tempered
4 _____ (adj.) able to accept what other people do and think
5 _____ (adj.) concerned about unimportant details

The fish owner
6 _____ (adj.) calm

The cat owner
7 _____ (adj.) clever

The reptile owner
8 _____ (noun) crazy people

The bird owner
9 _____ (adj.) strange or unusual
10 _____ (noun) a person who tries to impress other people by showing how good he or she is at doing sth

e Think of pets you have or have had, or people you know who have pets. Do you agree with the article that pets and their owners become more alike over time?

2 GRAMMAR ellipsis and substitution

a Complete the sentences from the text with an auxiliary verb. What is their function in the sentences?

1 "I'm becoming a little more bad-tempered as I get older, and so _____ he."
2 "I certainly enjoy my food as much as he _____."
3 "Am I happier because of Garfield? I think I probably _____."
4 "I've had bearded dragons calmly sitting and watching TV when I _____."
5 "It's not so much me who thinks that, but I think some of my friends _____."

b ➤ p.154 Grammar Bank 9A. Learn more about ellipsis and substitution, and practice them.

3 PRONUNCIATION weak and strong pronunciation of auxiliary verbs and *to*

a (5 9)) Read the dialogues and underline the auxiliaries or *to* when you think they are stressed. Listen and check. Then practice saying the dialogue.

A Do you like dogs?
B No, I don't, but my husband does.
A So does mine. We have three German shepherds.

A I took a cruise to Alaska last summer.
B Lucky you. I'd love to do that. Did you see any whales?
A No. I wanted to, but I got seasick, and I mostly stayed in my cabin.

A Allie doesn't have any pets, does she?
B She does have a pet. She has a hamster.
A Ugh. I don't like hamsters.
B Neither do I. They're too much like mice.

b Answer the questions with a partner.

1 Are auxiliary verbs stressed (S) or unstressed (U) in the following?
   • in question tags
   • in short answers
   • in *wh-* questions
   • in negative sentences
   • when they are used for emphasis
   • with *so* and *neither*
   • when they are the last word in a sentence
2 What vowel sound do unstressed auxiliaries usually have?
3 How is *to* pronounced
   a) when it's unstressed   b) when it's stressed?
4 When is *to* stressed?

c ➤ **Communication** Match the sentences **A** p.120 **B** p.122. Match the sentence halves.

4 VOCABULARY the natural world

a Work with a partner. How many of the quiz questions can you answer?

Animals, birds, and insects

1 What do you call a young…?
  a dog _____
  b cat _____
  c horse _____
  d cow _____

2 Which creatures live in…?
  a a nest _____
  b a hive _____
  c a stable _____
  d a kennel _____
  e a tank _____
  f a cage _____

3 What animals make the following noises?
  a squeak _____
  b bark _____
  c neigh /neɪ/ _____
  d meow _____
  e roar _____
  f grunt _____

b ➤ p.166 Vocabulary Bank *The natural world.*

c Choose five circles. Tell your partner something about a person you know who…

- goes hunting or fishing regularly
- has an unusual pet
- doesn't eat meat or fish because of their principles
- is allergic to bee or wasp stings
- has a dog that barks incessantly
- is often in the doghouse with their spouse
- has been bitten by a snake
- is an animal rights activist
- has a fear of animals
- is a member of an organization that protects the environment
- doesn't believe in wearing fur
- has been attacked by a wild animal
- can't eat shellfish
- breeds animals
- has a bark that is worse than their bite

5 LISTENING

a What animals are considered pests in your country? What animals that live in your country can be dangerous?

b (5 10)) (5 11)) Listen to two extracts from different news broadcasts, one about a woodpecker and one about snakes. What do the stories have in common?

c Read summaries of the two stories. Can you remember any of the missing words? Listen again and complete the summaries with one word in each blank.

1 The first morning after Louisa Hobson returned home from a business trip, she was awoken by the sound of a 1_____ .

It wasn't pecking on 2_____, as you would expect, but at a neighbor's metal drainage pipe. The noise would start at 3_____ each morning and go on for hours.

In desperation, Louisa decided to ask friends on Facebook how to 4_____ the bird.

A lot of people were 5_____ that Louisa would want to harm the bird. She didn't know that it was a 6_____ species and actually thought of it as a 7_____ .

Then a friend suggested getting a plastic 8_____ to scare it away, and Louisa decided to try it. After that, the bird was gone.

2 In August, 1992, a huge 1_____ hit Southern Florida. Because of the force of the storm, an exotic pet dealer's 2_____ was destroyed and many of the 900 Burmese 3_____ snakes living there escaped to the wetlands.

Today, their population has 4_____ and thousands of them are loose.

These snakes pose a threat to small animals whose population has been 5_____ by more than 98 percent. The snakes have even been known to swallow larger animals, such as 6 _____ and 7_____ .

No one knows exactly how many of these snakes are in the Everglades, but their numbers are estimated to be between 8_____ and 9_____ .

Wildlife officials are encouraging people to 10_____ and kill the snakes. The important thing is to prevent them from 11_____ to other areas.

d Are any species of wild animal a problem where you live? What is being done about it?

6 SPEAKING

a (5 12))) Listen to some short extracts of people discussing the issues below and complete the phrases with an adverb.

> **Common adverb collocations**
> 1 Now that's something I feel _____ _____ about…
> 2 Well, I don't feel _____ _____ about it either way.
> 3 I have to say I am _____ against zoos nowadays…
> 4 Oh no, I _____ disagree with you there…
> 5 Well, I couldn't disagree with you _____.
> 6 Well, I don't _____ agree with you…
> 7 Well, I'm _____ convinced that the animal does not want to be there…
> 8 Well, I'm _____ sure that kids could get the same amount of pleasure from seeing animals in the wild.

b Work in groups of three or four. You are going to debate some of the issues below. Each choose a different issue, for which you will start a debate. Plan what you are going to say, making a few notes to help you.

Animal debates

People should not be allowed to keep very aggressive breeds of dog such as Rottweilers as pets.

In a civilized society there is no place for entertainment that involves cruelty to animals.

Animal rights activists are correct when they object to animals being used in experiments.

Zoos nowadays serve no useful purpose and should be outlawed.

It is hypocritical for people who call themselves animal lovers to eat meat and fish.

People who live in apartments should not be allowed to have pets that require exercise.

Hunting as a sport should be banned.

Animals raised for food should be kept in humane conditions.

c Hold your debates. On which topic, as a group, do you most strongly a) agree b) disagree? Try to incorporate language from **a**.

7 (5 13))) **SONG** *Talking Bird* ♫

G nouns: compound and possessive forms
V preparing food
P -ed adjective endings and linking

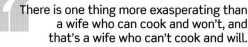

There is one thing more exasperating than a wife who can cook and won't, and that's a wife who can't cook and will.

Robert Frost, American poet

9B A recipe for disaster

1 VOCABULARY preparing food

a Imagine you are in a restaurant and are given the menu below. Study it for a couple of minutes, and choose what to have. Compare with a partner.

Ben's Bistro

starters

cobb salad	$7.95
grilled chicken, avocado, blue cheese, and arugula with raspberry vinaigrette	
steamed mussels	$9.95
with coconut and chili peppers	
grilled sardines	$8.50
with parsley, lemon, and garlic	

main courses

thai chicken curry	$17.95
stir-fried chicken, Thai spices, peppers, onions, cashew nuts, and coconut milk with jasmine rice or egg noodles	
pork sausages	$15.95
with garlic mashed potatoes and onion purée	
herb crusted lamb chops	$17.50
with potatoes, steamed green beans, and balsamic sauce	
smoked salmon	$15.95
with mashed potatoes, poached egg, and hollandaise sauce	
baked eggplant	$14.95
stuffed with basmati rice, pecorino cheese, and pistachios	

desserts

plum and almond tart	$8.95
with amaretto custard	
apple and blackberry pie	$9.50
with vanilla ice cream	

please note that the menu is subject to change
a service charge of 15% will be added to your bill

b Complete the chart with words from the menu. Try to find at least three for each column.

Ways of preparing food	Vegetables	Fruit	Sauces and dressings	Fish and seafood

c What fruits, vegetables, and fish / seafood are really popular in your region / country? Do you know how to say them in English?

d ➤ **p.167 Vocabulary Bank** *Preparing food.*

2 PRONUNCIATION
-ed adjective endings and linking

a Write the words in the chart according to how the *-ed* ending is pronounced.

baked   boiled   chopped   grated   grilled   mashed
melted   minced   peeled   scrambled   sliced   steamed
stir-fried   stuffed   toasted   whipped

-ed = /t/	*-ed* = /d/	*-ed* = /ɪd/

b (5 14))) Listen and check.

c (5 15))) Practice saying the phrases below, linking the two words together. Listen and check. Why are the words linked?

baked apples	scrambled eggs	stuffed eggplant
boiled eggs	sliced onions	toasted almonds
peeled oranges	steamed asparagus	

d (5 16))) How do you think you say these phrases? Listen and check.

chopped tomatoes   stir-fried tofu   grilled tuna

e What adjectives can you put in front of these items to describe the way they are cooked, for example *fried eggs*?

eggs   meat   chicken   vegetables

3 LISTENING

a (5 17)) Listen to three people describing cooking disasters and complete the information in the chart.

	Who were they cooking for?	What ingredients do they mention?	What went wrong?	What happened in the end?
Speaker 1				
Speaker 2				
Speaker 3				

LEXIS IN CONTEXT

b (5 18)) Listen to some extracts from the listening. What do you think the missing words are? How do you think they are spelled and what do you think they mean?

1 I imagined them enjoying the food and _____ each bite.

2 …the water was already boiling and the salt quickly _____.

3 I _____ the steaks in the honey for a few hours…

4 The steaks were too sweet, _____, and _____!

c Have you ever had a cooking disaster, or experienced somebody else's? What was the dish being made? What went wrong?

4 SPEAKING

a Work in groups of three. Imagine you have friends coming over this evening, and there is nowhere near where you can eat out or order takeout. All you have in the house (besides oil, salt, flour, sugar, etc.) are the ingredients below. Decide what you're going to serve and how you're going to cook it.

onions

lettuce

a lemon

chicken breasts

walnuts

canned tomatoes

cheese

eggs

apples

b In groups, discuss the questions.

1 Who is the best cook in your family? What dishes do they make particularly well?

2 Do you like cooking? Why (not)? What (if anything) would you cook…?
   a if you were alone at home   b if you had friends coming over

3 Do you have a dish that is your speciality or that you often make? How do you make it?

4 Do you enjoy reading cookbooks to find new recipes?

5 GRAMMAR

nouns: compound and possessive forms

a Circle the right phrase in each pair. If you think both are possible, explain what the difference between them is.

1 a recipe book / a recipe's book
2 a tuna salad / a salad of tuna
3 children's portions / children portions
4 a coffee cup / a cup of coffee
5 a chef hat / a chef's hat
6 a can opener / a cans opener
7 James' kitchen / James's kitchen
8 a John's friend / a friend of John's

b ▶ p.155 Grammar Bank 9B. Learn more about nouns, and practice them.

6 READING

a Read the introduction to a book called *My Last Supper* and find the answers to the questions.

1 What is the "My last supper" game?
2 Who plays the game in the book?
3 Do you recognize any of the chefs? Have you dined at any of their restaurants?

b Read the introduction again and answer the questions with a partner.

1 Why does Anthony Bourdain think chefs are good at the "My last supper" game?
2 Why does he think their answers are surprising? Do you agree?
3 What impression does he give of a typical chef's character? Do you think it is accurate?
4 What, according to Anthony Bourdain, is the difference between cooking and eating? Do you agree?

MY LAST SUPPER

INTRODUCTION

BY CHEF ANTHONY BOURDAIN

CHEFS have been playing the "My last supper" game, in one version or another, since humans first gathered around the flames to cook. Whether late at night, after their kitchens had closed, sitting at a wobbly table on the periphery of Les Halles in nineteenth century Paris and drinking vin ordinaire, or while nibbling bits of chicken from skewers in after-hours izakayas in Tokyo, or perched at the darkened bar of a closed New York City restaurant, enjoying vintages they couldn't otherwise afford, someone always piped up, "If you were to die tomorrow, what single dish, what mouthful of food from anywhere in the world or any time in your life would you choose as your last?"

I've played the game myself, hundreds of times, with my crew in Manhattan, line cooks in San Francisco and Portland, chefs from Sydney to Kuala Lumpur to São Paulo — and with many of the subjects in this book. It's remarkable how simple, rustic, and unpretentious most of their selections are. These are people who, more often than not, have dined widely and well. They know what a fresh white truffle tastes like. The finest beluga for them holds no mysteries. With chefs traveling so much these days, many have enjoyed every variety of edible exotica. Which is to say, chefs know good stuff. And they get a lot of it.

And yet, when we ask ourselves and each other the question, what would we want as that last taste of life, we seem to crave reminders of simpler, harder times. A crust of bread and butter. Poor-people food. When we think of what we would eat last, we revert from the loud obsessive dominating control freaks we have become to the children we once were. Not that all of us were happy children, but we were children just the same. If cooking professionally is about control — about manipulating the people, the ingredients, and the strange physical forces of the kitchen universe to do our bidding, always anticipating, always preparing, always dominating one's environment — then eating well is about submission. About letting go.

Ferran Adrià

Jamie Oliver

Guillaume Brahimi

Raymond Blanc

Lidia Bastianich

Glossary

Les Halles the traditional central market of Paris, which was demolished in 1971

izakaya a type of Japanese drinking establishment which also serves food to accompany the drinks

c Now look at the questions and some of the answers. Whose choices do you most agree with?

THE QUESTIONS

1 What would your last meal on earth be?
2 What would the setting for the meal be?
3 Would there be music?
4 Who would your dining companions be?

d Read the answers again and complete the sentences in your own words.

1 Ferran Adrià and Guillaume Brahini differ from the others in their choice of food because…
2 The most commonly chosen setting is…
3 Jamie Oliver and Tetsuya Wakuda are the only chefs who wouldn't…
4 Raymond Blanc would particularly like to have his partner Natalia with him because…

LEXIS IN CONTEXT

e Read the article again and underline any words for items of food or drink that you did not know. Compare with a partner, and check their meaning with a dictionary. Are any of these words ones that you wouldn't consider to be English?

f Now find words in the text to match the definitions below.

Introduction	1 _____	*verb* take small bites of sth, especially food
	2 _____	*noun* a long, thin piece of metal that is pushed through pieces of meat or vegetables to hold them together while they are cooking
	3 _____	*adj.* that can be eaten
	4 _____	*verb* have a very strong desire for sth, especially food
	5 _____	*noun* the hard outer surface of bread
Lidia Bastianich	6 _____	*adj.* fully grown and ready to be eaten
Ferran Adrià	7 _____	*noun* a lot of different dishes served in small quantities
Tetsuya Wakuda	8 _____	*verb* capture a fish
Raymond Blanc	9 _____	*verb (formal)* have dinner

g With a partner, answer the four questions, and explain your choices.

7 WRITING

➤ **p.116 Writing** *A complaint.* Write a letter of complaint.

THE ANSWERS

Tetsuya Wakuda

LIDIA BASTIANICH ITALIAN

1 My last meal would consist of a plate of sliced San Daniele prosciutto with some ripe black figs; linguine with white clam sauce; a plate of Gran Padano; and perfectly ripe juicy peaches.
2 The setting would be in my house overlooking the Adriatic, while the waves crashed against the rocky shore.
3 *Scheherazade* would be playing in surround sound.
4 I would like my family and closest friends with me.

JAMIE OLIVER BRITISH

1 I would have a big pot of spaghetti all'arrabbiata made with three types of chilies — my perfect comfort food. If I were going to have dessert, it would be homemade rice pudding with roasted peaches. The rice pudding would be served very cold and topped with the hot caramelized peaches.
2 I would be in my house in Essex, cuddled up on the sofa with my wife. There would be some silly show on television and a fire going. The window would be open just a crack, with the fresh air cooling the back of my neck after all those chilies.
3 Just the TV playing in the background.
4 My wife Jools would be sitting beside me.

FERRAN ADRIÀ SPANISH

1 I love seafood, so my last meal would be a tasting menu that featured a variety of seafood, prepared in many different ways, and inspired by the cuisine at Kiccho Restaurant in Kyoto, Japan. I would finish the meal with fruit from the Amazon that I had never tasted before.
2 I wouldn't like to have my last meal on earth, but if there were no alternative I would have it at Kiccho. The restaurant is a Japanese house with a beautiful Zen garden.
3 I would like to listen to fusion music, and the same Berber music that they have in Yahout restaurant in Marrakesh. To see Berber musicians performing transports you to ancestral times and places, while at the same time it sounds so progressive and modern.
4 My companions would be my wife, my family, and my friends.

GUILLAUME BRAHIMI FRENCH

1 Definitely a multicourse feast, starting with oysters and caviar, followed by some foie gras, then a nice piece of rib eye steak, and lastly some cheese.
2 At home. As a chef, I'm home too little, so it is always a great luxury to be in my house, seated in my favorite chair, with my children bouncing and playing around me.
3 I love opera. I'd like to hear my favorite of all time, Verdi's *La Traviata*.
4 My family. I have three daughters ages one, four, and seven, and am very close to my family in France. We're a very Latin bunch, so it would involve lots of talking, hugging, tears, and laughter.

TETSUYA WAKUDA JAPANESE

1 My passion is fishing and boating. Since my favorite food in the world is tuna, I want my last meal to be like this: I would be on the boat, fishing; we would catch a tuna, let it settle for a few days, and then eat it. I would prepare it many ways — sashimi, carpaccio, lightly seared, tartare.
2 On a boat of any size, any place; it doesn't matter to me as long as I am on the water.
3 There would just be the sounds of the water and the wind.
4 I would be with my sailing teacher and my fishing teacher.

RAYMOND BLANC FRENCH

1 I imagine the food would be something humble and simple, something very casual with comfortable flavors like a big fat local saucisse de Morteau with some Gruyère to accompany it, and a crusty traditional baguette. That would be just fine.
2 We would definitely be in France, somewhere near where my parents live in Besançon.
3 The Rolling Stones come to mind. Afterwards I am likely to need peace and quiet, so Arvo Pärt, the Estonian composer, would perform his *Spiegel im Spiegel*. That would be perfect.
4 I would dine with my friend René, who has been my best friend since I was two. My two sons would have to be there, since they are not only my sons but my best friends as well. My partner Natalia would bring a little humor to the whole process. Being Russian, she has a great knowledge of the grieving process. The Russians love their dead, and mourn them openly for years. Their cemeteries are in the woods, and they plant trees there to shade the graves. Once a year they go to them with vodka and bread and let their grieving out.

1 ◼◄ VIDEO THE INTERVIEW Part 1

a Read the biographical information about Chantelle Nicholson. What part have Josh Emmet, Gordon Ramsay and Marcus Wareing played in her career?

Chantelle Nicholson is a New Zealand chef and she's worked for award-winning restaurants such as the Savoy and the Berkeley. She originally started out pursuing a law degree then worked in banking before following a career path in the culinary industry. She received her first cooking opportunity when Josh Emett, then of the Savoy, discovered her through the Gordon Ramsay Scholarship competition and offered her a job. She worked for several years as a sous-chef at the Marcus Wareing restaurant in London, and she considers him her mentor.

b (5 19)》 Watch or listen to Part 1 of an interview with her. Mark sentences 1-5 below **T** (true) or **F** (false).

1 There were 12 applicants for the first round of the Gordon Ramsay Scholarship.
2 Chantelle believed that Marcus Wareing was a great mentor because he had a good business sense and was a perfectionist.
3 People are treated differently according to the things they order off the menu.
4 Some ingredients are considered more important than others at the restaurant.
5 The restaurant focuses on making ingredients taste differently than they really do.

c Now listen again and say why the **F** sentences are false.

Glossary
foodie *informal* a person who is very interested in food and cooking
the Gordon Ramsay scholarship a scholarship for young chefs set up by the celebrity chef Gordon Ramsay, where the winner gets work experience and a cash prize
Josh Emett the head chef at the Savoy Grill (at the Savoy Hotel in London)
Marcus Wareing well-respected British chef who ran the Savoy Grill and now runs several other highly prestigious London restaurants
beetroot a dark red root vegetable

◼◄ VIDEO Part 2

a (5 20)》 Watch or listen to part 2. What does she say about…?

1 the difference between a sous-chef and a head chef
2 the hours she works
3 things that cause stress in the kitchen
4 why she doesn't cook at home very much
5 her last meal on earth

b Answer the questions with a partner.

1 What impression do you get of Chantelle's attitude toward her job?
2 Is it a job that would appeal to you?

Glossary
delicacy a type of food considered to be very special
scallops a kind of shellfish
Tarte Tatin a French cake usually made with apples or pears

2 LOOKING AT LANGUAGE

> 🔍 **Distancing**
> Chantelle often uses language to distance herself when she is answering questions by using certain words or phrases, e.g., "I guess in a sense," "I mean, "etc. that don't add meaning but which we use to soften and distance the things we say.

a (5 21)》 Listen to some extracts from the interview and complete the phrases.

1 _____ my parents when I was younger.
2 _____ , it was always something that I was interested in from an early age and I used to be the kitchen quite a lot.
3 ...he's quite, _____ I wouldn't want to work for any other chef of that high caliber really.
4 So in that sense he's a great kind of mentor, _____ .
5 We, _____ , we're more about Marcus, Marcus is a person that's very respectful of ingredients and basically treats, _____ , will treat a carrot the same way as a piece of foie gras...
6 Basically a sous-chef is, _____ a second chef...

3 🎥 VIDEO ON THE STREET

a (5 22)》 You are going to hear three people talking about food. What three questions are they asked? Who is most / least positive about the cuisine in their country? Which is the most popular foreign cuisine?

| Victor | Jackie | Ezra |

b Listen again and answer the questions.

Victor
1 What examples does he give of American cuisine?
2 What does he say about food in California compared to other parts of the country?
3 What does he mean when he says "buzz words"? What examples does he give?

Jackie
4 What does she say about the cuisine in New York City?
5 What's her favorite type of cuisine? Why?

Ezra
6 What does he say about food in New York compared to other areas in the US?
7 What does he like about his favorite cuisine?

c (5 23)》 Listen and complete the phrases with two words. What do you think they mean?

> **Useful phrases**
> 1 I have a _____ _____ defining what American cuisine is.
> 2 Living in a rather, I suppose, _____ _____ ...
> 3 I am a very heavy _____-_____ .
> 4 If you're in New York, American food is a lack of a better term is a _____ _____ ...
> 5 You have Italian, Chinese, Thai, _____-_____ , wherever you go.

4 SPEAKING

Answer the questions with a partner. Practice using distancing to give yourself time to think, and where possible the useful phrases.

1 What's your favorite type of cuisine? Why do you like it so much?
2 Do you think people from your country are good cooks?
3 Do you think the cuisine in your country is healthy?
4 What are the different types of restaurants in your city? Which ones do you go to most often?
5 In general, do you believe that food in expensive restaurants is worth the price tag?

G adding emphasis (2): cleft sentences
V words that are often confused
P intonation in cleft sentences

10A The promised land?

"We can have no "50–50" allegiance in this country. Either a man is an American and nothing else, or he is not an American at all.

Theodore Roosevelt, American President"

1 LISTENING & SPEAKING

a Can you think of some reasons why people decide to go and live in another country, or in another city in their country? Can you imagine doing it yourself?

b Talk to a partner. What do you think are the pros and cons of...?
• living in a country which is not your own
• living in a city in your country which is not your own

c (5 24)) (5 25)) You are going to listen to two people who emigrated to another country. Take brief notes in the chart.

d Compare the information in the chart. Who do you think feels more positive about their adopted country?

Poland

Renata

Spain

	Renata, from Poland, who lives in Spain	Jung-hwa from South Korea, who lives in the US
1 Why did they go there in the first place?		
2 How long have they been living there?		
3 What is the positive side of living there?		
4 What is the downside?		
5 What do they miss most about their home country?		
6 Do they think they'll ever go back to their country? Why (not)?		

LEXIS IN CONTEXT

e Look at some expressions that Renata and Jung-hwa used. In what context did they use them? What do you think they mean?

Renata
1 It was **a bit of a fluke** really.
2 ...**the paperwork**, which would have been very complicated.
3 But **bit by bit** we managed to find jobs and somewhere to live.
4 Of course — **loads of** things!

Jung-hwa
5 I had no idea how things were going to **unfold**.
6 I'm still **living the dream**...
7 ...the best place to see **people at their best and worst**.

f Talk to a partner.
1 Do you have any friends who have emigrated to another country or who are foreigners who have come to live in your county? Where have they gone to or come from?
2 How do you think they would answer the questions that Renata and Jung-hwa answer in **d**?

South Korea

Jung-hwa

the US

2 GRAMMAR adding emphasis (2): cleft sentences

a Sentences 1–4 below convey ideas which the speakers expressed, but they phrased them in a slightly different way. Can you remember what they actually said?

1 In fact, my husband first came up with the idea of moving here.
"In fact, it _____."

2 If you're prepared to work hard you can get what you want, and that's what I like best.
"What _____."

3 I first came here because I always wanted to improve my English and live abroad.
"The reason _____."

4 My attitude toward communication has definitely changed a lot.
"One thing _____."

b (5)26)) Listen and check. Now look at the pairs of sentences. What's the difference between them?

c ► p.156 Grammar Bank 10A. Learn more about cleft sentences, and practice them.

3 PRONUNCIATION & SPEAKING intonation in cleft sentences

> **Cleft Sentences**
>
> Cleft sentences beginning with *What...* or *The person / place*, etc. typically have a fall-rising tone at the end of the *what...* clause.
>
> *What I hate about my job is having to get up early.*
>
> *The reason why I went to Japan was because I wanted to learn the language.*
>
> Cleft sentences beginning with *It...* typically have a falling tone in the clause beginning with *It.*
>
> *It was her mother who really broke up our marriage.*
>
> *It's the commuting that I find so tiring.*

a (5)27)) Read the information in the box and listen to each example sentence twice.

b (5)28)) Listen and repeat the sentences below, copying the intonation patterns.

1 What I don't understand is why she didn't call me.
2 The thing that impresses me most about Jack is his enthusiasm.
3 The reason why I left early was because I had an important meeting.
4 The place where I would most like to live is Thailand.
5 It was the neighbors that made our lives so difficult.
6 It was then that I realized I'd left my keys behind.

c Complete the sentences in your own words. Then use them to start conversations with your partner.

What I would find most difficult about living abroad is...
What I love about the summer is...
What I least like about this town is...
The person I most admire in my family is...
The place where I would most like to live is...
The reason why I decided to come to this school was...
What I love about...
What I hate about...
The reason why I...

4 READING & SPEAKING

a You are going to read an extract from *The Joy Luck Club*, a best-selling book by Amy Tan about first and second generation immigrants, which has also been made into a movie. Before you read, answer the questions below with a partner.

1 Do you know any second generation immigrants to your country?

What country did their parents originally come from?

Do the parents in the family still keep up their language and culture? What about the children?

2 Do you think some children of immigrants might have a conflict of identity? Why (not)?

b Now read an extract from the book. To what extent do you think Waverly is having an identity crisis? What does her mother feel about it?

> *The Joy Luck Club is the story of four Chinese mothers and their first-generation Chinese-American daughters; two generations of women struggling to come to terms with their cultural identity. Here Lindo Jong, one of the mothers, talks about her daughter, Waverly.*

LINDO JONG

Double Face

1 My daughter wanted to go to China for her second honeymoon, but now she is afraid.

"What if I blend in so well they think I'm one of them?" Waverly asked me. "What if they don't let me come back
5 to the United States?"

"When you go to China," I told her, "you don't even need to open your mouth. They already know you are an outsider".

"What are you talking about?" she asked. My daughter likes to speak back. She likes to question what I say.

10 "Aii-ya," I said. "Even if you put on their clothes, even if you take off your makeup and hide your fancy jewelry, they know. They know just watching you walk, the way you carry your face. They know you do not belong."

My daughter did not look pleased when I told her this,
15 that she didn't look Chinese. She had a sour American look on her face. Oh, maybe ten years ago, she would have clapped her hands — hurray! — as if this were good news. But now she wants to be Chinese, it is so fashionable. And I know it is too late. All those years I tried to teach her!
20 She followed my Chinese ways only until she learned how to walk out the door by herself and go to school. So now the only Chinese words she can say are *sh-sh, houche, chr fan* and *gwan deng shweijyau*. How can she talk to people in China with those words only? Pee-pee, choo-choo train,

25 eat, close light, sleep. How can she think she can blend in? Only her skin and her hair are Chinese. Inside — she is all American-made.

It's my fault she is this way. I wanted my children to have the best combination: American circumstances and
30 Chinese character. How could I know these two things do not mix?

I taught her how American circumstances work. If you are born poor here, it's no lasting shame. You are first in line for a scholarship. If the roof crashes on your head,
35 no need to cry over this bad luck. You can sue anybody, make the landlord fix it. You do not have to sit like a Buddha under a tree letting pigeons drop their dirty business on your head. You can buy an umbrella. Or go inside a Catholic church. In America, nobody says you
40 have to keep the circumstances somebody else gives you.

She learned these things, but I couldn't teach her about Chinese character. How to obey parents and listen to your mother's mind. How not to show your own thoughts, to put your feelings behind your face, so you
45 can take advantage of hidden opportunities. Why easy things are not worth pursuing. How to know your own worth and polish it, never flashing it around like a cheap ring. Why Chinese thinking is best.

No, this kind of thinking didn't stick to her. She was
50 too busy chewing gum, blowing bubbles bigger than her cheeks. Only that kind of thinking stuck.

"Finish your coffee," I told her yesterday. "Don't throw your blessings away."

"Don't be so old-fashioned, Ma," she told me, finishing
55 her coffee down the sink. "I'm my own person."

And I think, How can she be her own person? When did I give her up?

c Read the extract again. Then with a partner choose a, b, or c.

1 Lindo thinks her daughter will not be mistaken for a native-born Chinese mainly because of the way she ____.
   a speaks
   b looks
   c moves
   d dresses

2 Lindo's daughter ____.
   a wishes she had learned to speak Chinese
   b never behaved like a Chinese person
   c has forgotten all the Chinese she ever knew
   d became less Chinese as she grew older

3 What Lindo most likes about the American way of life is that ____.
   a you don't have to accept your fate
   b education is free for everybody
   c you can choose your religion
   d other people always help you

4 Which of these is *not* an aspect of Chinese character, according to Lindo?
   a hiding your real feelings
   b doing what your parents tell you to do
   c showing off
   d being aware of your strengths

5 Lindo gives the example of the chewing gum to show that ____.
   a her daughter was stupid as a child
   b American habits were very easily acquired by her daughter
   c the American way of life is inferior to the Chinese
   d young people don't pay attention to adults

LEXIS IN CONTEXT

d Look at the following verbs in the text and guess their meaning.

blend in (l.25)
sue (l.35)
obey (l.42)
pursue (l.46)
polish (l.47)
flash around (l.47)
stick to (l.49)

e Whose problems do you identify with most, the mother's or the daughter's? Why?

5 VOCABULARY words that are often confused

a The words *foreigner*, *outsider*, and *stranger* are often confused. What is the difference in meaning?

b Look at some other words that are often confused. For each pair, complete the sentences with the right word. (You may need to change the form.)

1 **suit** /sut/ | **suite** /swit/
   a The hotel upgraded us and gave us a _____ instead of a double room.
   b You should definitely wear a _____ to the interview — you'll make a better impression.

2 **beside | besides**
   a Let's not go out tonight. I'm tired, and _____ I want to read.
   b They live in that new apartment building _____ the school.

3 **lay | lie**
   a Please _____ down and relax. This will only take a minute.
   b If you _____ her on the sofa gently, I'm sure she won't wake up.

4 **actually | currently**
   a The inflation rate is _____ two percent.
   b I thought I wouldn't enjoy the movie, but _____ it was very funny.

5 **announce | advertise**
   a It is rumored that the President will _____ the latest recipient of the Medal of Honor this week.
   b The company is planning to _____ the new product both on TV and online.

6 **affect | effect**
   a How does the crisis _____ you?
   b What is the main _____ of the crisis?

7 **ashamed | embarrassed**
   a As soon as the plumber arrived, the leak stopped! I was so _____.
   b When my teacher told my father I had cheated on the test, I felt so _____.

8 **deny | refuse**
   a The accused does not _____ being in the house, but he insists that he did not touch anything.
   b The man continues to _____ to answer the question.

9 **compromise | commitment**
   a I know we will never agree about what to do, but we should try to reach a _____.
   b The company's _____ to providing quality at a reasonable price has been crucial to its success.

10 **economic | economical**
   a I think we should buy the Toyota. It's nicer looking, and it's much more _____ on gasoline.
   b I don't agree with the government's _____ policy.

c Complete the sentences with words from **b**. Then with a partner say if you think they are more true of men or women, or equally true of both.

1 They let personal problems _____ them at work.
2 They feel _____ when they have to talk about feelings.
3 They are afraid of making a long-term _____ to a relationship.
4 They tend to buy things because they are _____ on TV.
5 They often say they can do something well when _____ they can't.
6 They _____ to admit they are wrong in an argument.

6 🔊 5 29)) SONG *The Outside* ♫

10B Sports on trial

1 READING & SPEAKING

a Look at the photos. Do you do any of the activities, or have you ever done them? Is / Was your experience positive or negative?

b Read an article comparing four types of workouts. Then, according to the text, work as quickly as you can to match one or more workouts with each of the statements below.

For which of the workouts are these statements true?

1 There are two different varieties.
2 You can easily get addicted.
3 You can easily get bored if you don't vary what you do enough.
4 Some specific muscles become stronger.
5 You work on the lower body more than the upper body.
6 It takes the longest time to show any benefits.
7 Having the right instructor strongly influences your enjoyment.
8 It is difficult to actually improve.
9 You can aggravate an existing injury if you don't do it properly.
10 You may not actually improve your level of fitness.
11 You will learn to stand better.
12 You will lose weight the quickest.

c Read the text again. For each pair of workouts, which do you think, according to the article, was the winner?

LEXIS IN CONTEXT

d Look at the definitions below. Can you remember what any of the words are? Find the ones you can't remember in the text.

1 _____ *noun* one long step (also vb *to walk with long steps*)
2 _____ *noun* the row of small bones that are connected together down the middle of the back
3 _____ *noun* a period of physical exercise that you do to keep fit
4 _____ (to) *adj.* likely to suffer from
5 _____ *noun* a place where two bones are joined together in the body
6 _____ *verb* the act of putting your arms or legs out straight and contracting your muscles
7 _____ *noun* an exercise in which you lie on your stomach and raise your body off the ground with your hands until your arms are straight
8 _____ *noun* an exercise for making your stomach muscles strong, in which you lie on the floor on your back and raise the top part of your body
9 _____ *noun* the main part of the body apart from the head, arms, and legs

BATTLE OF THE WORKOUTS

Running or aerobics? Yoga or Pilates? Making the decision to get in shape is easy — choosing how to go about it is the difficult part. Peta Bee offers some advice.

RUNNING VS. AEROBICS

RUNNING

How quickly will it make a difference? After two to three weeks if running three or more times a week.

How many calories does it burn? Around 612 per hour if you run six miles per hour. You will burn more calories running off-road as your legs have to work harder on soft ground.

Will it keep me motivated? Running on a treadmill like a hamster can be tedious: run outside, changing your route and terrain whenever you can. As you improve your level of fitness, challenge yourself more by entering fun runs.

What are the specific benefits? The basic running action strengthens the hamstring, quadriceps, iliopsoas muscles at the front of the hip, calf, and the gluteus maximus muscles each time you take a stride forward. The pumping action of your arms will strengthen the upper body to some extent. And it's among the best forms of aerobic exercise.

What are the risk factors? Your feet absorb three to four times your body weight every time they strike the ground, and a shock reverberates up through your legs and into your spine. Good running shoes help to cushion the blow and reduce the risk of injury to the knees and other joints.

AEROBICS

How quickly will it make a difference? After four to five weeks of twice-weekly classes.

How many calories does it burn? 374 per hour.

Will it keep me motivated? It depends on your instructor. Classes that stick to exactly the same format every week can become too predictable for both muscles and mind. As with all class-based workouts, there is little scope for progress, so there will come a time when you will want to try something different.

What are the specific benefits? Aerobics classes incorporate an element of dance that will improve coordination and spatial awareness.

What are the risk factors? Low-impact aerobics — at least one foot remains in contact with the floor at all times — are preferable to high-impact classes for anyone prone to back and joint problems.

WINNER

YOGA VS. PILATES

YOGA

How quickly will it make a difference? After eight weeks of three sessions per week.

How many calories does it burn? 102 per hour for a general, stretch-based class. Power yoga burns 245 per hour.

Will it keep me motivated? Yoga is all about attaining a sense of unity between body and mind rather than setting and achieving personal goals. However, you will feel a sense of accomplishment as you master the poses, and there are many different types to try.

What are the specific benefits? In a study for the American Council on Exercise (ACE), Professor John Porcari found that women who did three yoga classes a week for eight weeks experienced a 13 percent improvement in flexibility, with significant gains in shoulder and torso flexibility. They were able to perform six more push-ups and 14 more sit-ups at the end of the study compared to the beginning.

What are the risk factors? Don't fall for the line that celebrities get fit on yoga alone. According to the ACE, even power yoga constitutes only a "light aerobic workout."

PILATES

How quickly will it make a difference? After five to six weeks of three sessions per week.

How many calories does it burn? 170–237 per hour.

Will it keep me motivated? Once you start noticing positive changes in the way you move and hold your body, Pilates is hard to give up.

What are the specific benefits? Widely used by dancers and top athletes, it improves postural awareness and strength. Studies have shown that Pilates exercises can develop the deeply embedded traversus abdominal muscles, which support the torso.

What are the risk factors? Another study found the cardiovascular benefits of Pilates to be limited. Even an advanced 55-minute session raised participants' heart rates to a maximum of only 62 percent (below the recommended 64–94 percent said to constitute an aerobic workout) and was deemed the energy equivalent of walking 3.5 miles an hour. If you have back pain, make sure your instructor is also a physiotherapist, as poor technique can make matters worse.

`WINNER`

From The Guardian

e Match the verbs on the left with their collocates in the text. Which two verbs are similar in meaning?

master	a sense of unity
challenge	the poses
attain	calories
perform	personal goals
set / achieve	six push-ups
burn	yourself more by entering fun runs

f Think of a sport or activity which you have done or know something about. What is it good for? What is it not so good for? Tell your partner about it, answering the questions in the text.

2 VOCABULARY

word building: adjectives, nouns, and verbs

a Without looking back at the text, complete sentences 1 and 2 with a word made from *strong*.

1 The pumping action of your arms will _____ the upper body to some extent.

2 Widely used by dancers and top athletes, it improves postural awareness and _____.

b Complete the chart.

Adjective	Noun	Verb
strong		
long		
deep		
short		
wide		
high		
weak		
thick		
flat		

c Complete the sentences with words from **b** in the right form.

1 I often have to _____ new pants because they're usually too long for me.

2 Can you measure the _____ and _____ of the living room? I want to order a new carpet.

3 I'm more or less the same _____ as my sister, but my brother's much taller than us.

4 People's joints tend to _____ as they get older.

5 **A** What's the _____ of the water here?
   B About thirty feet, I think.

6 If you want to _____ the sauce, add butter and flour.

7 People do sit-ups to try to _____ their stomach.

8 He's almost unbeatable. He doesn't have any real _____.

9 This road needs to be _____. It's far too narrow.

10 My grandfather suffers from _____ of breath. He used to be a heavy smoker.

3 GRAMMAR *comparison*

a Right (✓) or wrong (✗)? Correct the mistakes in the highlighted phrases

1 The more exciting the game gets, the crowd gets louder.
2 The players on their team can run much faster than the players on our team.
3 Richards got a little more votes than Brown did for the Most Valuable Player award.
4 I don't enjoy sports so much as my brother does.
5 There are much more seats in Yankee Stadium than in Carnegie Hall.
6 The cheaper the tickets, the best.
7 The baseball game lasted twice as long as we expected.

b ➤ p.157 Grammar Bank 10B. Learn more about comparison, and practice it.

c In groups of three, discuss each of the topics below for at least two minutes.

• The nicer the food is, the worse it is for you.
• The more expensive the clothes are, the longer they last.
• The older you get, the less tolerant you become.
• The more interesting a job, the less well paid it is.
• The smaller the country, the more patriotic the people are.
• The bigger the family, the more fun the children have.

FOUL PLAY
What's wrong with sports?

In his book, *Foul play*, sports journalist Joe Humphreys challenges the idea that sports are a positive influence on athletes, spectators, and the world as a whole.

According to Humphreys:

1 Sports bring out the worst in people, both fans and athletes. They do not improve character or help to develop virtues such as fair play and respect for opponents. ☐☐

2 Sports don't make you happy. Spectators as well as athletes have higher than normal levels of stress, anxiety, and hopelessness because of their involvement with professional sports. ☐☐

3 Sports are like a religion in their ability to "move the masses." ☐☐

4 Doping is no worse than any other kind of cheating and really no different from using other kinds of technology to gain an advantage, e.g., high-tech running shoes. ☐☐

5 It's ridiculous to expect professional athletes to be role models. ☐☐

6 Sports occupy a disproportionately high place in the media, often making the headlines in newspapers and on TV. ☐☐

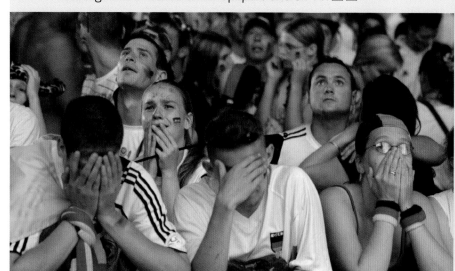

4 SPEAKING & LISTENING

a Look at the information about the book *Foul Play*. Check (✓) the points you agree with or put an ✗ beside the ones you disagree with. Be ready to say why you agree / disagree.

b In groups of three or four, discuss each point, explaining why you agree or disagree and giving examples where possible. Try to decide whether as a group you agree or disagree with the statements.

c (5 30)》 Now listen to Ron Kantowski, a sports journalist in Las Vegas, talking about the topics in **a**. Mark the statements A if he agrees, PA if he partially agrees, and D if he disagrees. Do his opinions coincide with what you said in your groups?

d Listen again and write a brief summary of each of the reasons he gives.

5 PRONUNCIATION homographs

a Read the information box about homographs.

> 🔍 **Homographs**
>
> Homographs are words that are spelled the same but have different meanings and can be pronounced differently, e.g:
> **bow** /baʊ/ = move your head or the top half of your body forwards and downwards, as a sign of respect or to say goodbye
> **bow** /bəʊ/ = 1 a weapon used for shooting arrows 2 a hair decoration made of ribbon
> There are not very many words like this, but the common ones are sometimes mispronounced, and learning the correct pronunciation will avoid misunderstandings.

b Look at the sentences which contain homographs. Match them with pronunciation **a** or **b**.

close   a /kloʊz/ or b /kloʊs/?

1 ☐ It was a really close race, and they had to use a video replay to see who won.

2 ☐ What time does the ticket office close? We need to get our tickets for the game on Saturday.

upset   a /ˈʌpsɛt/ or b /ʌpˈsɛt/?

3 ☐ The lowest-ranked baseball team in our division pulled off an amazing upset when they played the top team and defeated them five to four.

4 ☐ He was really upset because he missed an easy shot that would have won the basketball game for the team.

minute   a /ˈmɪnət/ or b /maɪˈnut/?

5 ☐ He was disqualified because they found a minute quantity of a banned substance in his blood sample.

6 ☐ He scored a goal just one minute before the referee blew the final whistle.

tear   a /tɛr/ or b /tɪr/?

7 ☐ If you tear a muscle or a ligament, you may not be able to train for six months.

8 ☐ As she listened to the national anthem play, a tear rolled down her cheek.

content   a /ˈkɑntɛnt/ or b /kənˈtɛnt/?

9 ☐ Professional athletes never seem content with their contracts. They're always trying to negotiate better terms.

10 ☐ The content of the program was a two-hour analysis of the game.

wound   a /wund/ or b /waʊnd/?

11 ☐ He wound the tape tightly around his ankle to prevent a sprain.

12 ☐ You could see his head wound bleeding as he was taken off the field.

use   a /yuz/ or b /yus/?

13 ☐ If you use a high-tech swimsuit, you will be able to swim much faster.

14 ☐ It's no use complaining; the umpire's decision is final.

c (5 31)》 Listen and check. Practice saying the sentences.

GRAMMAR

a Right (✓) or wrong (✗)? Correct the mistakes in the highlighted phrases.

1 He's my brother's friend.
2 Do you have a cans opener?
3 She has far more money than I do.
4 What's the name of the store where you bought that skirt?
5 He's not nearly as stupid as he looks.
6 I'd love to drink a coffee cup.
7 The sky got more and more dark, until it seemed as if it were night.
8 São Paulo is the largest city of Brazil.

b Circle the right phrases. Check (✓) if both are possible.

1 *The capital city of Japan | Japan's capital city* is Tokyo.
2 I found an old *photo album | album of photos*.
3 We'll be *at Tom's | at Tom's house* at 9.
4 The best place to hide valuables is in the *children bedroom | children's bedroom*.
5 She's *far more | much more* intelligent than her brother.
6 I've never been to Patagonia, but my sister *did | has*.
7 I think her latest novel is *by much | by far* the best book she's written.
8 It's only *a few | a little* more weeks before we go back to the US.

c Rewrite the sentences using the **bold** word.

1 I didn't bring sunscreen because the weather forecast said rain. **REASON**
   The _____ because the weather forecast said rain.
2 I spoke to the head of customer service. **PERSON**
   _____ the head of customer service.
3 I don't like the way my boss blames other people. **WHAT**
   _____ the way my boss blames other people.
4 I only said that I thought she was making a big mistake. **ALL**
   _____ I thought that she was making a big mistake.
5 A boy from my school was chosen to carry the Olympic torch. **IT**
   _____ was chosen to carry the Olympic torch.

VOCABULARY

a Write the words for the definitions.

1 _____ _____ *noun* a thing you use to cut vegetables on
2 _____ *verb* to cook at a very low heat
3 _____ *verb* to move sth around, e.g., a sauce using a spoon
4 _____ *verb* to fill, e.g., a vegetable with another type of food
5 _____ *verb* make liquid as a result of heating
6 _____ *noun* a flow of cool air
7 _____ *noun* the row of small bones that are connected together down the middle of your back
8 _____ *noun* a building where horses are kept
9 _____ *adj.* (of fruit and crops) fully grown and ready to be eaten
10 _____ *noun* a young cow

b Complete the sentences with a verb.

1 If you're hungry, there's some pasta left over from yesterday. You could _____ it in the microwave.
2 To make an omelet, first break two eggs into a bowl and then _____ them lightly with a fork.
3 Ouch! That hurt! I think a wasp just _____ me!
4 Relax! Don't _____ it so seriously — it's not the end of the world.
5 We thought that the painting my grandmother left me was worthless, but it _____ out to be a very valuable work by a well-known Mexican painter.
6 The mouse _____ loudly when I accidentally stepped on it.
7 You'd _____ more calories if you did power yoga instead of normal yoga.
8 _____ yourself a realistic goal, and then gradually work toward it.

c Complete the sentence with a word formed from the **bold** word.

1 Animal _____ are trying to get a worldwide ban on experiments involving animals. **ACTIVE**
2 The real _____ of the movie is its witty dialogue. **STRONG**
3 I need to get someone to _____ my new jeans. I'm no good at sewing. **SHORT**
4 The pole-vaulter Sergei Bubka was the first man to clear the _____ of six meters. **HIGH**
5 I'm not ready to get married just now because I feel it's too big of a _____. **COMMIT**
6 Cover the mousse with _____ cream and then decorate with grated chocolate. **WHIP**
7 I run the air conditioner in my room nearly all summer, but it isn't very _____. **ECONOMY**

CAN YOU UNDERSTAND THIS TEXT?

a Read the article once. What technological advances described in the article have affected sports? Do you know of any others?

b Read the article again. Then mark the sentences **T** (true) or **F** (false).

1 Some competitive ice skaters have created a new technology for designing skates.

2 Haptic sports clothing helps athletes improve their performance through instructional videos.

3 European rugby teams are only using RFID tags to assess games.

4 Instant play without RFID tags can transmit coordinates of players and the ball at 2000 times per second.

5 The "Hawk-Eye" system is used to improve players' performances in the games.

6 Live cameras and microphones are being used today to give fans a more intimate view of the game.

c Choose five new words or phrases from the text. Check their meaning and pronunciation and try to learn them.

CAN YOU UNDERSTAND THIS INTERVIEW?

a Do you ever eat too much? If so, when was the last time? Do you know why you overate?

b (5 32)) You are going to hear an interview with Dr. Brian Wansink, an expert in food psychology. Then put a check (✓) next to the things he says.

☐ The largest number of respondents said they over ate because they were hungry.

☐ When people were given bad popcorn and they weren't hungry, they ate more from the bigger bag.

☐ Candy can cause serious health problems and heart-related diseases.

☐ Simple things like the placement of food can affect the way people eat.

☐ When a person eats with someone who's a fast eater, they are more likely to consume more calories than if they ate alone.

☐ People can't tell if they're full because of the way the human brain is programmed.

☐ Mindless eating is something that cannot be changed.

c Do you know anyone who eats "mindlessly," that is, without paying attention to how much they're eating? Can you identify any cues that cause them to eat that way?

How is technology affecting sports?

Technology plays a major role in sports: it has changed the way athletes perform, the way professional sports are officiated, and the way fans watch the game.

Because athletes are always looking for an edge against the competition, many are taking advantage of the latest trends in technology. For example, some competitive ice skaters are taking their experience on the ice to the design table. They have developed a new way to make skates using a process called rapid prototyping, using CAD (computer-assisted design). This process allows athletes to get a custom pair of boots made in record time and be on the ice with them faster than ever before.

Even more remarkable is a state-of-the-art clothing line that allows athletes to coach themselves. Unlike a video or instructional pamphlet, the "Haptic Sports Garment" senses your every move and lets you know which areas you need to improve. The garment uses vibrations to help improve posture, target key muscle groups and even help maintain optimal speeds.

Years ago, the instant replay was considered a giant technological leap, because for the first time, it allowed judges and fans to watch video of a disputed play almost immediately after it happened. But there is no longer a need for instant replay with the new RFID tags (Radio Frequency Identification Technology), which European rugby teams are experimenting with. This amazing micro-location technology can transmit the exact coordinates of the ball and players at an astounding 2000 times per second. It can also be used to calculate movement, speed, accuracy, and even force of impact. It essentially eliminates the guess work from officiating.

The "Hawk-Eye" system is an example of successful technology that has been used in professional tennis for several years now. High-speed cameras mounted around the stadium, combined with a 3D (three-dimensional) model of the tennis court, can track the position of the tennis ball in 3D space. This not only affects the game itself, but also the ability of players to self-analyze at a new level of detail.

Where will technology take us next? Will there one day be tiny live cameras and microphones inserted into basketballs, footballs, and baseballs that allow fans to get an even closer view of the action? Will we all one day be playing video games with holographic players on a life size field? It may all sound far-fetched but the technology is there, and it may be on the market sooner than you think.

Writing A job application

ANALYZING A MODEL TEXT

a You see the following advertisement on a world music festival website. Would you be interested in applying for the job? Why (not)?

Festival staff required to work at the *World Music Festival*, a world music festival event in California from July 12th to 14th

Responsibilities

To ensure the safety and comfort of the public and to assist in the running of a successful festival.

To reduce any crowd-related problems, including maintaining a state of calm to minimize any injury.

To prevent unauthorized access to the site by members of the public.

Requirements

You must be aged 18 or over on the date of the festival and be eligible to work in the US.

You must be physically fit and healthy and able to work under pressure.

You should have a high level of English, and some experience dealing with the public.

How to apply

Email your cover letter and resume to Jane Richards (J.Richards@bkyworldmusic.org).

b Read the first draft of an email written in response to the advertisement. What information does Kurt give in the three main paragraphs?

To:	J.Richards@bkyworldmusic.org
From:	Kurt Fischer
Subject:	Application

Dear ~~Miss~~ *Ms.* Richards,

~~My name is Kurt Fischer.~~ I am writing to apply for a staff position advertised in the World Music Festival website.

I am a final year student at the University of Campinas and I am pursuing a degree in physical education. I have a high level of spoken English (C1 on the CEFR), as I lived in the United States during six months as part of a exchange program between my school and a High school in Utah. I made many American friends during this period but we lost touch when I came home.

As you will see from my resume, I have some relevent experience because I have worked for the last three summers helping to organize a tennis tournament in my town, Ouro Preto. I was in charge of selling tickets at the entrance gate, so I am used to handing money and, on ocasion, having to refuse people entry. The tournament organizer would be happy to provide a reference. He is, in fact, distantly related to my mother.

I am very enthusiastic on world music, and would welcome the chance to be part of this event. I believe I would be suitable for the job advertised as, apart of my experience, I am a very cheerful and outgoing person and get along well with people. Friends describe me as being calm and pacient, and I think I would be able to cope if I had to deal with angry or difficult members of the public. I would definitely know how to look after myself if I got into a fight!

I attach a resume, and if you require any further information, I would be happy to provide it. I would also be grateful if you could send me an information regarding acommodation during the festival.

I look forward to hearing from you.

Yours sincerely,

Kurt Fischer

c Read the draft again and try to improve it.

1 Cross out three sentences (not including the example) which are irrelevant or inappropriate.

2 Try to find and correct 12 mistakes in spelling (including capital letters), grammar, and vocabulary.

d Do you think the festival organizers would have given him an interview if he had sent his first draft?

USEFUL LANGUAGE

e Look at 1–10 below. Without looking back at the draft, can you remember how Kurt expressed these ideas in a less informal way? Use the **bold** word(s) to help you. Then look at the text again to check your answers.

1 This letter is to ask you to give me a festival staff job. **APPLY**
I am writing to apply for a staff position.

2 I'm a senior at college and I'm doing P.E. **FINAL YEAR / PURSUE**
_____

3 I can speak English very well. **HIGH**
_____

4 I've done this kind of job before. **RELEVANT**
_____

5 My job was to sell tickets. **CHARGE**
_____

6 I'd love to work at the festival. **WELCOME**
_____

7 I think I'll be good at this job. **SUITABLE**
_____

8 If you need to know anything else, I'll tell you. **REQUIRE / PROVIDE**
_____

9 Let me have some information about accommodations. **GRATEFUL**
_____

10 Hope to hear from you soon! **FORWARD**
_____

PLANNING WHAT TO WRITE

Brainstorm the content

a Read the job advertisement below and underline the information you will need to respond to. Then make notes about
- what personal information you think you need to include.
- any relevant experience or qualifications you have.
- what aspects of your personality you think would make you suitable for the job, and how you could illustrate them.

Do you want to work for us?
Are you the right person for the job?

We are looking for fun, energetic, experienced people of any age to work as camp counselors at our day and residential summer camps in July and / or August. Children are between 7 and 15 years old and participate in a wide range of sports and activities from swimming and water sports to survival skills and cooking.

Do you enjoy working with children? Are you good at working on a team? Do you have any relevant experience or qualifications? Do you speak English either as a first language or fluently?

You can earn between $300 and $400 per week (food and accommodations provided). Minimum contract: one month.

Interested? Send an email with your cover letter and resume to Richard Cunningham at summercamp@bt.com

---

b Compare notes with a partner, and discuss how relevant you think each other's information is, what you think you should leave out, and what else you might want to include.

TIPS for writing a cover letter / email to apply for a job, grant, etc.
- Make sure you use appropriate sentences to open the letter.
- Organize the main body of the letter into clear paragraphs.
- Make sure you use a suitable style:

Don't use contractions or very informal expressions.

Use formal vocabulary where appropriate, e.g., *require* instead of *need*, *as* instead of *because*.

The use of a conditional can often make a request sound more polite, e.g., *I would be grateful if…, I would welcome the chance to…*
- When you say why you think you are suitable for the job, don't "oversell" yourself. Be factual and positive, but not arrogant.
- Make sure you use the appropriate phrases to close the letter.

WRITING

You have decided to apply for the job advertised above. Write a cover letter or email. It should be approximately 250 words.

DRAFT your letter.
- Write an introductory sentence to explain why you are writing.
- Paragraph 1: give relevant personal information.
- Paragraph 2: talk about relevant experience and qualifications you have.
- Paragraph 3: explain why you think you would be suitable for the job.
- Write a closing sentence.

EDIT the letter, cutting any irrelevant information, and making sure it is the right length.

CHECK the letter for mistakes in grammar, spelling, punctuation, and register.

◄ *p.7*

Key success factors
- getting and keeping the reader's attention
- using rich and precise vocabulary

ANALYZING A MODEL TEXT

a You are going to read an article about childhood covering the areas below. What information would you include if you were writing about your country?

- What are the main differences between a child's life 50 years ago and a child's life now?
- Why have these changes occurred?
- Do you think the changes are positive or negative?

b Now read the article. Did the writer include any of your ideas? With a partner, choose what you think is the best title from the options below and say why you prefer it to the others.

How childhood has changed

Changing childhood

My childhood

Children's lives have changed dramatically over the last 50 years. But do they have a happier childhood than you or I did?

It's difficult to look back on one's own childhood without some element of nostalgia. I have four brothers and sisters, and my memories are all about being with them, playing board games on the living room floor, or spending days outside with the other neighborhood children, racing around on our bikes, or exploring the nearby woods. My parents hardly ever appear in these memories, except as providers either of meals or of severe scoldings after some particularly hazardous adventure.

These days, in the US at least, the nature of childhood has changed dramatically. First, families are smaller, and there are many more only children. It is common for both parents to work outside the home and there is the feeling that there just isn't time to bring up a large family, or that no one could possibly afford to have more than one child. As a result, today's boys and girls spend much of their time alone. Another major change is that youngsters today tend to spend a huge proportion of their free time at home, inside. This is due more than anything to the fact that parents worry much more than they used to about real or imagined dangers, so they wouldn't dream of letting their children play outside by themselves.

Finally, the kinds of toys children have and the way they play is totally different. Computer and video games have replaced the board games and more active pastimes of my childhood. The irony is that so many of these devices are called "interactive." The fact that you can play electronic games on your own further increases the sense of isolation felt by many young people today.

Do these changes mean that children today have a less idyllic childhood than I had? I personally believe that they do, but perhaps every generation feels exactly the same.

c Answer with a partner.

1 What is the effect of the direct question in the introduction? Where is it answered?

2 What does the first main paragraph (not including the introductory sentence) focus on? What examples are given?

3 What are the changes that the writer has focused on in the third main paragraph, and what reasons have been given for the changes? Do you agree?

4 Underline the discourse markers that have been used to link the points in the second and third main paragraphs, e.g., *First…*

> **Using synonyms**
>
> When you write, try not to repeat the same words and phrases too often. Instead, where possible, use a synonym or similar expression if you can think of one. This will both make the text more varied for the reader and help the article link together. A good monolingual dictionary or thesaurus can help you.

d Find synonyms in the article for…

1 at the present time _____ / _____

2 children _____ / _____ / _____

3 alone, without adults _____ / _____

4 games _____

> **Using richer vocabulary**
>
> You can make your writing more colorful and interesting to read by trying to use a richer range of vocabulary instead of the most obvious words.

e Without looking back at the article, try to remember how the words in italics were changed to make the article more enjoyable to read.

1 Children's lives have changed *in a big way*

2 …being in the street with the other *children who lived near us*

3 …*going* around on our bikes…

4 …after some particularly *dangerous* adventure.

5 My parents *don't* appear *very often* in these memories…

6 …think that no one *has enough money* to have more than one child.

7 …that children have a less *happy* childhood than I had?

◀ *p.19*

PLANNING WHAT TO WRITE

Brainstorm possible content

a Look at the test question below.

> Many aspects of life have changed over the last 30 years. These include:
>
> **marriage**
>
> **dating**
>
> **the role of women or / and men**
>
> Write an article for an online magazine about how <u>one</u> of these areas has changed in your country and say whether you think these changes are positive or negative.

With a partner brainstorm for each topic…

1 what the situation used to be like and what the big changes are.

2 whether the situation has changed a lot in your country.

3 whether you think the changes are positive or negative and why.

Now decide which area you are going to write about and which ideas you want to include.

> Remember that this is an article, not an essay. You don't necessarily want to include the most important points, but the ones that you could say something interesting about, or where you can think of any interesting personal examples.

b Think of a possible title for your article.

TIPS for writing an article

• Give your article an interesting title.

• There is no fixed structure for an article, but it is important to have clear paragraphs. Use discourse markers to link your points or arguments.

• Make sure you use a suitable style, neither very formal nor informal.

• Make the introduction reasonably short. You could use a question or questions which you then answer in the article.

• Try to engage the reader, e.g., by referring to your personal experience.

• Try to vary your vocabulary using synonyms where possible.

WRITING

You are going to write the article in approximately 250 words.

DRAFT your article, with

• a brief introduction, which refers to the changes and asks a question.

• two or three main paragraphs saying what the situation used to be like, and how it has changed.

• a conclusion, which refers back to the question in the introduction, and says whether you think the changes are positive or negative.

EDIT the article, cutting any irrelevant information and making sure it is the right length.

CHECK the article for mistakes in grammar, spelling, punctuation, and register.

Key success factors

- being able to express a reasonably sophisticated opinion
- using a range of vocabulary to describe what you are reviewing (plot, dialogue, characters, etc.)
- being able to summarize

ANALYZING A MODEL TEXT

a Which of the following would normally influence you to read a certain book?

- A friend of yours recommended it.
- It's a best seller — everybody is reading it.
- You saw and enjoyed a movie based on it.
- You were told to read it at school.
- You read a good review of it.

b Read this newspaper book review. In which paragraph do you find the following information? Write 1–4 in the boxes, or DS if the review doesn't say. Does the review make you want to read the book?

- [ ] The strong points of the book
- [ ] The basic outline of the plot
- [ ] What happens in the end
- [ ] Where and when the story is set
- [ ] The weaknesses of the book
- [ ] Whether the reviewer recommends the book or not
- [ ] How good the English translation is
- [ ] Who the author is
- [ ] Who the main characters are
- [ ] How much the book costs
- [ ] Who the book is suitable for

Don't spoil the plot; Say what you think

When writing a book or movie review, give your reader a <u>brief</u> idea of the plot (without giving away the whole story!). Try to make your description as concise as possible to leave you space to give your own opinion.

The Girl Who Played with Fire

The Girl Who Played with Fire is the second novel in the Millennium trilogy by Swedish writer Stieg Larsson. A thriller, set in modern-day Sweden, it immediately became an international best seller.

In this book the same main characters from the first book reappear, journalist Mikael Blomkvist and the extraordinary girl Lisbeth Salander, a freelance investigator. This time Lisbeth herself becomes the suspect of a triple murder. Three people are shot on the same day, and her fingerprints are found on the murder weapon. She goes quickly into hiding, and Mikael, whose life she saved in the previous book, is determined to prove her innocence. Devastated by the fact that two of the murder victims were colleagues of his, but convinced that Lisbeth cannot possibly have been involved, he works first on his own, and then with the police, to discover what really happened. Meanwhile Lisbeth, carefully keeping out of everyone's sight, is making her own investigations…

The great strength of this book, and what makes Larsson's books so different from other recent detective fiction and thrillers, is the character of Lisbeth. Most famous fictional detectives or investigators tend to be either middle-aged policemen with marital problems, female forensic scientists, or middle-aged male intellectuals. Lisbeth, however, is a young slightly autistic girl from a broken home, who is also a computer genius. She is an intriguing character, and in this book we find out a lot more about her, among other things who her father is, and why she spent her teenage years in a psychiatric hospital. My only criticism of the novel would be that the early sub-plot about Grenada is not very relevant and could have been cut.

Not only is this a complex and absolutely gripping novel, but it also tackles real problems in society, and most unusually I think for a sequel, is even better than its predecessor. For all lovers of crime novels and thrillers the Millennium trilogy is a must.

c Look at these extracts from the second paragraph. Which words did the author leave out to make it more concise? Then read the rules for **Participle clauses** to check.

> **Because he is devastated by the fact** that two of the murder victims were colleagues of his, but **he is convinced that** Lisbeth cannot possibly have been involved, he works first on his own, and then with the police, to discover what really happened.
> Meanwhile Lisbeth, **who is carefully keeping out of everyone's sight**, is making her own investigations…

Participle clauses

The writer uses participles (*devastated, convinced, keeping*) instead of a subject + verb. Past participles replace verbs in the passive, and present participles (*-ing forms*) replace verbs in the active. The subject of the clause is usually the same as the subject of the main clause.

Participle clauses can be used:

- instead of a conjunction (*after, as, when, because, although*, etc.) + subject + verb, e.g., *Devastated by the fact*… instead of *Because he is devastated*…
- instead of a relative clause, e.g., *carefully keeping* instead of *who is carefully keeping*.

d Rewrite the highlighted phrases to make them more concise using participle clauses.

1 As she believes him to be the murderer, Anya is absolutely terrified.
2 Simon, who realizes that the police are after him, tries to escape.
3 It was first published in 1903, and it has been reprinted many times.
4 It is set during World War I, and it tells the story of a young soldier.
5 When he hears the shot, Mark rushes into the house.

e Underline the adverbs of degree in these phrases from the review. What effect do they have on the adjectives?

> Lisbeth, however, is a young, slightly autistic girl from a broken home…
> Not only is this a complex and absolutely gripping novel…

f Use your instinct. Cross out any adverbs that don't fit in these sentences. Check (✓) if all are possible.

1 My only criticism is that the plot is **somewhat** / **slightly** / **a little** implausible.
2 The last chapter is **really** / **very** / **absolutely** fascinating.
3 The end of the novel is **fairly** / **pretty** / **quite** disappointing.
4 The denouement is **somewhat** / **incredibly** / **extremely** thrilling.

g Where all the adverbs are possible, is there any difference in meaning or register?

 p.41

PLANNING WHAT TO WRITE

Brainstorm the content

a Think of a book or movie that you have read or seen recently. Write a paragraph of approximately 100 words explaining who the main characters are and summarizing the plot, but without giving away the ending. Use the present tense, and try to include at least one participle clause.

b Exchange your paragraph with other students to see if they can identify the book or movie.

TIPS for writing a book / film review

- Organize the review into clear paragraphs.
- Make sure you use a suitable style, neither very formal nor informal.
- Use the present tense when you describe the plot. Using participle clauses will help to keep it concise.
- Try to use a range of adjectives that describe as precisely as possible how the book or movie made you feel, e.g., *gripping, moving*, etc. (see page 39). Use adverbs of degree to modify them, e.g., *absolutely gripping*.
- Remember that a positive review will include some criticism as well as praise.

WRITING

A student magazine has asked for reviews of recent books and movies. You are going to write a complete review.

DRAFT your review. It should be approximately 250 words.

- Paragraph 1: The title of the book or movie, and the author or director. Where and when it is set.
- Paragraph 2: The plot, including information about the main characters.
- Paragraph 3: What you liked, and any criticisms you may have.
- Paragraph 4: A summary of your opinion and a recommendation.

EDIT the review, making sure you've covered all the main points and making sure it is the right length.

CHECK the review for mistakes in grammar, spelling, punctuation, and register.

Key success factors
- being able to construct an argument
- being able to link points together in a logical sequence
- using appropriate discourse markers to connect, contrast, and balance points

ANALYZING A MODEL TEXT

a You have been asked to write the following essay:
Text messaging is an important advance in communication — or is it?
With a partner, discuss three reasons you think text messaging represents an important advance in communication and three reasons why it does not. Order them 1–3 according to their importance.

b Read the model essay and see if the writer has mentioned some or all of your arguments. Does the writer put the main argument first in both paragraphs?

c Look at the three introductory paragraphs below and choose which one you think is best for the essay. Compare with a partner, and discuss why you think it is the best, and why the other two are less suitable. Then do the same with the concluding paragraphs.

Introductory paragraphs

1 Since the first text was sent in 1992, text messaging has become one of the most popular forms of communication, especially among the younger generation, with billions of messages being sent every year. But has this technology really improved interpersonal communication?

2 Text messaging clearly has important advantages and disadvantages. In this essay, I am first going to analyze the advantages of this technology, and then I will outline some important disadvantages before finally drawing my conclusions.

3 Can you imagine life without sending and receiving texts? Probably not, as this cheap and convenient technology has become such a crucial tool for organizing our social lives and communicating instantly with our friends and family. How did we manage before it was invented?

Concluding paragraphs

1 In conclusion, text messaging has important advantages and disadvantages, but on the whole, I believe that it has improved our lives in a significant way.

2 In my view, text messaging has improved communication considerably and it is highly useful, for example, if you are trying to contact someone in a very noisy place, such as a concert, where it would be impossible to hear a phone call. In conclusion, it is an indispensable piece of technology.

3 To sum up, although text messages are a cheap and useful way of communicating, they have arguably led to young people being less able to express themselves correctly in writing. On the whole, I believe that text messaging does not represent an advance in communication.

Texting is an important advance in communication – or is it?

"Just think of it as if you're reading a long text-message."

Introduction

Arguments in favor

Being able to send short, written messages via cell phone has clearly advanced communication in certain respects.

The greatest benefit of texting is that it allows us to communicate instantly with other people wherever they are, but without interrupting them in the way that a phone call would, and allowing them to reply whenever it is convenient for them to do so. In addition, sending a text, for example to arrange where to meet someone, is a quick, concise, and efficient way of communicating, as people normally only include the key information. Finally, text messaging is a very cheap form of communication, which is a particular advantage for young people or for people who are traveling, when cell phone conversations can be prohibitively expensive.

Arguments against

On the other hand, however, there are strong arguments to suggest that text messaging has had a negative effect on how we communicate. One downside is that there is a tendency for people to use texts as an excuse to get out of conversations which might be uncomfortable to have either face-to-face or on the phone. Another drawback is that people increasingly text while they are with other people, suddenly breaking off a conversation and focusing on their phone screens. However, perhaps the most important and worrying downside of texting is the effect it is having on written communication. Teachers worldwide complain that the idiosyncratic language of text messages, such as abbreviated words and the use of letters and numbers to convey meaning has led to a generation of young people being unable to spell or form correct sentences.

Conclusion

Introductions and conclusions

In an essay it is important that the introduction engages the reader's attention. It should introduce the topic, but should not include the specific points that you are going to mention in the body of the text.

A good introductory paragraph describes the present situation and gives supporting evidence. It should refer to the statement or question you have been asked to discuss. This can often be done in the form of a question to the reader which the subsequent paragraphs should answer.

The conclusion should briefly sum up the arguments you have made, and can include your personal opinion. The opinion you express should follow logically from the arguments you have presented.

USEFUL LANGUAGE

d Complete the missing words. Some (but not all) are in the model essay.

Expressing the main points in an argument

+	
1 The greatest **b**_____ is that	texting allows us to communicate instantly with other people.
2 **First and most im**_____	

−	
3 One **d**_____ of texting is that	people use texts as an excuse to get out of conversations.
4 Another **dr**_____ to text messaging is that	

Adding supporting information to a main argument, or introducing other related arguments

5 In **a**_____,	sending a text is a quick, concise, and efficient way of communicating.
6 **What is m**_____,	
7 **Not o**_____ that, but	
8 **Another point in f**_____ **of** this technology is that	

Describing cause and effect

9 Text messaging can **r**_____ **in** / can **l**_____ **to**	an inability to write correctly.
10 Other problems can arise **because of** / **d**_____ **to**	text messaging.

Weighing up arguments

11 **On the wh**_____,	I believe that it does not represent an advance in communication.
12 **A**_____ **in a**_____,	
13 **All things c**_____,	

◀ p.61

PLANNING WHAT TO WRITE

Brainstorm the content

Budget airlines have revolutionized travel — but at what price?

The growth of online shopping has greatly improved life for the consumer.

a Look at the essay titles above, and with a partner choose one of them. Brainstorm the pros and cons. Then decide on three main arguments on each side that are relevant to the title.

b Write an introduction for the essay. Follow this pattern:

1 Write an introductory sentence about how budget airlines or online shopping affect our lives nowadays.

2 Write a second sentence supporting the first one.

3 Ask a question that you intend to answer in the essay.

c Compare your introduction with a partner. Together, make a final version.

TIPS for writing a discursive essay in which you put forth both sides of an argument

- Brainstorm points for and against and decide which two or three you think are the most important.

- Use a neutral or formal style.

- Write a clear introduction that engages the reader. You could end with a question you are going to answer.

- Link your ideas together with varied discourse markers and linking phrases, e.g., *due to*, *this can lead to*, etc. because an essay should show the development of a logical argument; it's not just a list of random ideas and opinions.

- Make sure your conclusion is a summary of what you have previously said and refers back to what you were asked to write about. It is important that this is not just a repetition of your arguments. It is a summary of what you believe your arguments have proven.

WRITING

Write the essay in approximately 250 words.

DRAFT your essay in four paragraphs:

- introduction
- arguments in favor of budget airlines or online shopping
- arguments against budget airlines or online shopping
- conclusion, saying whether you think the advantages outweigh the disadvantages or vice versa

EDIT the essay, cutting any irrelevant information and making sure it is the right length.

CHECK the essay for mistakes in grammar, spelling, punctuation, and register.

Key success factors
- being clear and concise
- making sensible recommendations based on your observations

ANALYZING A MODEL TEXT

a The owners of a language school are doing some research into student satisfaction, and have asked several students to interview all the students at the school and write a report. Read their report and then, from memory, tell a partner what the school's main strengths and weaknesses are in each area.

b Without looking back at the model text, try to remember how some of the highlighted phrases below were expressed in a less informal way. Go back and check the text for those you can't remember.

1 What this report is for is…
The _____ is…

2 …is to find out how happy students are with the classes and facilities.
…is to _____ with the classes and facilities.

3 In general, students thought the teachers were very good.
In general, students _____.

4 About class sizes, most students think that there should no more than 12 students in a class.
_____, most students think that there should no more than 12 students in a class.

5 As for how long the classes last, they officially last an hour…
As for _____, they officially last an hour…

6 We suggest buying more computers…
We suggest _____ more computers…

7 Most students are extremely positive…
_____ are extremely positive…

8 …that if you make the changes we suggest, it will be an even better place to study.
…that if _____, it will be an even better place to study.

English Time Language School:
A report

Introduction
The aim of this report is to assess student satisfaction with the classes and facilities at the English Time Language School, and to make suggestions for improvements.

Testing and registration of new students
Most students were satisfied with the testing process for new students. However, they complained about the long lines at registration. We believe it would be preferable either to have more staff available to deal with registration, or to give students a specific day and time to register.

The classes
In general, students rated the teachers very highly. Their main criticisms had to do with class sizes and the length of classes. With regard to class sizes, most students think there should be no more than 12 students in a class. As for the duration of classes, they officially last an hour, but in practice they are usually only 45 minutes because of latecomers. We propose that all students who arrive more than five minutes late should have to wait until the break for admittance.

The self-study center
It is generally thought that the self-study center, while useful, has two major drawbacks. There are not enough computers, and at peak times they are always occupied. Also, the center closes at 7 p.m., so students who come to the later classes cannot use the center at all. We suggest purchasing more computers and extending the center's hours to 9 p.m.

The cafeteria
The cafeteria was replaced last year by vending machines for drinks and snacks. Although it is true that people often had to wait to be served, most students greatly preferred the cafeteria and would like it to be reopened.

Conclusion
Overall, the majority of students are extremely positive about the school, and feel that if the suggested changes are implemented, it will be an even better place to study.

USEFUL LANGUAGE

c Complete the missing words.

Some common expressions for generalizing

1 Generally **sp**_____, people think…

2 In **g**_____, people think…

3 The general **v**_____ is that certain improvements need to be made.

4 It is generally **co**_____ / **thought** …

5 **Ov**_____, the majority of students think…

d Rewrite the following sentences.

Making suggestions

1 Please buy new computers
We suggest
_____
_____

2 You should improve the registration process.
It would be advisable
_____
_____.

3 Why don't you make the classes smaller?
We propose
_____
_____

4 You really should extend the center's hours.
I strongly recommend
_____
_____

5 It would be much better if classes lasted an hour.
It would be far preferable for classes
_____
_____.

◀ p.67

PLANNING WHAT TO WRITE

Brainstorm the content

a Read the following task and all the relevant information. Then with a partner decide

1 how many headings you will need and what they should be.
2 how to express the relevant information in your own words.
3 what suggestions for improvements could be made under each heading.

b Together, suggest improvements to the study trips beginning with a different expression each time.

> Your language school has just started four-week study trips to the US. You have been asked by the principal of the school to get feedback from all the students who participated and write a report detailing what students were positive about, what problems they had, and making suggestions for improving future study trips.
>
> You have made notes covering the views of the majority of participants:
>
> People with families much happier than ones who stayed in the dormitories, because they were able to speak to the families.
>
> School OK and classes good but almost everyone complained about the lunch (just a sandwich). Some thought six hours a day too much.
>
> People not very interested in some weekend cultural programs. Trips to New York City and Philadelphia great, Gettysburg and Valley Forge boring.
>
> On all trips too much sightseeing and not enough time for shopping!

TIPS for writing a report

- Look carefully at who the report is for and what they need to know. This will help you choose what information you have to include.
- In the introduction, state what the purpose of the report is.
- Decide what the sections are going to be within the areas of the report and think of headings for them.
- For each paragraph, state the situation (strengths and weaknesses) and then make a recommendation.
- If on a test you are given information on which to base your report, try not to use exactly the same words.
- Try to use a variety of expressions for generalizing and making suggestions.
- Use an appropriate professional style, avoiding very informal expressions.

WRITING

You are going to write the report. It should be approximately 250 words.

DRAFT your report, using the headings and suggestions you worked on in the planning stage.

EDIT the report, deciding if there is any information that should be left out and making sure the report is the right length.

CHECK the report for mistakes in grammar, spelling, punctuation, and register.

Key success factors
- constructing an argument
- sustaining your case with examples
- showing that you have considered the opposing viewpoint

ANALYZING A MODEL TEXT

a You have been asked to write the following essay:

Tourism always does a place more harm than good.

Discuss the question with a partner. Do you think that the effect of tourism on a country, city, or region is in general more positive or more negative? Why?

Topic sentences
In a well-written essay, the first sentence of a paragraph establishes what the paragraph is going to be about. This is sometimes called the "topic sentence."

b Read the topic sentences below one by one and, in pairs, imagine how the paragraph will continue. Do you think the essay will be in favor of or against tourism?

A The infrastructure of an area is also often improved as a result of tourism.

B It is often claimed that popular tourist destinations are spoiled as a result of over-development.

C Tourism remains one of the world's great growth industries.

D Badly behaved tourists can often be a source of annoyance for the local population.

E Another point in favor of tourism is that governments are becoming aware of the need to protect tourist areas in order to attract visitors.

F The main positive effect of tourism is on local economies and employment.

c Now read the model essay and fill in the blanks with a topic sentence. There is one sentence you don't need.

Tourism always does a place more harm than good

1 _____ People today are traveling farther and farther, no longer just in the summer but throughout the year. Although some people argue that mass tourism has a negative effect on destinations, in my view its influences are generally positive.

2 _____ Tourists need places to stay and things to do, and this creates a wide range of skilled and unskilled jobs for local people. Vacationers also spend a great deal of money, which stimulates the economy of the region as well as benefiting the country as a whole.

3 _____ For example, when tourists start visiting an area, roads and public transportation tend to improve, or an airport may be built, all of which benefit local people as well as tourists.

4 _____ Not only is this leading to better conservation of historic buildings and monuments in towns and cities, but also of areas of natural beauty and endangered habitats in rural areas.

5 _____ For instance, many people argue that tourist development just leads to a proliferation of ugly hotels and apartment buildings. This may have been true in the past, but nowadays there are many more restrictions placed on both planners and builders to ensure that the character and architectural harmony of the place is maintained.

To sum up, I believe that tourism has, on the whole, a positive influence provided its development is properly planned and controlled. Tourist destinations have a lot to gain from visitors and the business they bring. In my opinion, it is possible for both tourists and local people to benefit, and for popular tourist destinations to have a sustainable future.

d Read each paragraph again, including the correct topic sentence. Answer the questions with a partner.

1 Where does the writer state his opinion about tourism?

2 How many arguments are given to support his view?

3 What is the purpose of paragraph 5?

> **Using synonyms and richer vocabulary**
>
> When you are writing an essay, remember to vary and enrich your vocabulary by using synonyms where appropriate.

e Find synonyms in the essay for the following words and expressions:

1 tourists   ——————— ———————
2 effects   ———————
3 for example   ———————
4 to profit from   ———————

USEFUL LANGUAGE

f Complete the missing words in the expressions. Some (but not all) are in the model essay.

> ### Giving personal opinions
>
> 1 I **f**———————— that…
>
> 2 I **b**———————— that…
>
> 3 In my **v**———————— the influences of tourism are generally positive.
>
> 4 In my **o**————————…
>
> 5 **P**————————, I think that…
>
> ### Expressing opposite arguments
>
> 6 Some people **ar**————————…
>
> 7 It is often **cl**———————— that popular destinations are spoiled by tourism.
>
> 8 There are **th**———————— who say…
>
> ### Refuting them
>
> 9 This **m**———————— **h**———————— been true in the past, but nowadays…
>
> 10 There are a number of **fl**———————— in this argument.
>
> 11 That is simply not the **c**————————.

PLANNING WHAT TO WRITE

Brainstorm the content

a Read the essay titles below. For each one, decide which side of the argument you are going to take, and think of three or four reasons.

Drivers should be charged for using highways and roads linking major towns and cities.

Marrying someone from a different country will always be more problematic than marrying someone from your own country.

b Compare with a partner. Decide which you think are the three most important reasons. Decide if there are any typical opposing arguments which you could refute.

c Choose which of the essays you are going to write. Write topic sentences for the main paragraphs. Show your topic sentences to a partner and see if you can improve each other's sentences.

TIPS for writing a discursive essay where you take one side of an argument

- Organize your essay into paragraphs, with a clear introduction and conclusion (see page 110).
- Begin each paragraph with a clear topic sentence and then develop the idea.
- Use synonyms to avoid repeating yourself.
- Use a variety of phrases for giving your opinion, or introducing an opposing argument and refuting it.

WRITING

You are going to write one of the essays above. It should be approximately 250 words.

DRAFT your essay in four paragraphs:
- an introductory paragraph where you introduce the topic and state your opinion.
- three or four paragraphs giving your reasons.
- if relevant, a paragraph stating one or more common counter-arguments, and refuting each one.
- a conclusion, stating what your arguments have shown.

EDIT the essay, making sure your arguments link together and making sure it is the right length.

CHECK the essay for mistakes in grammar, spelling, punctuation, and register.

◀ *p.81*

Key success factors
- being able to summarize the issue clearly
- maintaining an assertive but respectful tone
- being clear and reasonable about what you expect to be done

ANALYZING A MODEL TEXT

a Have you ever had a very bad experience at a restaurant or a hotel? What happened? Did you make a complaint either in person or in writing? What response did you get?

b Read the model letter. What exactly is the complaint about?

c With a partner discuss which phrase is better for each blank and why.

1. a I'm sorry to say
   b I am afraid to say
2. a did not live up to our expectations
   b was a complete disaster
3. a was supposed to provide
   b was going to give us
4. a it didn't happen
   b this was not the case
5. a fed up
   b dissatisfied
6. a we were told
   b they told us
7. a to our great disappointment
   b really irritatingly
8. a a pack of lies
   b totally inaccurate and misleading
9. a we are owed an apology
   b you ought to say sorry
10. a some form of compensation
    b a lot of money back

Dear Sir or Madam,

I am writing to complain about a Caribbean cruise we booked through your company.

¹_____ that the Island Excursion Cruise (booking reference CI38591) ²_____ and did not reflect the description on your website.

According to your website, the cruise ³_____ "all the comforts of a five-star hotel." Unfortunately, ⁴_____ and it left us and the other guests feeling extremely ⁵_____.

When we first boarded the ship and went to our cabin, there was an extremely unpleasant odor coming from the bathroom. When we complained to the cruise manager, ⁶_____ that there had been a problem with the ship's sewage-treatment system, and so it couldn't be helped. Hoping to make the best of things, we headed to the buffet, which was advertised as "a pan-Caribbean taste sensation." When we got there, ⁷_____, we found hot dogs, hamburgers, some wilted salad, and little else. To add insult to injury, on the third day of the cruise, we discovered that our two tablet computers, kept in the room safe, were somehow stolen out of that safe. When we informed an officer of the ship about it, we received apologies and excuses, but nothing more.

I feel strongly that the description of your on-board facilities on your website should be changed, as it is ⁸_____. We were extremely disappointed by the experiences we had on ship, and under the circumstances we believe that ⁹_____ and that we should receive ¹⁰_____.

I look forward to hearing your views on this matter.

Sincerely,

USEFUL LANGUAGE

d Without looking back at the letter, try to remember how the writer expressed the following in a more formal way.

1 In this letter I want to complain…

_____

2 It said on your website…

_____

3 The bathroom smelled really bad.

_____

4 I really think that you should change the description on your website…

_____

5 I'd like to know what you think about this.

_____

PLANNING WHAT TO WRITE

Brainstorm the content

a Read part of an email to Hannah from a friend. What exactly is the "Board first" service? What problem did she have?

Hi Hannah,

Just got back from Florida. That's the last time I fly with GreenAir!

It says on their website that there's this "Board first" service, meaning that if you pay $40 extra per person you can get on the plane first. Since I was with the kids, I thought it'd be worth the extra money so we could all sit together. Anyway when it was time to board we went through the gate first, but instead of going directly onto the plane, it turned out that the plane was miles away from the gate, and there was a bus to take us there. So what happened? All the people who hadn't paid the extra money got onto the same bus, and then got off the bus before us! So we paid $120 for nothing — we were almost the last ones on the plane and couldn't sit together!

I'm going to email GreenAir and complain. It's a complete rip-off! And if they don't do anything about it, I'll file a complaint with the Department of Transportation.

Apart from that, the vacation was great. Florida was a dream…

◄ *p.91*

b You are going to write the email to GreenAir. With a partner…

- underline the relevant information in the email.
- summarize exactly what it is that you are dissatisfied with.
- think of reasons why your complaint is justified.
- discuss what would be reasonable for GreenAir to do to compensate you for the inconvenience.
- decide what other details you think might be important to include in the email, e.g., the date and the flight number, and invent them.

TIPS for writing an email or letter of complaint

- Make a note of all the relevant details you want to include before you start drafting your email.
- Decide what action you want the person you are writing to to take.
- Use appropriate expressions for opening and closing the email.
- Use a formal style, and be clear and assertive but not aggressive.
- Try to use a variety of expressions for generalizing and making suggestions.
- Use the passive, e.g., *we were told, we are owed an apology*, etc. to make it more impersonal or to make it clear that you are not accusing individuals.

WRITING

You are going to write an email to the airline. It should be approximately 250 words.

DRAFT your email, explaining why you are writing, what the complaint relates to, giving the details, and asking for some action from the airline.

EDIT the email, making sure you are happy with the content and tone throughout, and making sure it is the right length.

CHECK the email for mistakes in grammar, spelling, punctuation, and register.

Communication

1B WHAT CAN YOU SEE? Students A + B

Look at the picture below. Write down on a piece of paper what you see. Allow yourself about 30 seconds for this.

◄ *p.8* and continue choosing your answers.

1B WHO AM I? Students A + B

a For each section, find out which personality type you are.

1 more a and b = **planner**   3 more a and b = **head**
  more c and d = **spontaneous**   more c and d = **heart**

2 more a and b = **facts**   4 more a and b = **introvert**
  more c and d = **ideas**   more c and d = **extrovert**

b With your four types, find out which of the categories below you fit into. Then read the description of your personality type.

c Now find out what your partner's personality type is, and read the description.

BIG THINKER = Spontaneous + Ideas + Heart + Extrovert
How they see themselves talkative, curious, logical, self-sufficient
What they are like ingenious, bored by routine, can be rude, rebellious, critical of others

COUNSELOR = Planner + Ideas + Heart + Introvert
How they see themselves gentle, peaceful, cautious
What they are like relaxed and creative, deeply private, can be difficult to get to know

GO-GETTER = Spontaneous + Facts + Head + Extrovert
How they see themselves inventive, enthusiastic, determined, alert
What they are like resourceful, tough-minded, may become frustrated by routines and constraints

IDEALIST = Spontaneous + Ideas + Heart + Introvert
How they see themselves bright, forgiving, curious
What they are like generally easygoing, flexible, can be stubborn, may refuse to compromise

INNOVATOR = Spontaneous + Ideas + Heart + Extrovert
How they see themselves imaginative, sociable, sympathetic
What they are like energetic, sensitive, creative, sometimes illogical, rebellious, unfocused

LEADER = Planner + Ideas + Head + Extrovert
How they see themselves bright, independent, logical
What they are like organized, good at solving large-scale problems, can be critical and aggressive

MASTERMIND = Planner + Ideas + Head + Introvert
How they see themselves logical, thorough, bright
What they are like efficient, independent, rarely change their minds, critical of those who don't understand them

MENTOR = Planner + Ideas + Heart + Extrovert
How they see themselves intelligent, outgoing, sensitive
What they are like articulate, warm, lively, extremely sensitive to people's needs, may become overbearing

NURTURER = Planner + Facts + Heart + Introvert
How they see themselves gentle, conscientious, mature
What they are like caring, may have trouble making decisions that could hurt others, tend to avoid conflict, others may take advantage of them

PEACEMAKER = Spontaneous + Facts + Heart + Introvert
How they see themselves steady, gentle, sympathetic,
What they are like sensitive to the feelings of others and the world around them, can be self-critical, often difficult to get to know

PERFORMER = Spontaneous + Facts + Heart + Extrovert
How they see themselves enthusiastic, sociable, sensitive
What they are like fun-loving, outgoing, often good motivators, can be unreliable

PROVIDER = Planner + Facts + Heart + Extrovert
How they see themselves sympathetic, easygoing, steady
What they are like warm, caring, traditional, tend to avoid conflict, not afraid to express their beliefs

REALIST = Planner + Facts + Head + Introvert
How they see themselves mature, stable, conscientious
What they are like loyal, straightforward, good at meeting deadlines, respect facts and rules, can be obsessed with schedules, critical of others, may not have faith in other people's abilities

RESOLVER = Spontaneous + Facts + Head + Introvert
How they see themselves understanding, stable, easygoing
What they are like independent, rational, good at finding solutions, natural risk takers, they enjoy an adrenaline rush, often focus on short-term results, sometimes lose sight of the bigger picture

STRATEGIST = Spontaneous + Ideas + Head + Introvert
How they see themselves bright, logical, individualistic
What they are like quiet, easygoing, intellectually curious, logical, may be critical or sarcastic, can be insensitive to the emotional needs of others

SUPERVISOR = Planner + Facts + Head + Extrovert
How they see themselves stable, practical, sociable
What they are like natural organizers and administrators, irritated when people don't follow procedures, other people find them bossy

3B GUESS THE SENTENCE
Student A

a Look at sentences 1–5 and imagine what the missing phrase could be. Remember ⊞ = positive verb and ⊟ = negative verb.

1 A lot of people say the book is better than the movie, but actually I _____. ⊞

2 It wasn't a particularly nice day for the barbecue but at least _____. ⊟

3 The sea was blue, the sun was shining, and the picnic was marvelous. All in all, it _____. ⊞

4 On the one hand, dogs are much better company than any other pets, but on the other hand you _____ at least twice a day. ⊞

5 Make sure your suitcase weighs less than 40 pounds, otherwise you _____. ⊞

b Read your sentences to **B**. Keep trying different possibilities until you get each sentence exactly right.

c Listen to your partner's sentences. Tell them to keep guessing until they get it exactly the same as yours.

6 I'm not sure you would enjoy the play, and in any case it will be very difficult **to get tickets**.

7 Some of the teachers aren't very stimulating, but on the whole I think **it's a good school**.

8 Laura's husband only thinks of himself and he always gets his own way. In other words, **he's totally selfish**.

9 I don't feel like going to Miranda's birthday party and besides, I don't **have anything to wear**.

10 It's no big surprise that Leo didn't do very well on his test. After all, he **didn't study at all**.

5B DO YOU HAVE "AFFLUENZA"?
Students A + B

If you answered "yes" to **any** of the questions, then you have the virus. The more "yes" answers, the worse you have it.

7A QI QUIZ Student A

a Read the answers to questions 1–5 and remember the information.

b Explain the answers to **B** in your own words. **B** will tell you the answers to 6–10.

1 What was Tutankhamun's curse?
There wasn't one. The story of the curse was made up by a reporter. When the British archaeologist Howard Carter discovered the tomb of King Tutankhamun in Cairo in 1922, a reporter who was writing for the British newspaper the *Daily Express* reported that there was an inscription above the door of the tomb that said, "They who enter this sacred tomb shall swiftly be visited by wings of death." In fact, there is no such inscription, but the story of the curse spread around the world and after that every time a member of the expedition died, people said it was because of the curse.

2 What do chameleons do, and why?
We all learn at school that chameleons change color as a form of camouflage, for example they change to gray so that they can hide on a rock, but in fact this is a total myth. Chameleons do change color, but not to match the background. They change color when they are frightened or after a fight and they sometimes change color due to changes in light or temperature.

3 What man-made structures can be seen from the moon?
No points if you said The Great Wall of China! In fact <u>no</u> man-made structures can be seen from the moon — even continents are barely visible. You <u>can</u> see the Great Wall of China from <u>space</u> (which starts about 62 miles from the earth's surface), as well as oceans, railways, cities, and even some buildings, but not from the moon.

4 What do kilts and whisky have in common?
The answer is that neither of them is Scottish in origin! Kilts were invented by the Irish and whisky by the Chinese.

5 Which metal is the best conductor?
Many people think that the answer is copper, but actually this is the second-best conductor. The best conductor is silver, but copper is more commonly used in electrical equipment simply because it is much cheaper.

7A WHAT A RIDICULOUS IDEA! Student A

a Read your sentences to **B**. He / She will respond with an exclamation.

- Did you know that you're not supposed to call a female actor an actress because it's considered sexist?
- I got a ticket from a policeman yesterday for talking on my cell phone while I was parked.
- My parents were robbed last night. They took all my mom's jewelry.
- I thought we could go to the movies and then have dinner at the new Italian place down the street.
- Did you know my parents were both born on exactly the same day?
- I really put my foot in my mouth at the party. I called Tom's wife "Anna," but that's his ex-wife's name!
- You won't believe it, but my sister just won $200,000 in the lottery!

b Respond to **B**'s sentences with an exclamation beginning with either *How…!* or *What (a)…!* Make sure you use expressive intonation, and link the words where appropriate.

Communication

7B FOUR WORKS OF ART
Students A + B

My Bed (1999) Tracey Emin

Away from the flock (1994) Damien Hirst

Balloon dog (yellow) (1994–2000) Jeff Koons

Felt suit (1970)
Joseph Bueys

7B STRESSING THE RIGHT WORD
Student A

a Read your sentence 1 to **B**. He / She will respond, giving one word extra stress. Continue with 2–6.

1 That girl really looks like your sister.
2 Did you say she was American?
3 Is the shoe store the one after the traffic lights?
4 Should we get her this bag then?
5 I thought you said you read the book?
6 I left your briefcase on your bed.

b Now respond to **B** with your number 7 below, giving extra stress to one of the words. Continue with 8–12.

7 He's not my dog. He's my girlfriend's / boyfriend's dog.
8 Sorry, I asked for a tuna salad.
9 I gave him the money. He'd never be able to pay me back.
10 It looks expensive, but actually it was really cheap.
11 I am going out. I haven't been out for a long time.
12 They lost 2–1 you mean.

8A GUESS THE SENTENCE Student A

a Look at sentences 1–7 and imagine what the missing phrase could be.

1 I would love _____ the boss's face when you told him you were leaving. [+]
2 There's no point _____. He never goes to parties. [+]
3 It's no good _____ pay you back. She's completely broke. [+]
4 We would rather _____ vacation in July, but in the end we had to go in August. [+]
5 I absolutely hate _____ I should do. I prefer to make my own mistakes. [−]
6 You'd better _____. There are cameras on this road. [−]
7 Jack completely denied _____ his ex-girlfriend again, but I don't believe him. [+]

b Read your sentences to **B**. Keep trying different possibilities until you get each sentence exactly right.

c Now listen to your partner's sentences. Tell them to keep guessing until they get it exactly the same as yours.

8 It's a very rewarding job that involves **working on a** team.
9 Lucy seems **to be seeing** Danny a lot recently. Do you think they're dating?
10 We hope **to have found** a new apartment by the end of the year.
11 Our plan is **to rent** a house in the north of Italy for two weeks in September.
12 There's absolutely **nothing to do** in this town. There isn't even a movie theater.
13 My father was the first person in my family **to go to** college.
14 I really regret **not having known** my grandfather. He died before I was born.

9A MATCH THE SENTENCES Student A

a Read your sentences to **B**. Make sure you stress auxiliaries and *to* where appropriate. **B** will choose a response.

1 Have you ever been to Canada?
2 I absolutely hate getting up early.
3 Is Lina coming swimming this afternoon?
4 Your brother lives in San Diego, doesn't he?
5 You do like cabbage, don't you?

b Now **B** will read you his / her sentences. Choose a response from below. Make sure you stress auxiliaries and *to* where appropriate.

☐ He is! He made the varsity team this year.
☐ I don't, but my sister does. I'm too lazy!
☐ No, there weren't. Where were you, by the way?
☐ She said she wanted to, but she wasn't sure if she'd be able to.
☐ We'd like to, but we're not sure if we can afford to.

c Practice all ten mini-dialogues again, making sure you get the stress right.

3B GUESS THE SENTENCE
Student B

a Look at sentences 6–10 and imagine what the missing phrase could be. Remember
$+$ = positive verb and $-$ = negative verb.

6 I'm not sure you would enjoy the play, and in any case it will be very difficult _____. $+$

7 Some of the teachers aren't very stimulating, but on the whole I think _____. $+$

8 Laura's husband only thinks of himself and he always gets his own way. In other words, _____. $+$

9 I don't feel like going to Miranda's birthday party and besides, I don't _____. $-$

10 It's no big surprise that Leo didn't do very well on his test. After all, he _____. $-$

b Listen to your partner's sentences. Tell them to keep guessing until they get it exactly the same as yours.

1 A lot of people say the book is better than the movie, but actually I **preferred the film**.

2 It wasn't a particularly nice day for the barbecue but at least **it didn't rain**.

3 The sea was blue, the sun was shining, and the picnic was marvelous. All in all, it **was a great day**.

4 On the one hand, dogs are much better company than any other pets, but on the other hand you **have to take them for a walk** at least twice a day.

5 Make sure your suitcase weighs less than 40 pounds, otherwise you **may have to pay extra**.

c Now read your sentences to **A**. Keep trying different possibilities until you get each sentence exactly right.

7A QI QUIZ Student B

a Read the answers to questions 6–10 and try to remember the information.

b **A** will tell you the answers to 1–5. Then explain the answers to 6–10 to **A** in your own words.

6 Which African mammal kills more humans than any other?

The hippopotamus. Most attacks occur because somebody in a rowboat accidentally hits a hippopotamus on the head and it decides to overturn the boat, or because a hippo leaves the water and tramples on people who are walking by the side of a river.

7 What would probably have killed you in an 18th-century sea battle?

A splinter. In spite of what you see in Hollywood movies, cannonballs didn't actually explode, they just smashed through the sides of the ship and made huge splinters of wood fly around the decks, and these splinters killed anyone they came into contact with.

8 What did the American Thomas Edison invent that English speakers use every day?

Of course Edison is famous for inventing the electric light bulb, but English speakers also have to thank him for suggesting the word "hello" as the best way to answer the telephone. Before "hello" was used telephone operators used to say "Are you there?" or "Who are you?" when they answered the phone. And the man who invented the telephone, Alexander Bell, actually preferred "Ahoy! Ahoy!," which is what sailors use to attract attention.

9 How does television damage your health?

Not by sitting too close to it! Until the 1960s televisions used to emit low levels of radiation, which made it dangerous to sit too close, but this is not the case anymore. The real damage caused to our health by TV is obesity, because of the lazy lifestyle it creates.

10 Why is a marathon 26.219 miles long?

Many people think that it is because this was the exact distance a Greek messenger ran from Marathon to Athens to announce that the Persians had been defeated by the Greeks. This distance was approximately 25 miles, and this is the reason why at the first three modern Olympic Games the marathons were roughly that length. However, the reason why the modern-day marathon is exactly 26.219 miles is because of the British Royal Family. In 1908 when the Games were held in London, the starting line was put outside Windsor Castle so that half of the royal family could see it from their windows, and the finish line was in front of the royal box in White City, London, where the rest of the royal family was waiting. The distance was exactly 26.219 miles, and this became the standard length of the marathon.

Communication

7A WHAT A RIDICULOUS IDEA!
Student B

a Respond to **A**'s sentences with an exclamation beginning with either *How…!* or *What a…!* Make sure you use expressive intonation, and link the words where appropriate.

b Read your sentences to **A**. He / She will respond with an exclamation.

- I was at home all morning waiting for the electrician to come and he didn't show up.
- We're going to New York on Friday for a long weekend.
- Jack's going to take Sue to the theater and then have a candlelight dinner at the new Italian restaurant.
- My sister got married on Saturday and it rained all day.
- Even though I got 70 percent on the test, the teacher refused to pass me.
- My daughter's goldfish died this morning.
- Maria's husband collects photos of Angelina Jolie. He has hundreds of them.

7B STRESSING THE RIGHT WORD Student B

a **A** is going to read you a sentence. Respond with your number 1 below, giving extra stress to one of the words. Continue with 2–6.

1 She is my sister.
2 No, I said she was Canadian.
3 No, it's the one before the traffic lights.
4 Personally, I still think she'd prefer that one.
5 I bought it, but I haven't read it yet.
6 Could you put it under my bed, please?

b Read your sentence 7 to **A**. He / She will respond, giving one word extra stress. Continue with 8–12.

7 Is that your dog?
8 Here you are. A tuna sandwich and a cola.
9 Did you lend John the money he needed to buy the car?
10 That coat looks really expensive.
11 You're not going out tonight, are you?
12 Chicago won 2–1 on Saturday.

8A GUESS THE SENTENCE Student B

a Look at sentences 8–14 and imagine what the missing phrase could be.

8 It's a very rewarding job that involves _____ team. ⊞
9 Lucy seems _____ Danny a lot recently. Do you think they're dating? ⊞
10 We hope _____ a new apartment by the end of the year. ⊞
11 Our plan is _____ a house in the north of Italy for two weeks in September. ⊞
12 There's absolutely _____ in this town. There isn't even a movie theater. ⊟
13 My father was the first person in my family _____ college. ⊞
14 I really regret _____ my grandfather. He died before I was born. ⊟

b Listen to your partner's sentences. Tell them to keep guessing until they get it exactly the same as yours.

1 I would love **to have seen** the boss's face when you told him you were leaving.
2 There's no point **inviting him**. He never goes to parties.
3 It's no good **expecting her to** pay you back. She's completely broke.
4 We would rather **have gone on** vacation in July, but in the end we had to go in August.
5 I absolutely hate **being told what** I should do. I prefer to make my own mistakes.
6 You'd better **not drive so fast**. There are cameras on this road.
7 Jack completely denied **having seen** his ex-girlfriend again, but I don't believe him.

c Now read your sentences to **A**. Keep trying different possibilities until you get each sentence exactly right.

9A MATCH THE SENTENCES Student B

a **A** will read you his / her sentences. Choose a response from below. Make sure you stress auxiliaries and *to* where appropriate.

☐ I love it. It's cauliflower I can't stand.
☐ No, but I'd love to if I ever got the chance.
☐ She isn't but her children are. She didn't want to.
☐ So do I. Luckily I don't often have to.
☐ Yes, and so does my sister.

b Read your sentences to **A**. Make sure you stress auxiliaries and *to* where appropriate. **B** will choose a response.

6 Are you going to go skiing during winter break?
7 Were there many people in class yesterday?
8 Do you do a lot of gardening?
9 Erica did say she was coming, didn't she?
10 Adam isn't particularly good at tennis, is he?

c Practice all ten mini-dialogues again, making sure you get the stress right.

Listening

🔵5))

Host Welcome to *Workplace* and on today's program we're looking at the results of two recently published surveys, which both deal with the same topic — happiness at work. John, tell us about the first survey.

John Well, this was done by a human resources consulting firm, who interviewed more than 1,000 workers, and established a top ten list of the factors that make people happy at work. The most important factor for the majority of the people interviewed was having friendly, supportive co-workers.

Host Mm..hm.

John In fact, 73 percent of people interviewed put their relationship with co-workers as being the key factor contributing to happiness at work, which is a very high percentage. The second most important factor was having work that is enjoyable per se, that is people actually liking what they do.

Host Uh-huh.

John The two least important factors were having your achievements recognized, and surprisingly, earning a competitive salary.

Host I see. So we're not mainly motivated by money?

John Apparently not.

Host Any other interesting information in the survey?

John Yes, for example 25 percent of the working people interviewed described themselves as "very happy" at work. However, 20 percent of employees described themselves as being "unhappy."

Host That's an awful lot of unhappy people at work every day.

John It is, isn't it? And there were several more interesting conclusions revealed by the survey. First of all, small is beautiful: people definitely prefer working for smaller organizations or companies with fewer than 100 employees. We also find out that, generally speaking, women were happier in their work than men.

Host Yes, we're a miserable bunch, aren't we?

John And part-time workers, who only work four or five hours a day, are happier than those who work full-time. The researchers concluded that this is probably due to a better work–life balance.

Host Are bosses happier than their employees?

John Yes, perhaps not surprisingly, the higher up people are in a company, the happier they are. So senior managers enjoy their jobs more than people working under them.

Host Uh-huh. Does the period of time you spend with the same company affect how happy you are?

John Well, according to the survey, happiness declines the longer people stay with the same company or organization. The most contented people were those who'd been with a company for less than two years, and the least contented were those who'd been in the same place of work for more than ten years.

Host So you can stay too long in the same place.

John So it seems. And lastly, according to the survey, apparently the happiest workers of all are those who are 55 years old or older, probably because they feel they're working at the peak of their abilities.

Host But I guess they haven't spent more than ten years in the same job.

John Exactly. So how long have you been here, Michael?

Host Eight years! Maybe I should start thinking about looking for a new job…

🔵6))

Host The second survey we're looking at on today's program is a *Sunday Times* survey that was all about the best UK companies to work for. Apparently, one of the best small companies to work for is *innocent drinks*. Well, I have with me in the studio Becka Walton, who works for *innocent drinks*. Becka, tell us what made you apply for the job at *innocent*.

Becka Well, I've always really liked them as a company, I've always followed their website and their weekly newsletter, I've always thought that they would be people that I would like to work for, so it was just a matter of keeping an eye on their jobs page and waiting for a position that I thought I could do.

Host Now, in a recent survey about what makes people happy at work, *innocent* was listed as one of the top companies to work for. You obviously think it is a happy company. Now why do you think that?

Becka Well, I can see how we would have scored very highly on that scale, I think there's a really big emphasis on a team environment at work, we're all mixed up so nobody sits according to the group of people that they work with, which means that you get to make friends in different areas of the business. Everybody's aware of the projects that people are working on, the pressures that they're under, so it makes for a really good team environment. I think that's important.

Host And how does that compare with other companies that you've worked for?

Becka Oh, I haven't really worked for any big companies before — *innocent* is the biggest company that I've worked for. I know friends of mine complain about really stuffy work environments, but the atmosphere at *innocent* is really informal, things are pretty relaxed and a lot of my friends are surprised that we don't have to dress up to come to work, often people don't even wear shoes, and we have a grassy floor in our office, and it's just kind of a relaxed place to work.

Host What would you change about the company if there was something that you could change?

Becka Oh, I, I'm not really sure how to answer that question, I think that, a thing that does come up when we survey people is the work–life balance, I think people are really passionate about their jobs, and that's a good thing, but it can lead to people working very long hours.

Host So you're overworked?

Becka I wouldn't go that far, but it would be easy to be overworked, yes.

Host You're obviously very happy with your work, but is there a high staff turnover rate? Do people generally stay for a long time?

Becka I know that Daisy, my first manager, was the first female employed by the company.

She stayed for ten years which is a long time, so I think that shows she was pretty happy. Obviously we have people on short-term contracts, but as a general rule I would say that people are happy and people do tend to stay at *innocent* for a pretty long time.

Host OK, in the other survey, the one about the ten things that make people happy at work, the issue of a competitive salary was the last on the list. What's your view on that?

Becka Well, I've thought about that and I hope it doesn't make me sound shallow, but I struggled to think of ten things that were more important than the money. I mean it's important to maintain a good work-life balance and to, I suppose, have fun at work and to enjoy the people you work with, but I think it's really important to feel like the financial compensation for what you do is adequate.

Host Mm…hm. OK. And finally, I should ask you, do you drink smoothies yourself and if you do, are they always *innocent*?

Becka I really love, I *really* love smoothies and if I didn't, it would be the wrong place for me to work, and naturally, they're always *innocent* smoothies. I think the working environment is reflected in the passion that we all have and I think that's because we know we have a really good product.

Host Thank you very much, Becka Walton.

🔵10))

In the spring of 1800, the court painter, Francisco de Goya was commissioned by the Spanish King Carlos IV, direct ancestor of King Juan Carlos, to paint a portrait of the royal family. At the time, the royal family was all staying at the summer palace of Aranjuez, near Madrid. First on the left is Prince Carlos, the King's second son, and next to him is his older brother Prince Fernando, who was the heir to the throne. Fernando grew up hating his parents, especially his mother, but in fact, he took after his mother in that he was very vain and authoritarian, and when he eventually became king he was extremely unpopular. The old woman just behind Prince Fernando is Maria Josefa, the King's sister. Single and childless, she died shortly after the painting was finished. Next to Maria Josefa is a young woman whose face we cannot see because she is looking away, and she is the "mystery person" in this painting. There are two theories about her identity. One theory is that she is Princess Maria Amalia, one of the King's daughters, who'd died in childbirth three years before the picture was painted. The fact that she's looking away would be to show that she was, in fact, dead. However, the other more popular theory is that she represents the woman that Crown Prince Fernando would one day marry. It would have been important to put her in the picture to show that the Prince would marry one day, and have a son to carry on the dynasty. If this theory is true, the woman would be looking away because she didn't actually exist at that time. In fact, Fernando did marry, not once but four times. The young girl next to the mystery woman is Princess Maria Isabel, the King's youngest daughter. She went on to marry and had twelve children. Next to her is the Queen, Maria Luisa. Goya made her the central figure in the painting because she had a very strong personality, and she completely dominated her husband the King. As a young woman she had been very beautiful. In middle age, as she is here, she was still very vain. She tried to compensate for the fact that her beauty was fading by wearing exquisite dresses and jewelery, as we can see in the picture. The little boy with the Queen is her youngest son, Prince Francisco. He was a very sensitive boy and he suffered all his life due to the fact that he looked incredibly like one of his mother's lovers. As a result, people assumed that he was not the King's son. The King, who is standing next to him, was a weak man. Although he came to the throne full of ideas and dreams, his wife and his advisors made sure that he never managed to achieve any of them and he died frustrated and disappointed. The King's brother is standing behind him, and on his right, although you can only actually see part of her head, is the King's eldest daughter Carlota. Her parents arranged a marriage for her when was very young. She was an ambitious girl and eventually became Queen of Portugal. The final group of three figures shows the Queen's brother, Don Luis de Parma, his wife, Maria Luisa and their first child, a baby boy. In fact, Maria Luisa was not only Don Luis's wife, she was also his niece, as she was the King's second daughter. In fact, Don Luis was supposed to have married the King's eldest daughter, Carlota, but he fell in love with Princess Maria Luisa, who was lively and intelligent, and he insisted on marrying her. The royal family didn't all pose together for the painting — it would have taken too long.

Instead Goya made individual studies of each family member and later used them to create this work. The painting took him two years to complete, and it was the last royal portrait he ever painted. Incidentally, he included himself in the painting — he is standing in the background on the left, behind the two princes. Carlos IV called this painting "the family all together picture," and it was originally hung in the Royal Palace in Madrid.

① 12))

Interviewer Where did your family originate from?

David My mom's side of the family is from what is now Croatia. When she was born it was in between Italy and Yugoslavia. And my dad's side of the family is from Italy.

Interviewer Why did you start researching your family tree?

David The reason that I started researching was because I have two older sisters and they're both ten and eleven years older than me. So, growing up I actually never met my dad's parents, my grandparents on my father's side. And my grandparents on my mother's side were very old. Luckily my grandmother lived until she was a hundred but I didn't really get to know my grandfather that well. So, just out of curiosity I was just trying to understand my immediate family, my grandparents and in talking to my mom, in talking to my father, just kind of learning that they themselves lead very interesting kind of journeys over here. And the more that I went to look into it, the more interesting the stories became to me.

Interviewer When you start researching, what's the first step the first thing you do?

David The first thing that I do when researching, or the first thing that I did when I started researching, for me it was very organic and I just started talking to my parents. And then they started talking, or, they introduced me to family that I had met when I was a child but I had talked to my cousin who's a judge in Italy, or my cousin in the Bronx who knows my dad's side of the family. So that was kind of my immediate. And then I started to branch out from there using

Ancestry.com or you know, different resources. You know, even just going to the public library and seeing if I could dig up documents that way.

Interviewer In practical terms, how important is the Internet in researching family history?

David I think the Internet obviously is extremely important. I mean, it just makes finding information and being able to look at so many different resources so much easier. Something that would take probably months or a year you could probably do in a few days or a few weeks online. And just the communities of people that you can be introduced to that have done similar things to you, I think that's a huge benefit as well. So you can start talking to people who give you advice, you know, just going to message boards and seeing what people have done in the past. And a lot of times hurdles that you might come across, they have already solved them for you, they have hints for you about how to get past them. So, I think that's, to me, has been the biggest help.

Interviewer How far back have you been able to trace your family?

David I've been able to go back about four generations with my family. I'm still searching and still talking with some family members in Italy about what information they know and trying to use local offices there to see if I can get marriage licenses, and birth certificates of my grandparents and their parents. But, it's, the further back you go it becomes a little bit more difficult. So, I'm at about four generations now.

① 13))

Interviewer Why did you go to Ellis Island?

David I felt, I feel Ellis Island was a good place because it was such a hub of activity and there is so much information that is at your disposal so again, it kind of allows you to see when your family came here, it's that initial stepping stone that they started with.

Interviewer How did you feel when you went there?

David It was the first time that I had been to Ellis Island and having grown up in New York that's kind of quite surprising that I had never been there. For me it was just, I felt like I was kind of walking through history a little bit and having it, it was much different, you know, when my great uncle was coming through, but it, you kind of still get the sense of the hope and the freedom that you know, knowing that my immediate family was trying to just leave such poverty and, you know, really seeing that American dream and having that hope, you kind of just get that sense of so many people were coming through here and this was just like I finally made it and you kind of feel that as you're walking around.

Interviewer And what did you find out about your family there?

David When I went to Ellis Island I was able to find on my dad's side when his great uncle came over a lot of the documentation that, or the documentation when he actually came over.

Interviewer And how did that make you feel when you found that?

David When I came across his documentation it was a very emotional moment. It made the whole, it made an aspect of the story very concrete for me just knowing that he, you know, did come across and he kind of went through the hallways of Ellis Island and you know, it allowed me to create in my own mind a very specific concrete event that happened. So, often times when you're doing research it can be very abstract and you're just kind of learning a piece of this and a piece of that. But seeing something very physical just kind of brought it home for me.

Interviewer And your dad's great uncle helped the rest of the family to come?

David My dad's great uncle actually sponsored the majority of my dad's family to come over so along with my grandparents, my uncle, my father, my other dad's, the other side of my father's family, his cousins, their parents, so he was the, kind of the first person that you know, when he came over he was I believe fifteen and just kind of working in the streets, working as an ice vendor, working construction. And slowly but surely he was able to bring the majority of the family, who at the time was living in Southern Italy which at that time there wasn't much going on in Southern Italy, to come over and you know, plant roots in New York.

Without him, I mean, I probably wouldn't be here 'cause my dad would have never come over and then my mom. So, you know, I think the courage that he had to come over, especially by himself, and to bring the rest of my family over was something very heroic to do.

Interviewer During all the research which you did into your family tree did you find out anything which surprised you?

David I did find some surprising stories. When my mom left, she had a passport just to go visit her sister in Italy and she basically left the country illegally and she seeked political asylum in Italy and she had to live in a refugee camp for about a year. And my aunt at the time, they wouldn't allow her a passport so she had to basically cross the border running through the woods with her two kids in the middle of the night. So, you know, as you start to just hear these even first account stories, second account stories, you know, just very interesting to understand the difficulties that your family had to go through sometimes to just create a better life for, you know, at the time they didn't know I was gonna be around.

Interviewer And what did you find out about how your parents met in New York?

David In talking to my parents, when my mom came over in 1960 and my father came over in 1961, even though they had very similar cultures they also had very, a lot of differences. So they didn't actually speak the same language and having met in English school I thought, you know, that was pretty surprising. Even though they both lived in New York it kind of brought a sense of how New York and the US really is a melting pot. And, you know, it took a little while for them to kind of, well, I guess my mom to warm up to my dad. But once they understood that a lot of their cultural backgrounds were very similar, you know, the whole family started to hang out and my mom became very close with my would be grandmother, or her would be mother-in-law.

Interviewer What would you say to somebody who is thinking of researching their family tree?

David I would recommend for anybody looking to start, who is possibly thinking about doing some research into family history to just start talking to your family. That's how I started and it's very easy, you know, assuming that your family is there and they have the history. You know, it's, it's a way to just kind of start and for me it's led down this path where I've decided to you know, research further and further. But I also did feel it was a bit of an obligation for me to understand so that I can pass it along to my kids and to my grandchildren. Because, you know, if I just would have never started asking my mom, I wouldn't be able to tell my kids about my uncle's coming over from you know, into, to America in the nineteen twenties and you know, working as an ice vendor, or my great uncle rowing across in the middle of the night to escape Yugoslavia. So to me it's led to a lot of information that now I've, you know, I can pass along, and, you know, to me it's, that, that aspect is important.

1 18)))

Interviewer Do you find it easier to understand native or non-native speakers of English?

Cristina Well, I've been in the United States for seven years now, and I've been exposed to a lot of different accents, not only people from the United States, but from different parts of the world, so I'm used to it. In terms of regional accents in the US, I still sometimes have trouble with Southern accents…they're a little more challenging for me, because I don't live in the South. The most stressful thing, I think, is talking on the phone, because you don't have the face-to-face interaction, so it can be tricky.

Interviewer Do you find it easier to understand native or non-native speakers of English?

Pun I find native speakers easier to understand, because they speak more clearly than non-native speakers. But, some native speakers can be difficult to understand too because they talk too fast. And even though I can usually understand native speakers better, I have more confidence when I'm talking to a non-native speaker because I know that *neither* of us speaks perfect English, so I'm not as worried about making mistakes or being embarrassed.

Interviewer How do you feel about having your English corrected?

Cristina Well, it hasn't happened much lately, but I don't mind, because that's how we learn, you know, we learn from our own mistakes. Sometimes when I'm tired, I might make a mistake with the third-person form, you know, but usually people are quite tolerant. And sometimes I catch my *own* mistakes, so I'm able to correct myself.

Interviewer How do you feel about having your English corrected?

Pun I love to have native speakers correct my English, because it helps to pinpoint my mistake. But some people can overdo it. For example, I had this co-worker at my job, and every time we had a conversation, he used to correct my mistakes — if someone corrects you constantly, you just don't want to speak anymore. But when they give me words that I didn't know before, then it's appreciated.

1 19)))

Interviewer Do you have any funny or embarrassing stories related to misunderstanding someone?

Cristina Yes, this happened a few years ago. I was trying to organize an evening out with some friends, and one of my friends picked a place for all of us to meet, and he said, "Let's all meet at Hideout." He meant H-I-D-E-O-U-T, you know, like a hiding place, which was the name of a bar. But I completely misunderstood him and thought he said "high doubt," two words, like H-I-G-H D-O-U-B-T. So, this caused a lot of confusion because I passed on the information to a bunch of other people and everybody got extremely confused and we couldn't find the place. We had to call him to find out where it was, and then we all figured out that I had misunderstood and gotten the name of the place wrong. Yeah, it took us a while, but in the end we all got together and had a good laugh. So it all worked out.

Interviewer Do you have any funny or embarrassing stories related to misunderstanding someone?

Pun Yeah, usually related to idioms. For example, I once took a business course, and the professor liked to use the phrase, "get a foot in the door." I didn't know what that expression meant and kept thinking, why do we need to put a foot in the door? Then a classmate told me it doesn't mean you REALLY stick your foot in the door, it means you initiate, or start, something…And here's another one: "sugar-free." I knew that "free" means no cost, but I kept seeing "sugar-free" things in stores. I thought that "sugar-free" meant they put in *more* sugar, like *extra* sugar, and it was free to the customer. But instead, it meant there was NO sugar at all. I was really surprised by that.

Interviewer Is there anything you still find difficult about English?

Cristina I find that certain idioms related to sports don't come easily to me because I don't know anything about baseball or basketball or American football, and there's quite a few idioms in American English that come from those sports, like "hit it out of the park" or "slam dunk." So even though I do understand them in context, I don't use them, because I don't always see the connection…Oh, and spelling. Romanian is a phonetic language, so spelling isn't necessarily as important as it is in English. Sometimes I have to write words out in English, maybe because I'm a visual learner. I have to visualize the letters in my head before I can spell the word.

Interviewer Is there anything you still find difficult about English?

Pun Hmm. Sometimes when I read a new word, I'm not sure where to put the stress, for example, I'll say STAtistics instead of staTIStics. And I always used to say aCAdemic…for the word acaDEMic. You see, the Thai language is very different from English, so sometimes it's hard. But mostly my problem is that I'm constantly monitoring my own speech because I'm afraid of making mistakes.

1 22)))

Interviewer What's your earliest memory?

Speaker 1 I was born on the Atlantic coast of New England, and my earliest memory is swimming between my mother and my father in the Atlantic Ocean.

Interviewer Oh, wow.

Speaker 1 Because I swam before I could walk. And it was wonderful.

Interviewer How amazing! How old were you then?

Speaker 1 I think I was like, actually, I must have been really, really young, maybe, maybe I'd already walked by that point, I must have been one and a half when I had that memory. Really young, it was really, it was a beautiful experience then, and remembering it makes me very happy.

Speaker 2 My earliest memory is of being completely by myself, lost in what seemed to be a great big forest, it probably wasn't. I was about 18 months old and we were living in Virginia, which is where I was born, and I was on a kind of a path in the middle of a really, really dark forest and I remember looking behind me and it was just darkness and big dark trees and the same ahead of me, and just having this feeling of being completely on my own, and calling out for my sister, Lynn, who was seven years older than me, who was supposed to be watching me and not being able to find her.

Speaker 3 I guess I was about three or maybe four, and I remember sitting on my father's shoulders and we were going to the zoo and there was an elephant, and the elephant took my ice cream.

Speaker 4 I remember it was 1966 and I was sitting at a bus stop with my grandmother, and I'd been given a brand new dime, it was brand new, it was so shiny, and it was beautiful, and I remembered deciding then and there that this was going to be my earliest memory, I was going to remember this day in 1966 when I was sitting there with this brand new dime. And then I remember the bus came, and when we went to get on, my grandma was a dime short, so that was the end of my dime.

Speaker 5 One of my very earliest memories is pulling away in a car looking out of the window seeing our dog Sam through a window, whimpering and looking really sad like he was already missing us. We were basically having to say goodbye to Sam because we were moving to an apartment where they didn't allow dogs. So we were having to say goodbye to him, and it was very sad, he was like whining and whimpering in his new home and we were pulling away. It was horrible.

1 23)))

Host Are our first memories reliable, or are they always based on something people have told us? What age do most people's first memories come from? John Fisher has been reading a fascinating new book about memory by Professor Draaisma called *How Memory Shapes our Past*, and he's going to answer these questions for us and more. Hello John.

John Hello.

Host Let's start at the beginning. At what age do first memories generally occur?

John Well, according to both past and present research, 80 percent of our first memories are of things that happened to us between the ages of two and four. It's very unusual to remember anything that happened before that age.

Host Why is that?

John There seem to be two main reasons, according to Professor Draaisma. The first reason is that before the age of two, children don't have a clear sense of themselves as individuals — they can't usually identify themselves in a photograph. And you know how a very small child enjoys seeing himself in a mirror, but he doesn't actually realize that the person he can see is in fact himself. Children of this age also have problems with the pronouns *I* and *you*. And a memory without *I* is impossible. That's to say, we can't begin to have memories until we have an awareness of self.

Host And the second reason?

John The second reason is related to language. According to the research, first memories coincide with the development of linguistic skills, with a child learning to talk. And as far as autobiographical memory is concerned, it's essential for a child to be able to use the past tense, so that he or she can talk about something that happened in the past, and then remember it.

Host I see. What are first memories usually about? I mean, is it possible to generalize at all?

John Early memories seem to be related to strong emotions, such as happiness, unhappiness, pain, and surprise. Recent research suggests that three quarters of first memories are related to fear, to frightening experiences like being left alone, or a large dog, or having an accident — things like falling off a swing in a park. And of course this makes sense, and bears out the evolutionary theory that the human memory is linked to self-preservation. You remember these things in order to be prepared if they happen again, so that you can protect yourself.

Host Are first memories only related to emotions, or are there any specific events that tend to become first memories?

John The events that are most often remembered, and they are always related to one of the emotions I mentioned before, are the birth of a baby brother or sister, a death, or a family visit. Festive celebrations with bright lights were also frequently mentioned, much more frequently than events we might have expected to be significant, like a child's first day at school. Another interesting aspect is that first memories tend to be very visual. They're almost invariably described as pictures, not smells or sounds.

Host First memories are often considered unreliable, in that perhaps sometimes they're not real memories, just things other people have told us about ourselves or that we have seen in photos. Is that true, according to Professor Draaisma?

John Absolutely! He cites the famous case of the Swiss psychologist, Jean Piaget…

1 24))

Host First memories are often considered unreliable, in that perhaps sometimes they're not real memories, just things other people have told us about ourselves or that we have seen in photos. Is that true, according to Professor Draaisma?

John Absolutely! He cites the famous case of the Swiss psychologist, Jean Piaget. Piaget had always thought that his first memory was of sitting in his stroller as a one-year-old baby when a man tried to kidnap him. He remembered his nanny fighting the kidnapper to save him. The nanny was then given a watch as a reward by Jean's parents. But many years later, I think when Jean was 15, the parents received a letter from the nanny in which she returned the watch to them. The nanny, who was by now an old woman, confessed in the letter that she'd made up the whole story, and that was why she was returning the watch. Of course Jean had heard the story told so many times that he was convinced that he'd remembered the whole incident.

2 4))

1 No relationship is an island; it's surrounded by friends and family, all of whom have something to say about it. In a study undertaken by Illinois University, researchers found that both men and women felt happier and were more committed to each other when their friends approved of their relationship. When friends tell a couple that they are a good match, and how much they enjoy going out with them, that couple starts believing that they really are a couple. Also when a couple stays together for a while, their two groups of friends start to make friends with each other, and as a result the couple's relationship gets stronger.

2 Cars are small, confined spaces, which makes them ideal to fight in. A survey conducted for a driving magazine found that one driver in ten will be arguing with a partner within 15 minutes of starting the trip. About 40 percent of the arguments are caused by men criticizing their partner's driving, and another 10 percent by the man taking control of the car stereo. At least disputes about map reading can now be resolved by GPS!

3 Relationship research would say that it's conclusively proven that like attracts like, in other words that we are generally attracted to people who are similar to us. This research shows that couples usually share religious and political beliefs and are about the same age. They are fairly similar in education, intelligence, and what they think matters in life. Most people also go for someone as good-looking or as plain as they are. You may, however, be familiar with the phrase "love is blind," suggesting that you can fall for anyone, if you get the chance to meet them. But psychologists argue that such "blindness" is temporary: after three months you can "see" again, and then you usually get over the person.

4 Today the Internet is one of the most popular ways for people to find dates. On the one hand, the opportunity to remain anonymous for a while is an advantage. People feel that they can express their emotions more readily online and get to know each other more quickly. On the other hand, people can lie more easily, the most common lies being about weight, age, and of course about already being married. But if you have reasonable expectations, online dating is a good way to start looking for dates. Increase your success by posting a picture and a truthful profile. Online dating agencies advise getting a picture taken that makes you look friendly, rather than seductive. Best of all, use a dictionary when writing your profile. The biggest turn-off, apparently, is profiles with poor spelling. But once you've found a date, will the relationship last? A study in the US of over 3,000 adults found that 15 percent knew someone in a long-term relationship that had started online and according to research the success rates of these relationships are very similar to offline methods of meeting people, such as meeting people at work or at a party.

5 Early loves are incredibly powerful and, with the Internet, increasingly accessible. A survey in *Time* magazine found out that nearly 60 percent of people interviewed still thought about their first loves. Dr. Nancy Kalish of California State University conducted another study which got randomly selected American adults to agree to be interviewed about their first loves. One third said they would reunite with their first loves if they could. Then, by advertising in the media, Dr. Kalish got data on 2,500 first love couples who got back in contact with each other. With the ones who were single when they found their lost loves, things moved quickly with 40 percent of them together again within three weeks, and most of them then getting married (and still together several years later). But there was a different story with the couples who were already in committed, usually happy relationships. Most of these people had casually Googled their old love on a whim with no plan for what to do if they found that person. 80 percent of these people ended up getting involved with their lost love again, and generally they became unhappy as a result. Dr. Kalish strongly warns people who aren't single not to do an online search for lost loves because of the destruction it can cause families and relationships.

6 You've just been dumped by your partner and you want revenge. But will it make you feel better? In a Canadian study, the most popular methods of revenge were flirting with friends or enemies of their ex, damaging their car, or breaking something they own, and writing nasty letters or emails. The question is, what will the revenge achieve? Another study by Stephen Hoshimura at the University of Montana asked people what act of revenge they had carried out, and what they had wanted to achieve, and how they felt afterward. The research showed that most people felt anxious and sorry afterward rather than feeling any happier. But most of all, they still felt angry. It seems that unfortunately, for most people, revenge is *not* sweet.

2 8))

In the book *History Goes to the Movies*, the author Joseph Roquemore rates movies according to their historical accuracy on a scale of one to five stars — five stars means a movie's very accurate, and no stars means it's very inaccurate. I'm going to look at two of the best-known movies that Roquemore features in his book. The first movie is the Oscar-winning movie *Titanic*, which was directed by James Cameron in 1997. The movie *is* historically accurate regarding the events leading up to the collision with the iceberg — the Titanic was sailing too fast and the captain ignored warnings about ice. The collision and sinking are also very accurately portrayed with amazing special effects. However, where the movies falls short is in its characterization. I have to say I entirely agree with Roquemore when he criticizes director James Cameron for what he calls "class-conscious overkill." What he means by that is Cameron depicts all the third-class passengers in the movie as brave and good, and all the first-class passengers as selfish, stupid, cowardly, or downright evil. And this can't have been the case. Then a large part of the movie focuses on the love story between Jack, a third-class passenger, played by Leonardo DiCaprio, and Rose, a first-class passenger, played by Kate Winslet. Obviously, these characters and their story are fictitious and were just added, presumably to sell the movie to a younger audience. But many historians have pointed out that a romance between Jack and Rose is totally improbable, because at that time there was complete class segregation on the ship. Roquemore also criticizes the movie's portrayal of Captain Smith. He's made out to be indecisive and basically useless throughout the disaster. But this contradicts everything which was said about him by survivors of the sinking. And for me, though, even more indefensible was the movie's portrayal of the ship's First Officer, William Murdoch. On the night of the sinking, he behaved heroically. In his hometown in Scotland there's even a memorial to him, but in the movie he's shown taking a bribe from a passenger (in exchange for a place in a lifeboat), shooting passengers dead, and finally shooting himself in the head. In fact, the movie studio 20th Century Fox, which produced *Titanic*, was eventually forced to admit that there was no historical evidence that Murdoch did any of these things, and that they'd included these details purely and simply to make the story more interesting. Roquemore gives *Titanic* three stars, describing it as "Great pyrotechnics — mediocre history." All in all, I think his assessment is about right. The main events are true but the characterization is definitely the weak point of the movie.

Moving on to the second movie, *Braveheart*, this is one of the movies that Roquemore gives five stars for historical accuracy. He gives the movie five stars because despite what he calls some "small fictions" he thinks *Braveheart* is, I quote, "true to the spirit of William Wallace." Well, that may be the case, but I'm afraid I have to take exception to the phrase "small fictions." The historian Elizabeth Ewan described *Braveheart* as a movie which "almost totally sacrifices historical accuracy for epic adventure." William Wallace is portrayed as a kind of poor primitive tribesman living in a village. In fact, he was the son of a rich landowner and he later became a knight. You'll remember too that in the movie Mel Gibson wears woad, a kind of blue face paint. Apparently, the Scots stopped wearing woad hundreds of years earlier. And while we're on the subject of costume, in the movie the Scottish soldiers wear kilts. No surprises there you might think, but in the 13th century, which is when the events of the movie are set, the Scots did not wear kilts, and in fact, they didn't start wearing them until four centuries later. Another of these "fictions" is that in *Braveheart*, William Wallace has a romance with the beautiful French princess, Isabelle. However, the historical reality is that Wallace never met Isabelle and even if he had, she would only have been nine years old at the time! Finally, anyone who's seen the movie will remember the famous battle scene. The battle was called the Battle of Stirling because it was fought on Stirling Bridge in Scotland. Basically, the reason why the Scots won the battle is because the English soldiers got trapped on the narrow bridge. In *Braveheart* the bridge does not appear at all in the battle. In fact, Mel Gibson originally planned to film the scene on the actual bridge, but he found that the bridge kept "getting in the way." Apparently, when he mentioned this to one of the Scottish history advisers on the movie, the man's reply was "Aye, that's what the English found." Mel Gibson defended all the inaccuracies in the movie saying that the movie's version of history was more "compelling cinematically." Admittedly, it *is* a very entertaining movie, and it does give you a strong feeling for William Wallace and how he must have inspired his countrymen, but I don't think you can give this movie five stars or even two stars for historical accuracy.

2 10)))

Interviewer You've written a number of screenplays for historical dramas, for example, *Rome*, why do you think there is so much demand for historical drama and film?

Adrian Well, film and TV is always about good stories. I know that seems a fairly obvious thing to say, but the thing about history is it's jam-packed full with good stories, many of which people know, part, or at least vaguely know. If you say, "I'm going to do a film about Robin Hood," you know that part of your audience at the very least will already have some knowledge of that story and they will think, "Oh yeah, I quite like that story, so maybe there's something in there that, for me in that film." And there are many other examples, Rome is a, you know, is a canvas full of stories that have, you know, lasted for 2,000 years. So, you know, many people have vaguely heard about Julius Caesar, some of them know that story very very well, and so on and so on, or Caligula or whoever. So history is just an endlessly useful way of telling great stories from the past in a way that means something in the present. In a perfect world, you get a double hit, you, you tell a classic story, but you also tell it in a way that makes it resonate with the present.

Interviewer Are historical films necessarily any more expensive than films set in the modern day?

Adrian Yeah, period is always more expensive. It's just something about the fact that you have to dress the film in a way that you don't have to dress a contemporary film. By "dress" I mean, not just dress people who have to wear costumes that are authentic to the period. If your film is set in 1800 they all have to look as though they were, you know, dressed exactly as in that period. That all costs money. But "dressed" also in terms of the way you make the houses look, the way you make all your decorations look, your furniture, everything has to be authentic to the period. You have to make sure there are no cars, no airplanes, every shot has to be weighed up to make sure that there's nothing in it which, which betrays the period. There's nothing more ridiculous than a period film where you

see a glaring anachronism, some detail that's horribly wrong. So unfortunately, all of that costs money and you have to have bigger crowds in many cases. *Rome* was a case in point. We needed big crowds. In the Senate you have to have, a certain number of Senators, all of them have to be dressed in, you know, in togas and so on. So I'm afraid it is just an expensive way of making films, yeah.

2 11)))

Interviewer How important is historical accuracy in a historical film?

Adrian The notion of accuracy in history is a really difficult one in drama because, you know, it's like saying, well, was *Macbeth* accurate, was a Shakespearean drama accurate. The thing is it's not about historical accuracy; it's about whether you can make a drama work from history that means something to an audience now. So I tend to take the view that in a way accuracy isn't the issue when it comes to the drama. If you're writing a drama, you have the right as a writer to create the drama that works for you, so you can certainly change details. The truth is nobody really knows how people spoke in Rome or how people spoke in the courts of Charles II or William the Conqueror or Victoria, or whoever. You have an idea from writing, from books, plays, and so on. We know when certain things happened, what sort of dates happened. I think it's really a question of judgement. If you make history ridiculous, if you change detail to the point where history is an absurdity, then obviously things become more difficult. The truth is that the more recent history you do, the more difficult it is not to be authentic to it.

In a way, it's much easier to play fast and loose with the details of what happened in Rome than it is to play fast and loose with the details of what happened in the Iraq War, say, you know. So it's all a matter of perspective in some ways. It's something that you have to be aware of and which you try to be faithful to, but you can't ultimately say a drama has to be bound by the rules of history, because that's not what drama is.

Interviewer Do you think the writer has a responsibility to represent any kind of historical truth?

Adrian Not unless that's his intention. If it's your intention to be truthful to history and you put a piece out saying this is the true story of, say, the murder of Julius Caesar exactly as the historical record has it, then of course, you do have an obligation, because if you then deliberately tell lies about it, you are, you know, you're deceiving your audience. If, however, you say you're writing a drama about the assassination of Julius Caesar purely from your own perspective and entirely in a fictional context, then you have the right to tell the story however you like. I don't think you have any obligation except to the story that you're telling. What you can't be is deliberately dishonest. You can't say this is true when you know full well it isn't.

Interviewer Can you think of any examples where you feel the facts have been twisted too far?

Adrian Well, I think the notion of whether a film, a historical film has gone too far in presenting a dramatized fictional version of the truth is really a matter of personal taste. The danger is with any historical film that if that becomes the only thing that the audience sees on that subject, if it becomes the received version of the truth, as it were, because people don't always make the distinction between movies and

reality in history, then obviously if that film is grossly irresponsible or grossly fantastic in its presentation of the truth, that could, I suppose, become controversial. I mean, if you know, I think that the only thing anybody is ever likely to know about *Spartacus*, for example, the movie, is Kirk Douglas and all his friends standing up and saying, "I am Spartacus, I am Spartacus," which is a wonderful moment and it stands for the notion of freedom, of individual choice and so on. So *Spartacus* the film, made in 1962, I think, if memory serves, has become, I think, for nearly everybody who knows anything about Spartacus the only version of the truth. Now in fact, we don't know if any of that is true really. There are some accounts of the historical Spartacus, but very very few and what, virtually the only thing that's known about it is that there was a man called Spartacus and there was a rebellion and many people were, you know, crucified at the end of it, as in the film. Whether that's irresponsible I don't know, I can't say that I think it is, I think in a way it's, *Spartacus* is a film that had a resonance in the modern era. There are other examples, you know, a lot of people felt that the version of William Wallace that was presented in *Braveheart* was really pushing the limits of what history could stand, the whole, in effect, his whole career was invented in the film, or at least, you know built on to such a degree that some people felt that perhaps it was more about the notion of Scotland as an independent country than it was about history as an authentic spectacle. But you know, again these things are a matter of purely personal taste. I mean, I enjoyed *Braveheart* immensely.

2 20)))

Host All of us are sensitive to sudden noise. We react if our neighbor suddenly turns on the radio full blast or if a dog starts barking loudly in the street. But are we aware of sounds which we are constantly surrounded by? The music in a restaurant, the noise of the subway. Do we even notice these sounds? And do we realize just how harmful they can be?

Here we are inside a well-known restaurant; you can actually hear the thumping of the music out in the street and people trying to talk above the noise. Let's talk to a waitress about the effect of the noise on her.

Host How long have-
Waitress Sorry, I can't hear you.
Host Let's go outside…How long have you worked here?
Waitress I've worked at this restaurant for a month now. Recently, I've been getting bad headaches, and sometimes I wake up with my ears buzzing. But I stay on the job because the money is good.
Host How long is your shift?
Waitress Eight to nine hours.
Host It's no wonder she's been getting headaches. The music level in there was 95 decibels. It's the equivalent of a jackhammer at 50 feet in the ground. One study shows that sustained exposure may result in hearing loss at 90 to 95 decibels. And according to the Occupational Safety and Health Administration (OSHA), the daily permissible noise level for 95 decibels is 4 hours. She's working twice the permitted time which explains the headaches and buzzing in her ears. So why does the restaurant play such loud music? Studies show that loud and fast-tempo music encourages customers to drink and chew more quickly. Some restaurants are using this to deliberately control their sound systems

and set noise levels to increase profits. So, yes, there may be a price to pay for the loud music, but the reward is cold hard cash.

Now we're inside the New York City Subway where millions of people pass through to get around the city. We can hear the subway cars on the tracks, doors opening and closing…

We can hear commuters talking, people's footsteps on the platform…

Let's listen a little closer. What else can we hear?

Let's talk to a train conductor who is exposed to these sounds on a daily basis.

Train Conductor We all wear these ear "muffs," they look like headphones but they're not. I find them uncomfortable and I don't really see the point in wearing them. I take them off sometimes because I like the sounds of the subway going along the track. There's almost something relaxing about it. Probably the reason I've been doing this for more than ten years.

Host What our conductor doesn't know is that a study recorded the noise levels in New York City's subway systems and found that the average maximum noise levels inside the subway cars were 95 decibels. On the platform, noise levels were higher at 100 decibels. The same study found that more than 30 minutes a day in the New York City subways has the potential to cause hearing loss. To put this into perspective, 100 decibels is equivalent to a jet take-off. Now imagine listening to a jet take-off over and over again. Experts say that hearing loss typically occurs gradually with extended exposure to loud noise. Over time, people exposed to loud noises can have trouble understanding what people are saying and things will begin to sound muffled. It can also cause a condition called tinnitus which is a constant ringing, roaring, buzzing, etc. in the ears. Around 37 million Americans are affected with this condition. However, hearing a ringing or buzzing may not necessarily mean you have permanent damage. Sometimes, your hearing may recover, but over time, constant exposure to loud noises will eventually cause permanent damage. And while sudden hearing loss is not as common, it can result from one-time exposure at above 120 decibels. The louder the sound, the shorter the permissible exposure time.

Let's see if commuters notice the noise levels in the subway.

Commuter 1 I guess it's a little noisy in here, but I think it's just as loud on the streets. Sometimes, I think the streets are louder.

Commuter 2 I'm not really focused on the noise because all I need to focus on is getting from one place to another and it's hard to do that sometimes in the middle of rush hour when there are all these people trying to fit into already packed subway cars.

Commuter 3 Yes, it's loud in here. And it gets even louder when there are performers playing music on the platform. I just want to commute in quiet sometimes, but it's a luxury, I know.

Commuter 4 The subway is loud. People try to talk above the subway sounds and when there are hundreds of people it's a lot of loud noise. I can't stand it sometimes.

Host So what do you do?

Commuter 4 That's when I put on my headphones and turn the volume up.

2 21)))

1 All I knew about the man with the beard and the Panama hat was that our paths crossed at about twenty past eight in the morning on the street I walked down daily. The rest of his story was my own invention, until I spoke to him last week. Eiran is a self-taught jeweler and artist. He passes me each day on his way back from the synagogue at the end of the street where he's training to be a rabbi.

2 I pass number 220 once or twice a day depending on my route and from time to time I see an older gentleman standing outside it leaning on the gatepost. I wonder when I pass him what he sees and what he has seen. When I talk to him he tells me his name is Clarence, and he's from Barbados. He arrived in Britain in 1957 and has been here ever since. He is in his 80s and has close family who live nearby.

3 As I leave for work in the morning, the man who cleans my street is usually positioned with his cart at the corner of the first junction I pass and he never fails to smile and say "Good morning." When I introduced myself to him, he told me that his name was Gerard and he's from Ireland. He moved to London when he was a child.

4 Always together, the young man and the dog who work at the hardware store are regularly to be found in the doorway of the shop, side by side, observing the comings and goings on the street. Shyan is from Iran and his dog is German. Both have lived in London for many years. Shyan tells me that he's not sure if he is a Londoner, but says that he kisses the ground every time he returns to the city from a trip abroad.

5 The bun shop at the end of the road is an old-fashioned bakery where you can get a no-nonsense cup of instant coffee and a doughnut covered in hundreds and thousands. When I pass it, the two ladies behind the counter are always busy feeding the local community. Tara is from St. Lucia though her accent has faded. Her nickname at work is Cleopatra because she spends so long on her hair. Rita is from the Philippines and she does not like eating buns.

2 25)))

Interviewer What made you want to be a translator?

Translator It was something that I'd done when I was in college, and when I moved to Mexico it was difficult to get a job that wasn't teaching English, so I went back to the US and I took a postgraduate course in translation. After taking the course I swore that I would never be a translator, I thought it would be too boring, but I kept doing translation work, and eventually I decided it was for me because I liked the idea of working for myself, and it didn't require too much investment to get started. And actually, I enjoy working with words, and it's very satisfying when you feel that you've produced a reasonable translation of the original text.

Interviewer Yes, what do you think is the most difficult kind of text to translate?

Translator Literary texts, like novels, poetry, or drama because you have to give a lot of consideration to the author, and to the way it's been written in the original language.

Interviewer In order to translate a novel well, do you think you need to be a novelist yourself?

Translator I think that's true ideally, yes.

Interviewer And is that the case? I mean are most of the well-known translators of novels, generally speaking, novelists in their own right?

Translator Yes, I think in English anyway. People who translate into English tend to be published authors, and they tend to specialize in a particular author in the other language.

Interviewer I see.

Translator And of course if it's a living author, then it's so much easier because you can actually communicate with the author and say, you know, like, "What did you really mean here?"

Interviewer Another thing I've heard that is very hard to translate is advertising, for example slogans.

Translator Well, with advertising, the problem is that it has to be something punchy, and it's very difficult to translate that. For example, one of the Coca-Cola™ ads, the slogan in English was "the real thing," but you just couldn't translate that literally into Spanish, it just wouldn't have had the same power. In fact, it became *Sensación de vivir*, which is "sensation of living," which sounds really good in Spanish but it would sound weird in English.

Interviewer What about movie titles?

Translator They're very difficult too. People always complain that they haven't been translated accurately, but of course it's impossible because sometimes a literal translation just doesn't work.

Interviewer For example?

Translator OK, well, think of, you know, the Julie Andrews movie, *The Sound of Music*. Well, that works in English because it's a phrase that you know, you know like "I can hear the sound of music." But it doesn't work at all in other languages, and in Spanish it was called "Sonrisas y lagrimas" which means "Smiles and tears," in German it was called "Meine Lieder — meine Traüme," which means "My songs, my dreams," and in Italian it was "Tutti insieme appassionatamente," which means I think "All together passionately" or I don't know, something like that! In fact, I think it was translated differently all over the world.

Interviewer Do you think there are special problems translating movie scripts for the subtitles?

Translator Yes, a lot. There are special constraints, for example the translation has to fit on the screen as the actor is speaking, and so sometimes the translation is a paraphrase rather than a direct translation, and of course, well, going back to untranslatable things, really the big problems are cultural, and humor, because they're just not the same.

Interviewer I see.

Translator You can get the idea across, but you might need pages to explain it, and, you know, by that time the movie's moved on. I also sometimes think that the translators are given the movie on DVD, I mean, you know, rather than a written script, and that sometimes they've simply misheard or they didn't understand what the people said. And that's the only explanation I can come up with for some of the mistranslations that I've seen. Although sometimes it might be that some things like humor and jokes, especially ones that depend on wordplay are just, you know, they're simply untranslatable.

Interviewer Right.

Translator And often it's very difficult to get the right register, for example with slang and swear words, because if you literally translate taboo words or swear words, even if they exist in the other language, they may well be far more offensive.

Interviewer What are the pros and cons of being a translator?

Translator Well, it's a lonely job I suppose, you know, you're on your own most of the time, it's hard work, you're sitting there and, you know, you're working long hours, and you can't plan things because you don't know when more work is going to come in, and people always have tight deadlines. You know, it's really rare that somebody'll call you up and say "I want this translation in three months." That just doesn't really happen.

Interviewer And the pros?

Translator Well, the pros are that it gives you freedom because you can do it anywhere if you have an Internet connection and electricity, and I suppose you can organize your time, because you're freelance, you know, you're your own boss, which is good. I like that.

Interviewer What advice would you give someone who's thinking of going into translation?

Translator I'd say that in addition to the language, get a speciality. Get another degree in anything that interests you, like economics, law, history, art because you really need to know about the subjects that you're translating into.

③ 5))))

Host And now it's time for our weekly dose of *Time Bandits*, the part of the show where we try to deal with your time issues. Today we're going to be talking to our time management guru, Richard. And now we're going to line 1, which is Jade from Chicago. Hi Jade.

Caller 1 Hi guys! OK, I have this friend who's always calling me and, well, she just won't let me get off the phone — I waste so much time just listening to her telling me every single thing she's been doing and every little problem that she has.

Host Uh-huh, I think that's a common problem for all of us — so Richard, what advice do you have for Jade?

Richard Well, say you'd love to talk, but you can't right now and you'll call back another time. How about that? Or say you only have five minutes and really mean it, I mean say goodbye when the five minutes are up. Use a finishing up expression like, "Oh, it's been great talking to you, but I really have to go now."

Caller 1 OK, thank you.

Richard No problem.

Host That's great advice Richard. I'll have to remember to use that with my mother-in-law. All right then, we're going to line 2 now. We're talking to Nick from St. Louis. Hi Nick.

Caller 2 Hi, there! What I wanted to say was I am a very punctual person, you know, it's something I pride myself on, and I really spend a lot of my time, I should say waste my time, waiting for people. Like, for example there's this friend of mine, and we'll often have like an informal lunch together or something, and I will always arrive on time, I will get to the restaurant on time, but I have to wait for him, well, it's at least ten minutes, sometimes more, for him to show up.

Host OK, Nick, thanks. Now over to you, Richard.

Richard Well, Nick, I really know what you mean, because I have friends like that too! I think the best thing to do, and I'm speaking from experience, is send your friend a text or email on the morning that you're getting together, and tell them you're a little short on time today so you don't want to hang around too much. And ask him or her to let you know if they're going to be late! That should get the message across.

Host That's great advice, Richard. OK then, moving punctually on to line 3 which is Judy from Sioux City, Iowa. Hello Judy.

Caller 3 Oh hello. Oh my. Well, it's my husband. He always expects me to help him find whatever he can't find, you know, usually his car keys or a particular shirt he wants to wear. Even when I'm busy, and I spend too much time helping him, and not getting around to doing what I'm supposed to be doing.

Host OK I see. Well Richard, what do you make of that?

Richard Rule number one, Judy. Never, ever, drop what you're doing to go and help. Now, if he shouts at you from another room, just tell him you can't hear what he's saying. Let him come to you. Pretend you're really busy even if you aren't.

Caller 3 Oh, I'll try.

Host That's fantastic, Richard. Thank you. Now, moving on to caller 4, who's Wendy from Columbus, Ohio. Wendy, what's your problem?

Caller 4 Hi. Every morning when I get up, I spend a lot of time just standing in front of the closet trying to decide what to wear. It's just such a waste of time, especially since I end up wearing the same thing again and again anyway.

Host I know how you feel, Wendy. Richard, what's your advice?

Richard OK. I think I can help you, Wendy. I got this advice from a friend of mine who works in fashion. She recommends you completely reorganize your closet. Set aside ten minutes one day, make a list of your five favorite outfits, and hang them all together.

Caller 4 Uh-huh.

Richard Then stick the list inside the door of the closet. And when you can't think of what to wear, just look at the list and wear one of the outfits. My friend swears it saves her a lot of time.

Caller 4 Wow! Thank you.

Host That's great advice, Richard. I should remember that myself. Now, we're almost out of time, so we need to take our last caller and that is Sue from Minneapolis. Hello Sue.

Caller 5 Oh, hi. Am I on?

Host Yes, you are. What's your problem?

Caller 5 I have kids and I work full time, so as you can imagine I don't have much spare time, and I'm often in a hurry when I go to the supermarket. And somehow I always manage to have someone in front of me in the line who seems to have all the time in the world, you know, who's really slow and, even more annoying, gets into a conversation with the cashier. Do you have any tips?

Host Any tips for Sue, there Richard?

Richard Of course, of course, well, first of all, don't complain aloud, because that could easily annoy the other person and make them take even longer. No, the thing to do is just politely interrupt and ask the cashier a question. Now that should bring the person ahead of you back to reality, and it will remind the cashier that there are other people waiting to check out.

Caller 5 All right.

Richard All right?

Host That's great advice, Richard. I think a lot of people could use that. Well, I'm afraid time's up for now, but thank you all for your calls…

③ 10))))

One of the most puzzling paradoxes in social science is that although people spend so much of their time trying to make more money, having more money doesn't seem to make them that much happier. My colleagues Liz Dunn and Lara Aknin — both at the University of British Columbia — and I wondered if the issue was not that money *couldn't* buy happiness, but that people simply weren't spending it in the right way to make themselves happier. Liz had the great idea of exploring whether, if we encouraged people to spend money in different ways, we could uncover the domains in which money might lead to happiness. We conducted a number of studies in which we showed that money *can* buy happiness, when people spend that money "prosocially" on others (for example, giving gifts to friends, donating

to charities, etc.) rather than on themselves (say, buying flat-screen televisions).

③ 11))))

So what are the psychological factors involved when it comes to individuals and the feelings they encounter when they are giving away their money? Does it matter how wealthy you are? We found that it was the relative percentage of their money that people spend on others — rather than the absolute amount — that predicted their happiness. We did a study to look at the happiness of 16 employees of a Boston-based company before and after they received bonuses of between $3,000 and $8,000. This showed that the size of the bonus that people received had no impact on their long-term happiness. It was the percentage of that bonus they spent on others that increased their well-being. In another study, we showed that spending as little as $5 over the course of a day, on another person, led to demonstrable increases in happiness.

In other words, people don't have to be wealthy and donate hundreds of thousands of dollars to charity to experience the benefits of prosocial spending; small changes — a few dollars reallocated from oneself to another — can make a difference. Of course many of us equate having money with happiness, and a large body of research does show that people become happier as they move from being very poor to lower middle class, but after this point the impact of income on happiness is much weaker.

Think of someone who makes $100,000 one year and $110,000 the next — do we really expect this additional income suddenly to make this person fulfilled, without a care in the world? Being informed about a raise certainly makes us happy, but the $10,000 doesn't make our siblings or in-laws any less difficult to deal with over the course of the following year. Although people believe that having money leads to happiness, our research suggests that this is only the case if at least some of that money is given to others.

We had one final question. We wanted to know whether *knowing* about the effect of prosocial spending might erase it, if people engaged in prosocial spending in a calculated manner in order to "get happy." We conducted a research project in conjunction with the *New York Times* in which readers who had been told about our findings were invited to complete a brief survey in which they reported their happiness, as well as how much money they'd spent on others and on themselves so far that day. Consistent with our previous research, we found that spending more on others was associated with greater happiness among this sample of approximately 1,000 *New York Times* readers, even though the respondents had been exposed to our previous findings.

③ 12))))

Interviewer Could you tell me who founded Women's World Banking and why?

Sarita The idea behind Women's World Banking came out in a meeting that was held in Mexico in 1975. It was a United Nations first International Year of the Women and really they were gathering women from around the world to discuss women and human rights and there was a small group that started to think if we could work on only one issue, because they were discussing domestic violence, you know, economic access, education, the whole plethora of human rights. So if we could only discuss one issue, sort of focus on one issue, put all our energies behind it, what would that be, what would be that catalyst? And they decided that it would be economic independence for women. So that if a woman has the access to financial independence, then she can choose, and she can have greater access to education, opportunity, well-being, and that's where the idea came about and Women's World Banking was really set up, the first mission was to give women all over the world greater access to the economies in their own countries.

Interviewer Where did the idea of microfinance come from?

Sarita The idea behind microfinance again goes back to the mid-70s. There had been, by that time, several decades of what we call "the Western World" giving massive amounts of aid to the developing world and a realization that a lot of it was not working, there were still many people who were left poor. So, you know, Muhammad Yunus is credited as being the father of microfinance. He's an economist living in Bangladesh, a very poor country, and he looked around and he said, "What is it that the poor lack? What is it that they need?" And the answer is obvious: they need money. And all of us, in order to get started, have had access to credit. So the poor can't get access to credit, they can't go to relatives to borrow because generally the relatives are as poor as they themselves are, and they certainly cannot go into a bank and borrow because they have no collateral.

Interviewer How did Dr. Yunus solve these problems?

Sarita There are really three innovations that he came up with that are brilliant in hindsight. One was, OK the poor have no collateral, but let's figure out a way to create collateral, which means collateral is basically if you're not going to pay back the loan that somebody's held responsible. So he came up with a lending methodology where there was a group of peers that were given the loan and they would be lending to each other and the group held each member accountable for paying back. The second innovation that he came up with is that it is very difficult for the poor to gather a lump sum to pay back a loan, but if you can break up that payment into very small regular payments that are coming out of your daily income, then it's feasible to pay back the loan. So what microcredit did was to break up the loan payment into these very sort of regular small payments. And the third was really an incentive system, that the poor were not encouraged to borrow a large amount, they only borrowed what they could use in their business and then pay back, and if they paid back successfully, then they were eligible for a larger loan.

Interviewer Do you have any examples of individual success stories?

Sarita Oh, I love talking about individual success stories, because this is what sort of gets us up in the morning and, you know, gets us to come to work and stay late, and do this, this work. Since I've been at Women's World Banking I've been to the Dominican Republic, Jordan, and India, so I'm happy to give you a story from each of the three countries. The DR is a more established economy, if you will, and so the woman I met had already had successive loans that she had taken from our partner in the DR and, uh, what she did was to start out, she was basically selling food from her kitchen, making excess food and selling it to the factory workers, took out a loan, sort of increased that business

and then set up a little cantina out of her living room. So that along with food, she was selling cigarettes, beer, candy, etc. That business did well, took out another loan and built a room on top of her house and started to rent it out. And so over seven years what she's been able to do is to completely build a new home for herself and rent out the old one and this is going to ensure income in her old age, because at some point she's going to be too old to work in the kitchen and to be, you know, standing on her feet behind the cantina counter and she's looking at these rental rooms that she has been able to put on as her, her old age security.

In Jordan, I'll tell you about a young woman that we met. You know, sort of the cultural norm in Jordan is that a fairly old husband can marry again and marry a fairly young woman, so the one that we met, her husband was now too old and sick so while he took care of having a roof over her head, she had absolutely no means of earning more money for herself or her kids, and at her socio-economic level it's not considered proper for a woman to go out and work. So the only thing that she was able to do, was she had taken a loan to buy cosmetics, and was selling them from her living room to her neighbors and this was considered to be an OK business for her because primarily she was dealing with other women, but it gave her that sort of extra money to use for herself.

And then in India where I was recently in the city of Hyderabad, and Hyderabad is this up-and-coming city, you know, it's gleaming. Indians themselves are thinking of it as the next cyber city. But across town they have slums, where even now, both men and women have not gone to school, they're not educated, and their only recourse is to work in the informal economy. So the family that we met, the husband was a vegetable cart seller, so he took his cart and went out into the more affluent neighborhoods. The son had dropped out of school to join his father to push a similar cart, and the mother had taken a loan to embroider saris. And she did this at home, sort of in her spare time and what she really wanted to do was to amass enough income so that she would cut out the middle man, because she basically got half of what the sari was worth, because she was handing it over to a middle man. So that if she could buy the materials herself, embroider it herself, and sell it herself to the store, she could in effect double her income without doubling her labor.

Host Hello, good afternoon and welcome to today's edition of the *Book Program*. Did you know that on every list of bestsellers, there's always one kind of book that's guaranteed to be there, and that's a self-help book? From how to make a fortune to how to bring up your children, there's a book that can give you advice on any problem you could possibly have. Today, our four regular guests have each chosen a best selling self-help book to talk about. First, Matt Crossley. What did you choose, Matt?

Matt Well, I have quite a few friends who are into psychology, and when I talk with them I always wish I could make an intelligent comment to show that I know something about psychology too — which, in fact, I don't. So I chose *The Bluffer's Guide to Psychology*. *The Bluffer's Guides* are a series of books that are supposed to help you to talk about a subject even if you don't really know anything about it. So there are *Bluffer's Guides* to economics, to opera, to wine, all kinds of things.

Host And what did you think?

Matt Well, I have to say I was really impressed. It's a light-hearted introduction to psychology, which is both funny but at the same time extremely informative and scientifically-based. My feeling is that even people who really do know about psychology would find it a good read, and speaking personally, it actually made me want to find out some more about certain things, like the gestalt theory....

Host So you'd recommend it?

Matt Absolutely! I now understand some of the terminology of psychology and a little about the main theories, but above all I had a great time reading it. I actually laughed out loud at one point just reading one of the glossary entries.

Host So, *The Bluffer's Guide to Psychology* is recommended reading. Anita, how about you?

Anita Well, I chose a diet book called *Neris and India's Idiot-Proof Diet*. I chose it mainly because India Knight is a columnist I like, and I often read her articles in *The Sunday Times*, which are usually very witty, and also because I see myself as kind of an expert on diet books. I mean I've read them all and I've tried them all over the last ten years.

Host And your verdict?

Anita Well, I'll just start by saying that I haven't actually tried out the diet yet, so I don't know if it really works, but I thought that the book was great. As Matt said about *The Bluffer's Guide*, this book made me laugh, which is not something you can usually say about a diet book. But for me the two best points were first of all that, it's written by two women who are overweight and they followed the diet themselves. Most diet books seem to be written either by men or by stick-thin women who've never had a weight problem in their lives. So the fact that the authors had tried out the diet themselves gave it credibility for me. And then the second reason is that more than half the book is these two women talking about all the reasons that made them put on weight in the first place, and I'm sure that all these psychological reasons are at the heart of most people's weight problems.

Host So, do you think you'll give the diet a try?

Anita Well, I don't know, maybe. The diet obviously worked for them, because they're honest enough to include "photos in the book." So…

Host Thank you Anita. So it's thumbs up for the *Idiot-Proof Diet*. Kate, what was your choice?

Kate Well, as you know James and I recently got married, and when I saw the title of this book, it's called *The Rules of Marriage* — "time-tested secrets for making marriage work," I thought, "That's the book for me."

Host I see. And was it?

Kate Definitely not. To tell you the truth, I was actually horrified. The book is supposed to be a kind of manual of dos and don'ts for what to do from the engagement onwards, and if you ask me it was something that could have been written fifty years ago, or more. The message is more or less that once you've *caught* your husband, you have to keep him satisfied in every possible way. And if you don't like it, then all they suggest is that you whine and complain to your girlfriends. According to this book, making a marriage work is entirely up to the wife. The husband doesn't have to do anything at all. The wife just has to try to be exactly what her husband wants her to be, and then everything will be just fine. I can't believe that in the 21st century such awful advice is being published and presumably, since it's a best-seller, being read by thousands of women.

Host So you wouldn't recommend *The Rules of Marriage*?

Kate Absolutely not! In fact, I think it should be banned.

Host So, now onto our last guest today, Daniel. And your book is…?

Daniel My book is Paul McKenna's, *I Can Make You Rich*. And I don't need to explain why I chose this book.

Host So do you think reading Paul McKenna's book will help make you rich?

Daniel No, I don't think so. In fact, I feel a little like Kate did about her book. I couldn't take it seriously at all. The book promises to help you see the world in a different way, which will make you "think rich" and eventually "live rich," all by doing mental exercises, which are supposed to help you find out what you want and focus on it. It comes with some kind of hypnosis-style CD, and I can't actually tell you much about it because I fell asleep after the first five minutes. Still, I suppose that means it's relaxing. But after reading it, my suggestion would be, if you want to get rich, start by not wasting money on buying this book.

Host So a big thumbs down for Paul McKenna too. Matt, Anita, Kate, and Daniel, thank you very much.

③ 23))）

It didn't take long for the withdrawal symptoms to set in. What was I supposed to do when I was standing in line waiting at the airport? And why did I feel my leg vibrating even though there was nothing in my pocket?

When we got to our destination we had other problems. For example, my wife and I went shopping at a mall one day. We decided to split up so she could shop for clothes and I could go to the electronics stores (predictable, I know). My wife said, "OK when you're done just text me…uh…"

We both looked at each other. What do we do? How on earth do we find one another? "Well, I guess this is good-bye," I said. "Forever."

My wife and I racked our brains for what seemed like hours, trying to come up with a reasonable method to locate one another. "When we're done why don't we meet at the car?" my wife offered, proudly. This is what prehistoric humans used to do — meet at the car.

Another time, we were downtown, relatively far from where we were staying. It was getting close to dinner time and we needed to find a restaurant.

"Why don't we go to that place that my friend was telling us about," my wife suggested.

"Sure. Where is it?" I asked.

"I don't know. Why don't we Google…oh."

To make a long story short, we turned around and drove home.

③ 24))）

So modern technology has its advantages – no question about that.

But there were positives during the no cell phone challenge as well. Two examples:

The first was when we took our kids to the Children's Museum. As I mentioned, my kids are five years old so let's use the term "museum" lightly. No art history or ancient artifacts here. More like finger paint and buttons to press that make burping noises. At one point, my kids went into a Play-Doh activity room. They sat down at a table and started to, well, squeeze. My first thought was – time to surf the web on my iPhone!

My second thought was: sigh.

So I had no choice but to sit down at the table and play with Play-Doh. And you know what? It was awesome. We made Play-Doh spaghetti and Play-Doh people. That Play-Doh time was a

family moment that I will probably remember for a lifetime, and if I'd had a cell phone with me it never would have happened.

A few days later I was sitting with my kids in an outdoor mall waiting for my wife who was shopping (again). This was another time when I would have no doubt pulled out my cell phone. But because I had no choice, instead I began to think. I looked at my kids and I realized how lucky we were to be on vacation, sharing this time together. I thought about the fond memories I had from vacations that I went on with my parents when I was a kid and as I looked at my kids I realized that we were now creating these memories for them.

As the week came to a close we returned home back to real life – jobs, bills, and yes, cell phones. No, I am not going to tell you that my wife and I threw out our cell phones at the end of our one-week experiment. But we did institute a rule – no cell phones during dinner, and perhaps more importantly, we gained some perspective and confidence to try and tune out the distractions and live our lives "in the moment."

So what do you say – the one week no cell phone challenge – are you up to it?

③ 26))）

Speaker 1 What's the question? Do I have any obsessions? Well, I don't consider them obsessions, but I do have a habit of organizing myself in ways that other people might consider obsessive. I've walked into a friend's apartment where I was staying for a week or two, and instantly alphabetized their collection of CDs or DVDs of maybe a hundred or so because if I was going to be there, and I needed to find a piece of music, it just means…it was a lot easier to find it when it's alphabetized.

Interviewer Are all your book collections and record collections at home alphabetized?

Speaker 1 Absolutely. It just saves…I do it once and it saves a lot of time when I'm looking for things afterward. It's just practical. I don't think it's obsessive.

Interviewer Do you have any personal obsessions, for example, you know, collecting things, exercise, neatness, that kind of thing?

Speaker 2 Well, I do, I have a real obsession with cleaning, and it's awful, it's the bane of my existence, it's absolutely terrible, you know, I cannot relax unless everything is absolutely, you know, clean and organized. I've had to dial it back a little bit because my husband's very laid-back and I just haven't been allowed to be as obsessed as I have been in the past, and of course having children stops the obsession a little bit because there are toys and stuff everywhere…

Interviewer Uh-huh. Where did the obsession come from?

Speaker 2 Well, I think it's just, it's a security thing, and I feel when everything's neat and clean I feel safe and comfortable, and I think it's because when I was in my early teens my parents split up, they divorced, and that's when it started, I started cleaning. We had a smoked glass coffee table with chrome legs and I used to clean that because I couldn't stand the fingerprints on it and that's where it began, that then escalated and I started cleaning the kitchen and the bathroom…

Interviewer Oh my goodness, as a teenager?

Speaker 2 Yes and then vacuuming came into the picture, and I started vacuuming, but ironically I have a couple of friends, and their obsession with cleaning started with the same thing, their parents split up, at about the same age, in their early teens, and they have obsessions with

cleaning, too. One who I work with, not very far from here today, and another girlfriend who, I took a class, we met during the class, and she has the same problems, so I don't know whether it's, there's anything to that.

Interviewer Do you clean when you're upset or do you…?

Speaker 2 Yes.

Interviewer Or do you just clean all the time… when you're upset?

Speaker 2 Particularly when I'm upset. It occupies me and everything is fine, but I have a handle on it now, and I'm a lot better than I used to be.

Interviewer Will you come over to my place and clean?

Speaker 2 Hah-hah, that's what everybody says.

Speaker 3 Well, my mother is completely, pathologically addicted to checking her hair in the mirror all the time, she has a real hang-up about her hair, she's completely obsessed with it. She spends hours and hours checking out her hair and…

Interviewer Does it interfere with her life?

Speaker 3 I think it's really time consuming and yes, I think it does, I mean she can get really upset, and if she goes to the hairstylist and has anything done, she gets really upset for days if it's slightly wrong, or she's really self-conscious about it.

Interviewer Just about her hair?

Speaker 3 Uh-huh.

Interviewer How long has this been going on?

Speaker 3 Ever since she was a child. I found out that her brother had curly hair when he was a child, beautiful curly hair, and big brown eyes, and I think he was kind of the favorite child, I think he was the favored one…

Interviewer And she has straight hair…

Speaker 3 And she has straight hair, and I think that's where it comes from. But she's absolutely, she's really hung up about it.

Speaker 4 There's a name for this condition but I can't remember what it is and I'm not sure what it's called but I count things. If I come into a room, I will count the number of lights on the ceiling. The only thing is, I don't know how many there really are, because I count things so that they turn out to be in multiples of three or nine, and I also count panes in windows, I will count panels in doors. But I like them always to add up to 3 or 30 or 90 so it's a pretty useless thing, but it's just something I do.

Speaker 5 Oh yes, my friend is obsessed with healthy eating, absolutely obsessed, and it makes going out for dinner with her really boring because you can't…anything on the menu she just goes on and on about how this is bad, that's bad, allergy to this, allergy to that, getting the waiter over to talk and, you know about certain things that are in each dish and it's just so, it really does interfere with like her social life, or having fun with her because she's just completely obsessed with what she eats and it's just, I don't know, it's kind of boring.

③ 28))）

Why is it that so many children don't seem to learn anything at school? A TV producer-turned-writer has come up with some very revolutionary ideas. A few years ago, TV producer John Lloyd thought up a formula for a new quiz show. The show is called *QI*, which stands for "Quite Interesting," and which is also IQ backwards. It's a comedic quiz show hosted by actor Stephen Fry, where panelists have to answer unusual general knowledge questions, and it's become unexpectedly popular with 15- to 25-year-olds. Along with co-author John

Mitchinson, Lloyd has since written a number of *QI* books, for example *The Book of General Ignorance*, and these have also been incredibly successful. Lloyd's basic principle is very simple: everything you think you know is probably wrong, and everything is interesting. The *QI Book of General Ignorance*, for example, contains 240 questions, all of which reveal surprising answers. So we learn, for example, that goldfish have very long memories, that you're more likely to be killed by an asteroid than by lightning, or that Julius Caesar was not actually born by Caesarian section. The popularity of these books proves Lloyd's other thesis: that human beings, and children in particular, are naturally curious and have a desire to learn. And this, he believes, has several implications for education. According to Lloyd and Mitchinson, there are two reasons why children, in spite of being curious, tend to do badly in school. First, even the best schools can take a fascinating subject, such as electricity or classical civilization, and make it boring, by turning it into facts which have to be learned by heart and then regurgitated for tests. Second, *QI*'s popularity seems to prove that learning takes place most effectively when it's done voluntarily. The same teenagers who will happily choose to read a *QI* book will often sit at the back of a geography class and go to sleep, or worse still, disrupt the rest of the class.

3 29))

So how could we change our schools so that children enjoy learning? What would a "QI school" be like? These are Lloyd and Mitchinson's basic suggestions. The first principle is that education should be more play than work. The more learning involves things like storytelling and making things, the more interested children will become. Second, they believe that the best people to control what children learn are the children themselves. Children should be encouraged to follow their curiosity. They will end up learning to read, for example, because they want to, in order to read about something they're interested in. Third, they argue that children should be in control of when and how they learn. The *QI* school would not be mandatory, so students wouldn't have to go if they didn't want to, and there would be no tests. There would only be projects, or goals that the children set themselves with the teacher helping them. So a project could be something like making a video or building a chair. Fourth, there should never be theory without practice. You can't learn about vegetables and what kinds of plants they are from books and pictures; you need to go and plant them and watch them grow. The fifth and last point Lloyd and Mitchinson make is there's no reason why school has to stop at 17 or 18. The *QI* school would be a place where you would be able to continue learning all your life, a mini-university where the young and old could continue to find out about all the things they are naturally curious about.

4 2))

Interviewer For most people, art for the last few centuries has meant paintings and sculptures, and suddenly there are all these new kinds of sculptures and installations, that for most people don't seem like art. First of all, could you please explain exactly what these kinds of sculptures and installations are?

Expert Um...well, installations are really mixed-media works that take up a whole gallery or space, while the modern sculptures you're referring to are assemblies of objects that may take up a little less space, but that you probably wouldn't think of as traditional works of art when you first see them.

Interviewer So how would you explain to people that installations are also art?

Expert Um...well, an installation, or this new kind of modern sculpture, is really no different from a painting or a traditional sculpture if you think about where the artist starts from. That is, they have an idea about something they want to communicate, and then they decide *how* to communicate that idea, so that could be in paint, or it could be in stone, or it could be in wood or metal, or it could be through an installation, which could be a kind of assembly of different types of objects. In all three methods, in all these different media, they would still be trying to say the same thing. They would then choose the medium that was suitable for them, or which they'd been trained in, or which was suitable for that particular idea they wanted to communicate. A lot of artists have been trained in how to make an installation perhaps more than they have been trained in drawing today.

Interviewer But I think a lot of people would think that while drawing and painting require a level of expertise that the average person doesn't have, when people look at some installations, they think, "Well, I could do that." They don't see that there's any expertise involved at all.

Expert Well, it's just different skills. For example, take Damien Hirst and *Away from the Flock*, which is a sheep in some formaldehyde, in a case. First of all, he had to have the idea, and this was a very original idea, no one had ever done anything like that before. He came up with the idea of an animal, a sheep isolated from its flock, and he came up with the idea of preserving this animal in formaldehyde, which is something that scientists have certainly done before, but artists hadn't. And then he had to research how the animal could be properly preserved in this substance, the formaldehyde, and how in ten or twenty years it would still be there and in good condition for people to look at, so there is a technical side to it as well. And then of course, he had to arrange it in a particular way, put the animal in a particular pose, so that it looks as if it's alive, although of course we all know that it isn't. And so it's a combination of an original idea and some very specific skills.

Interviewer And what is he trying to communicate to us through it?

Expert Um...well, as I said, the sheep looks alive, even though we all know it isn't, and so I think it's a kind of statement about death and life, just as lots of classical works of art, paintings, are about life and death, and it's not so different from those, it's just that it's expressed in a different way. I think the important thing is what it gets the viewers to think about and to reflect on, and that's the same with all art. I mean there isn't really any difference.

Interviewer OK, so I can understand that you need a certain amount of technical ability to create the sheep in formaldehyde, but what about the bed? I mean the bed is something that you look at and you think, "Yeah, that looks like my bed in the morning."

Expert Well, Tracey Emin's bed isn't actually her bed as it is in the morning when she gets up every day; it is a bed, and there are sheets and pillows, and lots of other objects, but she has assembled these objects to represent herself, this is an autobiographical piece just like a self-portrait, without her face or her body in it, but it still represents her. It's the story of her life, it's her relationship with all the men in her life and other people. You look on the floor and there are lots of pieces of her, there are

her slippers, her toy dog, and newspapers that she's read, and bottles of water. So it's a story of her life, and it's arranged in a very particular way, it's not random, not just like your bed or my bed, it's a bed that she's very specifically organized to communicate something about herself. I mean it's a different set of skills, from painting a self-portrait, but maybe it actually communicates a whole lot more to us, to viewers, than some self-portraits do, because we can actually look at it and understand, as contemporary viewers, a lot about her life. And incidentally, Tracey Emin is, in fact, extremely skilled at drawing, so if she'd wanted to draw a self-portrait, for example, she could have done that. But she chose this way of communicating her message.

4 14))

Interviewer What is it about New York that inspires you?

Patricia I was born here and raised nearby and so I have memories of New York City from my early childhood and to me it was always a magical place. Anything is possible here and everything seems to happen here. And as my aunt once said to me, she said, "People who live in New York even if they've only been here for one year, they feel like they own the place," and I think that it's because New York is almost more of an event than a place, where everything's changing and becoming something new all the time, and I think that's why it draws creative people and it's very inspiring.

Interviewer Do you always paint in situ or do you sometimes use photos?

Patricia I always paint in situ, almost always. I use sketches and I work a little from memory and from sketches. I touch things up a little in the studio sometimes or finish things. But I like to be in the location because it's always changing, and I take pieces of the scene, things that happen at different times, a bird flying by might be very beautiful or a person walking in the street and assuming a certain gesture or pose that's perfect for the composition. Things like that happen over the course of a painting and they can be just perfect. But a photo is very static and kind of flat and it doesn't interest me to work from that.

Interviewer Does that mean you have to work very fast?

Patricia Actually I do, I have learned to work very fast because there are so many things that change on the street including being blocked by trucks and I do often work very fast, the seasons are constantly changing. People think of the four seasons but really nature changes almost every day, or every day so if I started painting at one point, it's hard to finish it later in a different season or later on in the same season.

Interviewer What techniques do you use?

Patricia I use the traditional technique. I use oil paint and brushes and canvas.

Interviewer How long does it normally take you to finish a painting from start to finish?

Patricia Oh, there, every painting is different, they can take a few hours or a few years. I've worked on some paintings for years and years and sometimes I'll come back to a painting the following year when the season and the different light is right for that painting.

Interviewer As well as the city pictures you also paint outside New York in the countryside. What similarities and differences are there in painting the city and painting the countryside?

Patricia The city is very geometric, and I love, I happen to love geometry, I love angles, criss-crossing on the composition and different shapes, geometric shapes but the countryside, when I first started painting it was very difficult for me for that reason, because you don't have the perspective of the streets and the angles of the roofs and so on to lead your eye through the painting. It's, it was wonderful experience to learn how to make your eye move across a grassy field as opposed to down a street where it's so clear and easy kind of, to figure out.

Interviewer So what are the advantages and disadvantages of painting in the country and the city?

Patricia The countryside is a wonderful place for me to paint. I love it because I'm usually alone, pretty much alone there and I'm not distracted by passers-by. In New York City there are just so many distractions with people coming up to me and they're usually well-meaning but it's just an interruption, it's a distraction from my work. And the countryside is so beautiful that I love painting there.

Interviewer Do you ever paint portraits?

Patricia I do occasionally. I love painting portraits, but it's very rare to find someone who will sit for a few hours, for a couple of sessions, and I don't like to do portraits from photos. I've tried it and I don't like the results.

(4)15)))

Interviewer What kinds of things have influenced you as an artist?

Patricia I think one of the greatest influences on me was growing up on the banks of the Hudson, which is such a beautiful place in the different light and different times of year. I think that was a main influence on me to want to be a landscape painter. Also there were lots of paintings in the house where I grew up, and my parents loved painting very much and also my mother painted some, so I, especially after we all grew up, she painted, so, there were a lot of influences on me.

Interviewer What's your favorite time of day for painting?

Patricia Actually my favorite time of day is sunrise, but I don't always get up in time for that, so early morning and also late afternoon.

Interviewer Do you have a favorite time of year or season?

Patricia Yes, I do actually. I love to paint just before the spring when the air is so crisp and clear, and there aren't yet any leaves on the trees, so that I can really see down the streets, so there's something magical in New York about that time of year, around March and then then of course, when spring comes and the blossoms and the trees start to come out, it's just magical, but it lasts a very short time.

Interviewer Are there any other cities that you'd like to go and paint in?

Patricia Oh, there are thousands of cities I'd love to go to paint in, the ancient cities, the older cities, Paris, Amsterdam, Florence, Venice, many places in Sicily, in Greece, I'd love to go to Turkey and paint on the Mediterranean and any place where there's antiquity and where there's water or mountains. But it is hard to travel and paint, it's much better to go to one place and settle in and paint for a while in one place to get to really know the landscape. That's what I prefer to do.

Interviewer What do you think are the pros and cons of an artist's life?

Patricia I think to be an artist usually it requires a lot of sacrifice, and I know that sounds like a cliché, but it's true because it requires an enormous amount of time, it requires being free

to suddenly change your plans at a moment's notice. For example, being a landscape painter is completely insane, I could be going out the door with one painting under my arm to work on it and the weather could change and I'd be working on a different painting, or I could have plans with someone and suddenly change them, or drop the plans because the weather's right for a particular painting. That's a real big sacrifice in terms of your social life and also, of course, finances, if, as I do, I tend to put painting before anything else. Well, it's hard to earn money and be a dedicated artist at the same time, I think. They contradict one another to some degree.

(4)19)))

Interviewer We have in the studio Dr. Linda Blakey, who is helping us separate the medical facts from all the myths and old wives' tales that are out there. So, my first question, Linda, is there any truth in the belief that if you eat a large meal in the evening, you're more likely to gain weight than if you eat the same amount of food earlier in the day?

Doctor Well, there's a clear answer to that: if you're watching your weight, what matters is *what* you eat, not *when* you eat it. A calorie at midday is no different from a calorie at midnight, and the idea that your metabolism slows down in the evening is actually a myth. As a matter of fact, there is a medical condition called "night-eating syndrome," which affects two percent of the population, and people who suffer from it eat very little during the day, but often wake up and eat during the night. These people on average are no more overweight than people who do not suffer from this syndrome.

Interviewer So I can go out for a big meal in the evening and not feel guilty about it?

Doctor Absolutely — as long as you don't have a big lunch, too.

Interviewer Well, that's good. The next question I'd like to ask you about is catching colds. It's always seemed obvious to me that if you stay out in the cold and wind, you're more likely to catch a cold. But I also remember reading somewhere that this was a myth. What's the truth about that one?

Doctor Well, colds, we know, are caused by viruses, which you catch from an infected person, for example, when they cough or sneeze. Now for many years doctors believed that the only reason why it was more common to catch a cold in the winter was because people stayed indoors more, and so they infected one another. But recent research has found that being exposed to cold temperatures does in fact lower our body's defenses, so that means that if you get cold, you're more likely to become infected by a cold virus, or to develop a cold if you've already been infected. It's not a myth, it's true.

Interviewer OK. That all makes sense to me. Now something my parents used to tell me was that it's dangerous to take a bath or a shower during a thunderstorm, because I might get electrocuted. I've always thought it was crazy. Is it an old wives' tale?

Doctor In fact, that's actually true. Between ten and twenty people a year get an electric shock while taking a bath or shower during a thunderstorm, and some of them die as a result.

Interviewer Wow.

Doctor It's due to the fact that metal pipes are excellent conductors of electricity, as is tap water. So even though statistically it's not very likely to happen to you, especially if you live in a grounded building, you should probably avoid showering during a storm.

Interviewer OK, I'll remember that! Now the next one is something I'm always saying to my children: "Turn the light on. You can't possibly read in that dim light!" And they always tell me they can read perfectly well. But reading in dim light must be bad for their eyes, right?

Doctor Well, that's one that parents around the world have been telling their children for generations, but it actually has no real scientific basis. Reading in the dark or in dim light can cause a temporary strain on the eyes, but it quickly goes away once you return to bright light.

Interviewer Well, now I know. Now the next one affects me directly. Every summer in the mosquito season, I get really badly bitten, even when I put insect repellent on, but my wife never gets bitten at all. She says that mosquitoes don't like her. Is that possible?

Doctor It's irritating, isn't it?

Interviewer Yes.

Doctor As a matter of fact, it seems to be true. Female mosquitoes, which are the ones that bite, are attracted to the carbon dioxide we exhale, our body heat, and certain chemicals in our sweat. But some lucky people produce chemicals that either prevent mosquitoes from detecting them or that actually drive them away. Unfortunately, I'm not one of those lucky people either, but your wife obviously is.

Interviewer The last thing I would like you to clarify for us is the idea that bottled water is purer than tap water. Now I know it's one thing to drink bottled water if you're traveling in a country where the water hasn't been treated or isn't safe to drink. But what about here in United States?

Doctor We're all a bit suspicious of what comes out of our taps, and that's why sales of bottled water have risen so much over the last decade. But what many people don't realize is that bottled water isn't subjected to the same regular testing that tap water is, and in some tests a third of the samples of bottled water analyzed were contaminated. In any case a quarter of all bottled water sold is just filtered tap water.

(4)25)))

Interviewer Have you ever used alternative medicine?

Speaker A Yes.

Interviewer What did you use?

Speaker A Acupuncture.

Interviewer And did it work?

Speaker A Well, it actually did. I had a terrible time of, I lost my sense of taste and smell…

Interviewer Wow!

Speaker A …which started off with a cold and then I completely lost my sense of taste and smell for about three or four months, and it was very debilitating, and it was really pretty frightening.

Interviewer I can imagine.

Speaker A You suddenly realize that there is no point in eating at all because you can't enjoy any of it, and all the beauty of life kind of goes, it's an incredible thing of not having one of your senses. And somebody recommended acupuncture to me, and I went along and I said, "Do you think you can do anything about it?" and she said, "Yes, I think I can." She said, "So, here's a rose," which was in her room.

Interviewer Right…

Speaker A ..and she said, "Put your nose into it and tell me what you can smell." I put my nose into it and I couldn't smell anything at all, absolutely nothing at all. And she laid me down and half an hour of needles later, I got up and she said, "Try smelling that rose again," and I put my nose into it and there was this faint, faint smell of rose, which was the most beautiful thing I've ever smelled in my entire life.

Interviewer So that was it? You were cured?

Speaker A No, well, over the course of the next two weeks, very, very slowly it came back. I was walking down Cambria Avenue and a woman walked past and I went "Ooh perfume," and I literally turned and followed her, if she'd seen me she would have thought I was really weird because I practically had my nose in her hair, but anyway, it all came back.

Interviewer Wow!

Speaker B Ever since my children were born, well, even before my children were born, which is a really long time ago now, we've used alternative medicine, or as I like to call it, complementary medicine. We use homeopathy. And none of my children ever had an antibiotic while they were growing up, and I think that's something to be proud of. They *have* taken them since they've been adults, for various reasons, often because they have to work, but apart from that no antibiotics, and I don't think I've had any in the last thirty years or so.

Interviewer Kate, have you ever used alternative medicine?

Speaker C Well, the time I remember was during the birth of my second child. My first was a pretty dramatic experience, so I thought I'd go and find out if I could make it easier. I went to a homeopath who gave me a lot of pills, and said that when contractions started I should take one and then, you know, an hour later take another one, and an hour later take two, and within half an hour, I'd taken all three bottles and was still in agony.

Interviewer No.

Speaker C Yeah.

Interviewer They had no effect at all?

Speaker C No.

Interviewer So did you call the person? "These aren't working!"

Speaker C No, I never did, but I wouldn't recommend homeopathy for childbirth.

Interviewer I can understand why not.

Interviewer So Adam, what's your take on alternative medicine, do you have any experience?

Speaker D One, just one, and I was taking a very long flight from Miami to Vancouver and I don't like flying, though I don't take anything for it, but when I got there I was only there for just a few days and I wanted to enjoy my waking hours, and the jet lag was crazy so I bought some herbal sleeping pills.

Interviewer Oh, I see.

Speaker D So I didn't want to use really heavy, real sleeping pills, I've never used those, so I went to buy some herbal sleeping pills and put them in my bag and then I got there and I looked at the package and it said, "Take eight half an hour before bedtime," so I thought that was a lot, but that's what it said, so I took eight, but it was kind of like having a lot of grass in my mouth, it was like swallowing a lot of grass before bed and it didn't agree with me, so I was like burping up, like a lot of grass and I was burping so I wasn't sleeping, so I wasn't really convinced about them.

Interviewer So a great night's sleep.

Speaker D It was wonderful. A lot of grass.

🔵 **5 4** 🔊

I was in Warsaw in Poland for a week because I had rehearsals and a concert there, but on the Wednesday, Thursday, and Friday of that week I also had rehearsals in Berlin. I needed to be able to have the rehearsal in Warsaw in the morning, then fly to Berlin for the rehearsal there in the late afternoon, and then straight back to Warsaw late at night in time for the next morning rehearsal. The only way to get to Berlin and back in time was to fly. So I hired an air taxi. As soon as I left the rehearsal, there was a car waiting to take me to the airport, and when I arrived at the airport my heart sank because the weather was not so good, and the operations manager said, "Look, I'm terribly sorry. We can't fly at the moment because of the weather." Finally, the weather cleared and they said we could fly, so I was still hoping to make it in time for my rehearsal. However, we got into the plane and I didn't have a very good impression of it: it looked a bit old, and there was a little hole where the air was coming through where the door had been shut on my side.

🔵 **5 5** 🔊

I thought, "Well, never mind," and I put on my seat belt and finally we took off.

The weather was not good, and after about five or ten minutes I was terribly cold and I thought, well, I know it can be cold — and it was also very noisy-normally they give you headphones but for some reason they didn't, so the noise was very loud and it got very very cold, and then to my horror I realized that the co-pilot's door wasn't shut properly! By this point the co-pilot himself had realized that the door wasn't shut, so he turned to me and said, "Problema!" and then he started gesticulating to the pilot, who was already having difficulties because the weather was very bad and it was raining very hard and there was a bit of a storm. I was feeling extremely uncomfortable by now, wishing that I was on the ground, but then came the real drama because the pilot was trying to indicate to the co-pilot how to shut the door properly. Now what do you do if you're driving a car and you realize that you haven't shut the door properly? You usually stop, open the door again and then shut it with a bang or sometimes you don't even stop, you just while you're driving slowly, you do that. Anyway, this idiotic co-pilot, he proceeded to do precisely that. He then opened the door completely, in order to shut it properly, and I was just behind them, as this is a small plane so right in front of me was just open air, this open door — I was absolutely terrified, cold air rushing in, and then he tried to shut it properly, but presumably because of the pressure or the cold I don't know what he couldn't do so, and had he not had his seat belt on he would have fallen out of the plane, so he was holding on, partly for dear life, partly to try and shut it, unsuccessfully. The pilot was shouting at him but he couldn't correct the situation because, you know, he had to keep the plane in the air which was now extremely precarious and the plane was going up and down.

🔵 **5 6** 🔊

Then suddenly I felt that we were going right down and I prayed that we were going to land. To my relief we landed in one piece, so at least my life was no longer in danger, but as far as the rehearsal was concerned, I realized with horror that because of this emergency in the air the pilot had had to land at the nearest town, which was still quite a long way from Berlin. I had to phone the rehearsal people to say I was going to be late and I was feeling thoroughly miserable. However, we eventually took off and arrived in Berlin, and I did my rehearsal, and fortunately it had been the type of rehearsal where my lateness had not caused a real problem. Then on the way back, the pilots were waiting for me at the airport — this was now about ten o'clock at night or 9:30. So this time we took off, and I said, "Are you quite sure the door is properly shut? Quite sure?" and they said, "Yes, yes," and I said "We're very late now. I want you to get back to Warsaw as fast as possible," and they said "Yes, the wind is in our favor, this aircraft can go very fast. We should be back soon in Warsaw, don't worry, everything will go fine," so we took off, and things were, well, nothing was going particularly wrong, but I noticed that they were going rather slowly, but it was still so noisy that I couldn't communicate with them and ask, "Why are you going so slowly?" Eventually when we landed I said, "Why were you going so slowly? I told you to go as fast as possible," and the pilot said, "I'm terribly sorry, I didn't know this plane very well and we were having a fuel problem, so we were running out of fuel." So on the way there I'd nearly fallen to the ground through an open door, and now we'd been in danger of falling to the ground because of lack of fuel.

🔵 **5 10** 🔊

Interviewer Woodpeckers play an important role in controlling insect pests, yet they can be pests themselves when they cause structural damage to buildings and create disturbing noises. Woodpeckers are a protected species and by law cannot be harmed, despite the trouble they can cause homeowners. Louisa Hobson was such a homeowner. So, Louisa, tell us what happened.

Louisa Well I was out of town in the spring, traveling on business, and I don't know if this started while I was away, but as soon as I got home, the first morning, I was awoken very early by this pecking sound, and I could tell it was a woodpecker. It was so loud that I knew it couldn't have been pecking on normal wood. So I got up and looked for the source but couldn't find it at first. After a few days I discovered this woodpecker was pecking at my neighbor's drainage pipe.

Interviewer And this was a metal pipe, outdoors?

Louisa Right. And he would do this starting at 5:00 in the morning, and continue for hours, and even though I'm not usually home in the morning, we could hear him on weekends, throughout the morning. He was just focused on this one metal pipe.

Interviewer So what did you do, at first?

Louisa Well, I spoke to the neighbor, who didn't really know what to do, so then I decided to go on Facebook and send out a plea asking if anyone knew how to kill a woodpecker.

Interviewer Ah, and the response?

Louisa Oh, a lot of people were horrified that I would even think about hurting such a beautiful creature as a woodpecker.

Interviewer Sure.

Louisa I got some very angry messages. Then I realized it might sound bad to someone who's not living through it…but when you're being woken up at 5:00 every morning, you start to go a little bit crazy. You feel like it's an awful pest that you've just got to get rid of.

Interviewer And did you know, at the time, that woodpeckers are a protected species?

Louisa I didn't know that, so it's a good thing I didn't actually try to kill it.

Interviewer Did you receive any helpful suggestions?

Louisa Yes, actually, a friend suggested getting a fake owl…I'd always thought they were just bad decorations, but I discussed it with my neighbor, and he was willing to try it. So we got this plastic owl, and my neighbor affixed it to the outside wall, but it didn't help. But then he moved the owl closer to where the bird was. And after that we never saw the woodpecker again.

Interviewer So the owl really did work, and there was a happy ending.

Louisa Yes, thank goodness. But I tell you, I'm not a violent person, but I was ready to kill that woodpecker…it was driving me nuts!

5 11))

Announcer Did you know that tens of thousands of Burmese pythons live in Florida's Everglades? The story of how they got there is remarkable. In August 1992, Hurricane Andrew, a category 5 hurricane, hit Southern Florida hard. The immediate damages were obvious: it caused devastation in the area and claimed 40 lives. But no one imagined the storm's most frightening consequence, which would not become apparent for years.

When Hurricane Andrew hit, an exotic pet dealer's animal warehouse was destroyed… giant python snakes, native to Southeast Asia, were being kept in the warehouse, and many of the 900 Burmese Python snakes living there found their way into the Florida Everglades. Right now, thousands of these Burmese Pythons are on the loose in the wetlands of Florida… their population is growing, and officials fear they could eventually spread into other states.

Wildlife experts are worried. The snakes' size and power pose a huge threat to native animals and endangered species. Small animals, like rabbits, have disappeared from the Everglades, thanks to the Pythons, who just swallow up the smaller animals. The numbers of other mammals, such as opossums and raccoons, have dropped by more than 98 percent. An expert animal handler says:

Expert These pythons are massive. Recently, a college student captured an 18-foot, 8-inch Burmese python. He was lucky that it didn't kill him. The problem is that despite their size, they are not easy to catch. They hide in the waters and they are quick. If a python finds you before you find it, it tracks you with its tongue, and when it attacks, it will bite deep and hard.

Announcer Pythons have even been known to swallow deer and even alligators. And while attacks on humans are extremely rare, Burmese Pythons can pose a danger to people.

The actual number of Burmese Pythons in the Everglades is unclear. Estimates range from 10,000 up to 150,000. In order to control the increasing population, Florida wildlife officials have issued permits to reptile experts to hunt and kill the pythons. They hope this will prevent them from migrating to other areas. If you're not a reptile expert, the best thing to do is to stay away from one!

5 17))

Speaker 1 There was this girl who I had liked for a few months. She had no idea, of course. I was having lunch with her and another friend when the friend kept talking about what a great cook I was. I think he was trying to help me out. So I invited the two of them to come over for dinner and I decided that this was my big chance. I planned to cook my best dish, seafood pasta. I can usually make that in an hour, but that day, I was so nervous, and she kept insisting that she watch me cook that my hands kept shaking. I could feel my face turning red and I couldn't focus on the cooking. They were getting hungry and I just kept chopping onions, cleaning the squid, and peeling the shrimp because I couldn't look up and face her. And I also wanted things to be perfect. I imagined them enjoying the food and relishing each bite. It took me three hours to cook and by the time it was all done, they ate it in fifteen minutes. They didn't seem to notice how much effort I had put into it!

Interviewer Have you had any awful, memorable disasters in the kitchen?

Speaker 2 One particular one when I was cooking for my mother-in-law for the first time. She was visiting from Italy and so I wanted to make a classic Italian dish. I chose risotto. I was holding the salt shaker over the pot when the lid came off and it dumped into the risotto. I took out as much of it as possible, but the water was already boiling and the salt quickly dissolved. I put more water in, kept taking water out, but it was too late. My mother-in-law arrived and she tasted it and almost choked. She suggested I throw in some peeled uncooked potatoes to absorb the salt, which I did. Then I just kept adding in water. In the end we had mushy porridge and had to pick out the potatoes. She was really nice about it, but I'm sure she's never had risotto cooked that way in her life.

Interviewer Oh, that's a shame. Andrew, have you had a bad cooking experience?

Speaker 3 Um, well, it didn't really involve cooking as such, but it was certainly a bad food-preparing experience. I was cooking for my parent's 20th anniversary and I was only in high school. My mom is always telling me how honey is good for me and she puts honey on everything. My dad, on the other hand, loves meat. He loves a good steak. So, I decided to put their two favorite things together. I went to the farmer's market and bought really nice rib eye steaks and fresh honey. I came home and I marinated the steaks in the honey for a few hours and put them in the oven. You would think it would be delicious right? Well, it was the first time I realized that two things that can taste so good separately can taste so bad together! The steaks were too sweet, tough, and overcooked!

Interviewer So did your parents eat their dinner?

Speaker 3 Um, yes, but they put a lot of salt and pepper on it and ate it.

5 19))

Interviewer Who taught you how to cook?

Chantelle It would probably be my parents when I was younger. It was more, it was always something that I was interested in from an early age and I used to be in the kitchen quite a lot.

Interviewer How did you end up as a chef in London?

Chantelle One kind of afternoon when I was reading the, a foodie magazine in New Zealand, and it mentioned the Gordon Ramsay scholarship, and we had to submit a menu kind of a three-course menu and talk about the food, talk about what you'd done, so I thought, "Well, why not give that a go?" So I submitted an entry and then got a phone call kind of six weeks later saying I'd got into the semi final, which was basically 12 people, 11 of them all chefs, so I kind of felt a bit like a fish out of water, but you know, whilst I was there I met Josh Emmet, who was the head chef at the Savoy Grill, which was run by Marcus, and at the end of it he said "Well, you know, there's a job at the Savoy Grill if you want one," and it was just too good an opportunity to turn down, um, so it all kind of happened relatively quickly because I thought well, I can't turn this opportunity down. I was kind of at a point in my career where I was looking for another job anyway. So I just thought, "Well, I'll do it."

Interviewer Top chefs have a reputation of being difficult. What's Marcus Wareing like to work for?

Chantelle He is very, he's quite, I mean I wouldn't want to work for any other chef of that high calibre really. He's a very, he's a person that's very, he's got a real eye for detail, and a perfectionist. But he's also got a very good business sense, which is a great thing to learn from as well, because he oversees the whole operation. So in that sense he's a great kind of mentor, I guess. I mean if he gets upset with people, it's because of what's going on on the plate or in the restaurant. There's no kind of, there's no ego there at all, it's all about what goes out on the plate and what happens, and how the guests are treated, he's very much a person that people, when people come to the restaurant he wants them to have an amazing experience, no matter if they're kind of buying a £30 bottle of wine or £3,000 bottle of wine.

Interviewer Is this restaurant into the new trends in cooking, using science in the kitchen and things like that?

Chantelle We are more, not traditional but we use traditional techniques, classic techniques. We, I guess in a sense, we're more about, Marcus, Marcus is a person that's very respectful of ingredients and basically treats, you know, will treat a carrot the same way as a piece of foie gras in the sense they're both great things that need to be looked after and treated in the right way to get the maximum kind of flavor out of them, and I guess we're more about making a carrot taste like a carrot as opposed to making a carrot taste like a beetroot, which, in a sense, I think some people get a little carried away with.

5 20))

Interviewer You are the sous-chef here. Can you tell us, what exactly is the difference between a chef and a sous-chef?

Chantelle Basically a sous-chef is, it basically translates to a second chef, so you have the head chef and then you have the sous-chefs under the head chef, so they run the kitchen in the head chef's absence.

Interviewer How many hours do you work?

Chantelle We, they are long days for most people. I mean, we start at about 7:00 in the morning, and we normally finish, kind of, between 12:00 and 1:00 in the morning, so it's a long day, but in a sense it's something that you get used to the more you do it.

Interviewer Does it get very stressful in the kitchen?

Chantelle It can. The biggest thing is organization. It can be, it makes a big difference, kind of the way diners come in as well, if they all come in at once then it does get a bit, because you, you're always conscious of the fact that you don't want to keep people waiting too long but you don't want to, in the other sense, just push out the food, because they're here for the experience. So it can get stressful in some situations and when, if you cook something and something, and it's not right and you can't serve it, the time it takes to kind of begin the whole process again, a) for those, the guests that have ordered that particular dish, they have to wait a long time, but also it creates a backlog in a sense, so it can get stressful, but again it's something that's managed, and if you're organized and kind of a bit forward-thinking and always one step ahead, then it becomes, it minimizes the stress completely.

Interviewer And presumably the long hours don't help?

Chantelle Again the hours don't, don't help the stress because obviously the more tired people are, then the more stressed they can get. But in a sense the people that work here are quite, very focused, very, very passionate about what they do, you kind of have to be to be able to put in the time that we all put in. So the stress is, I think it's something that can be managed.

Interviewer Do you cook at home, if so, what kind of food?

Chantelle Ah, not much, I don't cook at home much, a) because I'm not really there a huge amount and b) when you have what we have here to go to a kind of small, small kitchen it's a bit, I find it a bit difficult, in a sense because you're used to having such great equipment and kind of ovens, and everything around you, and then you go back to a little flat and kind of trying to do it, it's just not quite the same. But then when I have time off, if I'm on holiday or something like that, I of course enjoy kind of going to a market or even a supermarket and getting kind of local ingredients and doing it that way.

Interviewer What would you have as your last meal on earth?

Chantelle Wow, it's a big question, probably would start with, something like foie gras, because it is such a kind of delicacy and then a seafood, probably scallops, main course would probably be some beef, a rib of beef with some beautiful vegetables, seasonal vegetables, then I'd definitely have to have cheese, I because I'm a big fan of cheeses, especially the European cheeses, they're just, that's one thing that I really love about the, kind of, the UK and Europe and then probably to finish, probably a pear Tarte Tatin.

(5 24))

Interviewer Why did you decide to come to Spain?

Renata Well, it's a bit complicated. It was a bit of a fluke really. In fact, it was my husband who first came up with the idea of moving here. He's from Peru, and when I met him he was studying catering in Poland, in Poznan where I live, and he could sort of speak a little Polish, but not very well. So it would have been very difficult for him to get a job in Poland. Not to mention the paperwork, which would have been very complicated, too. At that time, when we got married I mean, I had just finished university, where I studied Spanish, and I got a job teaching Spanish in a school. So we thought about what we were going to do because if we stayed in Poland, I would have had to be the one that worked. So as I spoke Spanish, and of course he did too, we decided to try living in Spain.

Interviewer When was this?

Renata About four years ago. We came with nothing, with just a bit of money and two suitcases — and that was it. But bit by bit, we managed to find jobs and somewhere to live. We were very lucky, the guy who rented us our first flat was a chef, and he gave my husband a job, and I managed to get a job teaching Spanish to Polish immigrants here.

Interviewer What's the plus side for you about living in Spain?

Renata What I like best is that if you're prepared to work hard, you can get what you want, you can get a good standard of living quite easily. Then the weather is nice, it's not as cold as in Poland — though actually I really miss the snow. Here in Valencia it never snows. Another good thing here is that you have the sea and mountains quite close by, which we didn't have in Poznan.

Interviewer What about the downside?

Renata The traffic. I absolutely hate driving here, nobody obeys the traffic rules, they drive really crazily. And what else? The food is different, but it's OK. My husband would say the noise, the people here are so noisy. In Peru, people aren't nearly as noisy — they live in their houses — if you want to see someone, you go to their house —

they're not in the street all the time like they are here. I agree with him. And I think people gossip a lot here too. They're always talking about what everyone else is doing, and I don't like that.

Interviewer There must be things you miss about Poland.

Renata Of course — loads of things! The food! My family and my friends. The little corners of my town that I love, my favorite cafes and cinemas. That's what I miss most.

Interviewer Might you go back to Poland one day?

Renata I personally would love to go back, but I'm not sure if we ever will. It would be very difficult, especially for my husband. But you never know — or maybe we'll end up in Peru!

(5 25))

Jung-hwa I've been living in New York City for just over five years now. The reason I first came here is because I always wanted to improve my English and live abroad. I came alone, and I didn't have any family or friends in the US. I had no idea how things were going to unfold. It was all terrifying and exciting at the same time. South Korea is a relatively homogenous country, so I was completely fascinated and shocked by the diversity in New York City. I was surrounded by people of different races who spoke languages that I had never heard before. Even if people were speaking English, I didn't notice because of all the different accents. It was all so different from what I had been used to back in Korea.

You see, what I like best about living here is that in some way I'm still "living the dream." I was only planning to stay a year, but five years later, I have a master's degree from NYU and I'm working as a teacher's assistant. I get to meet people from all over the world, and people have such different backgrounds that I find myself learning all the time. In South Korea, people are more conservative and cautious about expressing their views. One thing that has definitely changed a lot is my attitude toward communication. In the past, I always went for the politically-correct answer, and I had to spend some time looking for the "right" words to phrase my opinions. But I've gotten used to the idea of the "right to express oneself," and now I feel more comfortable with expressing my thoughts in a more straightforward and honest way.

The thing I love about living in New York City is the people, but it's also the same reason I get frustrated and fed up. I find that people, especially New Yorkers, have little patience. And as much as expressing oneself is a great thing, I find that some people take the "right to express oneself" a little too far. I think the New York City subway system during rush hour is a really good example and the best place to see people at their best and worst. I've seen people express their frustration and anger with other commuters by cursing and yelling. Sometimes, things will get really heated and fights will break out. That really surprises me because in Korea, no matter how crowded or packed it gets, people don't usually yell at one another.

All in all, I love living here and I've made some really good friends, but I still get homesick from time to time. I can easily communicate with my family or friends back in Korea using the Internet, but it doesn't completely get rid of my longing for home. And as much as I love the people, sometimes I feel like the pace in New York City can be overwhelming. I do often think about going home and returning one day.

(5 30))

Interviewer There's a deeply held belief that sports teach us valuable lessons about life and ultimately makes us better people. In your opinion, is that true?

Kantowski Call me old-fashioned, but I actually *do* believe that, having played sports myself when I was younger. There are some things that sports can teach you. Just in general terms, it teaches you to respect authority — for example, when there's a referee in the game, there's an authority figure. And it teaches you how to get along with others and cooperate. When I was a kid, we would play ball sometimes without supervision, and we'd have to get along by choosing up sides for the teams. When there was an issue with the rules, we'd have to get together and come up with a compromise. So, yes, I think there are a lot of lessons to be learned, especially when you're young, that help you later on in life.

Now, when it comes to individual sports, the effect is even more evident than in team sports. It takes an incredible amount of discipline, for example with tennis and golf and track, which aren't team sports. It's a matter of getting up early, training on your own, and all the repetition that you need to do, sometimes without supervision. A lot of people who aspire to be professional athletes can't afford a trainer or a coach, especially when they're young. So the discipline involved in individual sports is a valuable lesson in life as well.

Interviewer On the whole, would you say that sports bring about more happiness or unhappiness in the world?

Kantowski Well, as long as there's some perspective there, and you look at sports as a sort of temporary escape from real life, as entertainment — like going to a movie — if you have that kind of perspective, then I think sports can enhance your life. And life is *better* with diversions. With sports, a lot of people look forward to following their teams: it gives them a sense of family, a sense of community, and some wonderful memories. And as entertainment, sports have tremendous value.

But again, there has to be some perspective. When you go past the level of sports as entertainment, as diversion, as a pastime, when it gets into the obsession area, then it's probably *not* a good thing. People who get too carried away by whether their team wins or loses are not in a healthy situation. As long as you can look at sports as a diversion, it's fine. Part of the secret of life, and this certainly applies to sports, is to do it in moderation, and being a sports fan is no different. But overall, I would say sports create a great deal of happiness.

Interviewer Do you think there's a sense that sports have replaced religion in modern society?

Kantowski That's a great question. Probably for a lot of people, it has. I'm thinking of some of these major sporting events that draw worldwide interest, like the World Cup, for instance. You see the passion of the fans, and I think that passion is wonderful, as long as it doesn't carry over into fanatical levels. Again, we get back to that obsession thing, and once you've crossed that line where sports are no longer just entertainment, diversion, and pastime — when it crosses the line, then yes, it can border on religion for a lot of people.

Interviewer Do you think there's any difference between using technology to gain an advantage (for example high tech swimsuits) and doping, I mean taking performance-enhancing drugs?

Kantowski That's a profound question. I think if you're really honest about it, it's hard to see the difference. I mean, if you think about a sport like tennis or maybe golf, and you consider the advances in technology in the equipment, and if you go back to the 1930s and 1940s and think about the small wood tennis racquets and the wooden golf clubs…if those players had had today's equipment in their hands, it would have made a huge difference in their game, a *bigger* impact on their game than performance-enhancing drugs! The advances in technology have really done more to increase performance than drugs have. We're all quick to criticize, and there's a stigma attached to using drugs that doesn't exist with the equipment, but in a lot of ways they're similar. I think equipment, technology, diet, and education — all those things have done more to enhance athletic prowess and performance than drugs.

Interviewer We expect athletes to be positive role models. Is there any reason why we should?

Kantowski Years ago, people looked up to athletes, and they were our heroes. But there's no reason why they should be role models — they're in the public eye more than others, but they're human, like everyone else. All the money and adulation is difficult for these athletes to handle, paradoxically. Money and fame tend to bring down a lot of celebrities, like actors and rock stars, not just athletes. There's a lot of temptation and money involved that you don't see in other professions.

Also, there's more pressure nowadays, with the way the media has changed, and with social media. Everyone is looking for a sensational story, and athletes are more prone to being caught in scandals than ever before.

If it were up to me, parents and teachers, people like that, would be the real role models.

Interviewer Right. Do sports occupy a disproportionately high place in the media and have we lost all sense of proportion when it comes to sports?

Kantowski There *is* a disproportionate amount of interest in sports. There's an insane amount of hype around some of these big events, like the Super Bowl and the World Cup. The media knows that there's a captive audience, and more is better! You know, the first Super Bowl didn't even sell out, yet in today's world it's considered the most important event you can imagine, so it just shows how perspectives have shifted.

But the media *reflects* interest more than they create it — they're giving the public what they want. I'm not sure the media is totally to blame, either; it's just a form of economics.

1A discourse markers (1): connectors

result

> 1 It was freezing cold, **so** I wore a thick coat.
> 2 It snowed hard all night. **As a result**, the airport was closed the following morning.
>   We regret that you do not have the necessary qualifications, and **therefore | consequently** we are unable to offer you the job.

1 *So* is the most common way of introducing a clause of result.
2 *As a result*, *therefore*, and *consequently* (more formal than *so*) are often used at the beginning of a sentence or clause.
• When the marker is at the beginning of a clause, it is usually preceded by a comma, or comma + *and*.
• *Therefore* and *consequently* can also be used before a main verb, e.g., *We have therefore | consequently decided not to offer you the job.*

reason

> 1 I have stopped writing to her **because | as | since** she never answers me.
> 2 The plane was late **because of** the fog.
>   Flight 341 has been delayed **due to | owing to** adverse weather conditions.

1 *Because*, *since*, and *as* (more formal) are used to introduce clauses giving a reason and are synonyms. *As* is often used at the beginning of a sentence, e.g., *As the weather is so awful, we've decided not to go out.*
2 *Because of*, *due to*, and *owing to* also express the reason for something. They are usually followed by a noun.
• *Due to* and *owing to* are more formal than *because of*.

purpose

> 1 I took a language course **to | in order to | so as to** improve my English.
> 2 She closed the door quietly **so as not to | in order not to** wake the baby.
> 3 They moved to Quito **so (that)** they could see their grandchildren more often.
> 4 I'm not going to tell Ann **in case** she tells everyone else.

1 *To*, *in order to* and *so as to* introduce a clause of purpose and are all followed by an infinitive. *So as to* and *in order to* are more formal.
2 For negative purpose use *in order not to* or *so as not to*, NOT *She closed the door quietly not to wake the baby*.
3 You can also use *so (that)* + *can | could* + verb or *will | would* + verb to express purpose. You can leave out *that* in informal speech and writing.
• You must use *so (that)* when there is a change of subject in the result clause, e.g., *She put a blanket over the baby so (that) he wouldn't be cold.*
4 Use *in case* + clause when something is done in order to be ready for future situations / problems or to avoid them.

contrast

> 1 We enjoyed the concert, **but** we didn't have very good seats.
>   Agnes was attracted to the stranger, **yet** something in her head was telling her not to get close to him.
>   We enjoyed the concert. **However**, we didn't have very good seats.
>   Agnes was attracted to the stranger. **Nevertheless**, something in her head was telling her not to get close to him.
> 2 We enjoyed the concert **although | even though | though** we didn't have very good seats.
> 3 **In spite of** being attracted to the stranger, something in Agnes's head was telling her not to get close to him.
>   **Despite** her attraction to the stranger…
>   **Despite the fact that** she was attracted to the stranger…

1 *But* is the most common and informal way of introducing contrast, and is usually used to link two contrasting points within a sentence.
• *Yet* is used in the same way, but is more formal / literary.
• *However* and *nevertheless* are usually used at the beginning of a sentence, to connect it to the previous one. They are usually followed by a comma.
• *Nevertheless* (or *nonetheless*) is more formal / literary than *however*.
2 *Even though* is more emphatic than *although*. *Though* is more common in informal speech.

> ⚠ *Though* can also be used at the end of a phrase as a comment adverb, e.g., *He's very friendly — a little stingy, though.*

3 After *in spite of* and *despite* you must use a gerund, a noun, or *the fact that* + clause.

---

a Circle the right connector in each sentence.

(Even though) | *Despite* she's working really hard, I don't think she'll be able to catch up with the rest of the class.
1 We can't afford to take a vacation this year *as | so* we are broke.
2 Could we rearrange my schedule *so that | in case* I don't have so many classes on a Friday afternoon?
3 At the meeting Carla stuck to her guns *due to | in spite of* the fact that everybody was against her.
4 The restaurant chain has had a very difficult year. *Nevertheless | As a result*, they haven't had to close any of their restaurants.
5 He makes a good salary *though | since* the job itself is very monotonous.

b Circle the correct option according to register.

Sales have decreased over the last three months. *So* | (Therefore) we will not be taking on any new staff.
1 I've been off work for the last three days *because of | owing to* this nasty cough.
2 Jane texted me to say she's going to be a little late, *so | consequently* let's start without her.
3 The company has reported declining sales this year, *in spite of | but* they have so far managed to avoid any staff cuts.
4 I stopped at a gas station *to | in order to* fill up the tank.
5 I thought it was an amazing movie. It was really depressing, *though | however*.
6 We sincerely apologize for the delay, which was *due to | because of* the late arrival of the incoming aircraft.

c Combine the two sentences using the **bold word(s)**, making any necessary changes.

We always turn off the TV at night. We don't want to waste electricity. **so as**
We always turn off the TV at night so as not to waste electricity.
1 Our seats were a long way from the stage. We enjoyed the play. **In spite**

2 We were really late. The traffic was heavy. **because of**

3 I took the price tag off the bag. I didn't want her to know how much it had cost. **so that**

4 Keep the receipt for the sweater. Your dad might not like it. **in case**

5 Susanna is an only child. She isn't at all spoiled. **Even though**

6 Prices have increased. Production costs have risen. **due to**

◀ p.5

1B *have*

have

1 They **have** a large, rather dilapidated house in Florida.
2 He **doesn't have** lunch at home. **Are** you **having** lunch?
3 They**'ve been** married for 15 years.
How long **has** Anna **been going out** with James?
4 We're going to **have** the kitchen **repainted** next week.
I **had** my eyes **examined** when I got my new glasses.
5 He's **got** a lot to learn about raising children.

1 Use *have* as a **main verb** for possession.
Have with this meaning is a stative (non-action) verb and is not used in continuous tenses. Use auxiliaries *do* / *did* to make questions and negatives.
2 Use *have* + object as a **main verb** for actions, e.g., *have a snack, a drink, a meal*, etc.
Have with this meaning is a dynamic (action) verb and can be used in continuous tenses.
3 Use *have* as the **auxiliary verb** to form the present perfect simple and continuous. Make questions by inverting *have* and the subject, and negatives with *haven't* / *hasn't*.
• We also use *have* for other perfect forms, e.g., the future perfect, the perfect infinitive, etc.
4 Use *have* + object + past participle to say that you ask or pay another person to do something for you, e.g., *Where do you have your hair cut? Get* is a more natural alternative to *have* in the structure have *something done*. e.g., *Where do you get your hair cut?*
5 *Have got* is sometimes used in informal spoken English for possession. The meaning is exactly the same as *have*.
• *Have* here is an **auxiliary verb**, so make questions by inverting *have* and the subject and negatives with *haven't* / *hasn't*.
• *Have got* has a present meaning. We use *had* for the past, NOT *had got*.

have to

1 **I have to** learn to be patient with my younger cousins.
2 **Do we** really **have to** spend New Year's day with your parents again?
3 **I've got to** go now. I'm meeting my girlfriend for lunch.

1 Use *have to* to express obligation, especially obligation imposed by others, and rules and regulations. *Have to* is a main verb.
2 Use the auxiliary verbs *do* and *did* to form questions with *have to*.
3 *Have got to* is an alternative way to express obligation that is sometimes used in informal spoken English.
• *Have got to* is normally used for a specific obligation rather than a general or repeated obligation. Compare:
I've got to make a quick phone call (specific) and *I have to wear a suit to work* (general).
• We do not usually use *have got to* in questions. Instead, use *have to. Do you have to work tonight?* NOT *Have you got to work tonight?*
See **7A permission, obligation, and necessity** on page 150 for more information on *have to* and *have got to*.

a Right (✓) or wrong (✗)? Correct the mistakes in the highlighted phrases.

A You look exhausted.
B Yes, I've been having meetings all day with people. ✓
1 Are you going to have your nails done when you go to the salon?
2 **A** Why don't you want to come?
B I've got a lot of chores to do.
3 Has your husband to work tomorrow or is he taking the day off too?
4 The employees don't have to dress formally in this company — they can wear what they like.
5 How long have you been having your condo in New York?
6 What time are we having dinner tonight?
7 My parents had got many problems with my sister when she was a teenager.
8 I don't have a vacation for 18 months. I really need a break.
9 Have we got to do this exercise now, or can we do it later for homework?

b Rewrite the sentences using a form of *have*.

I started working for Microsoft in 2001 and I still work there.
I've been working for Microsoft since 2001.

1 She's an only child.
She _____.
2 We used to pay someone to take a family photograph every year.
We used _____.
3 Wearing a hard hat is obligatory for all visitors to this site.
All _____.
4 His last name is really long.
He _____.
5 He lacks the right qualifications for this job.
He _____.
6 It's not necessary for us to do it now. We can do it later.
We _____.
7 We knew almost everyone at the party — it was really enjoyable.
We knew almost everyone at the party — we _____.
8 When did you start having problems at school?
How long _____?
9 I need someone to fix the central heating system. I think the thermostat is broken.
I need _____.
I think the thermostat is broken.

◀ *p.8*

2A pronouns

generic pronouns

1 **You** can learn a language faster if you go to live in a country where it is spoken.
2 **One** should never criticize without being sure of the facts.
3 When **we** talk about an accent, **we** must not confuse this with pronunciation.
4 **They** always say that it's never too late to learn a new language.
  They should make it a requirement for people to learn two foreign languages at school.
5 If someone goes to live in a foreign country, **they** will have to get used to a different way of life.
  Could the person who left **their** bag in the library please come and see me?

1 We often use *you* to mean people in general.
2 We can also use *one* + 3rd person singular of the verb to mean people in general. *One* is more formal than *you* and is rarely used in spoken English.
3 *We* can also be used to make a general statement which includes the reader / listener.
4 In informal English, we also often use *they* to talk about other people in general, or people in authority, e.g., ***They*** *always say…* (they = people in general), ***They*** *should make it a requirement…* (they = the government).
5 We often use *they*, *them*, and *their* to refer to one person who may be male or female, instead of using *he or she*, *his or her*, etc.

reflexive and reciprocal pronouns

1 You need to take care of **yourself** with that cold.
  He's very egocentric. He always talks about **himself**.
2 I managed to complete the crossword! I was really proud of **myself**.
3 We decorated the house **ourselves**.
  There's no way I'm going to do it for you. Do it **yourself**!
4 I don't feel very comfortable going to the movies **by myself**.
5 My classmate and I don't talk to **each other** anymore.
  My mother and sister don't understand **one another** at all.

1 We often use reflexive pronouns when the subject and object of a verb are the same person.
  We don't usually use reflexive pronouns with *wash, shave, feel, relax, concentrate* NOT *relax yourself*.
2 We also use reflexive pronouns after most prepositions when the complement is the same as the subject.

> ⚠ After prepositions of place, we use object pronouns, not reflexive pronouns, e.g., *She put the bag next to her on the seat* NOT *next to herself*.

3 We can also use reflexive pronouns to emphasize the subject, e.g., *We decorated the house ourselves* (= we did it, not professional decorators).
4 *By* + reflexive pronoun = alone, on your own.
5 We use *each other* or *one another* for reciprocal actions, i.e., A does the action to B and B does the action to A.
• Compare *They bought themselves some new shoes* (= A bought some for A, and B bought some for B).
  They bought each other some new shoes (= A bought some for B and B bought some for A).

it and *there*

1 **It's** five miles to Chicago. **It's** 10 o'clock.
2 **It was** great to hear that you and Martina are getting married!
  It used to be difficult to buy fresh pasta here, but now you can get it everywhere.
3 **There's** a big crowd of people in the downtown area.
  There used to be a movie theater on that street, but there isn't one anymore.
  There are three meetings this week.

1 We use *it* + *be* to talk about time, temperature, and distance.
2 We also use *it* + *be* as a "preparatory" subject before adjectives. *It was great to hear from you* is more natural than *To hear from you was great*.
3 We use *there* + *be* + noun to say if people and things are present or exist (or not). You cannot use *It… here.* NOT *It used to be a movie theater on that street.*

---

a Circle the right pronoun. Check (✓) if you think both are possible.

> They hurt *one another* / (themselves) very badly when they fell off their motorcycle.

1 *One / You* can often tell where people are from by the way they dress.
2 Can you put my case on the rack above *yourself / you*?
3 Marga and her sister look so much like *each other / one another*. Are they twins?
4 Anna is very unselfish — she never puts *her / herself* first.
5 Either Suzie or Mark has left *her / their* bag behind, because there's only one in the back of the car.
6 When a person goes to live abroad, it may take *them / him* a while to pick up the language.
7 *They / One* say that eating tomatoes can help protect the body against certain diseases.

b Complete the sentence with a pronoun where necessary.

> In formal circumstances *you* should address people by their title and last name.

1 If anyone has not yet paid _____ tuition, _____ should go to registration immediately.
2 Isabel is very hot-tempered. She finds it very hard to control _____.
3 I wouldn't stay in that hotel. _____ say the rooms are tiny and the service is awful.
4 There is a total lack of communication. They don't understand _____ at all.
5 Mila gets distracted too easily. She doesn't concentrate _____ very well.
6 Are you going to have the apartment repainted or will you do it _____?
7 There are lots of bookshelves in the apartment, which is great as _____ can never have too many!

c Complete the sentences with *it* or *there*.

> *There* was a very interesting article about urban architecture in the newspaper yesterday.

1 Nowadays _____'s illegal to text while you're driving. _____ have been a lot of accidents caused by that.
2 Look. _____'s a spelling mistake in this word. _____ should be *j*, not *g*.
3 How many miles is _____ to San Diego from here?
4 _____'s scorching today. _____ must be at least 95 degrees.
5 _____'s no need to hurry. The train doesn't leave for a while.
6 _____'s not worth reading the newspaper today. _____'s absolutely nothing interesting in it.

◀ *p.15*

2B the past: narrative tenses, *used to* and *would*

narrative tenses: describing specific incidents in the past

> This **happened** when I **was** about five years old. My father **had gone away** on business for a few days, and my brother and I **were sleeping** in my parents' bedroom. Before we **went** to bed that night, I **had been reading** a very scary story about a wicked witch. In the middle of the night, I **woke up** suddenly and **saw** that a figure in a dark coat **was standing** at the end of my bed. I **screamed** at the top of my lungs.

- When we describe specific incidents in the past, we use **narrative tenses**, i.e., the simple past, past continuous, and past perfect or past perfect continuous.
- Use the simple past to talk about the main actions in a story (*We went to bed… I woke up… I screamed*).
- Use the past continuous to set the scene (*We were sleeping in my parents' bedroom*) and to describe actions in progress in the past (*Somebody was standing at the end of my bed*).
- Use the past perfect and the past perfect continuous to talk about the earlier past, i.e., things that happened before the main events (*My father had gone away…I had been reading a story*).

used to and *would*: describing repeated actions in the past

> 1 Every summer my family **rented** an old house in Newport, Rhode Island. My sister and I **used to walk** to the harbor every morning and watch the fishermen cleaning their nets.
> 2 Every night before we went to bed my mother **would tell** us a story, but she **would never read** them from a book — she **would always make them up** herself.
> 3 When I was a teenager, my friends **were always teasing** me because of my red hair.

1 We often use *used to* + infinitive as an alternative to the simple past to talk about things that we did repeatedly in the past.
- We can also use *used to* + infinitive to talk about situations or states which have changed, e.g., *I used to have much longer hair when I was younger.*
2 We also use *would* + infinitive as an alternative to *used to* to talk about things that we did repeatedly in the past.
- However, we <u>don't</u> use *would* with stative verbs, i.e., to talk about situations or states which have changed: NOT ~~I would have much longer hair when I was younger.~~
3 We can also use *always* + past continuous for things that happened repeatedly, especially when they were irritating habits.

> ⚠ When we describe past habits or repeated past actions we tend, for stylistic reasons, to use a mixture of *used to*, *would*, or the simple past (with adverbs of frequency). *Used to* and *would* make it clear that you are talking about something that happened regularly and often convey a sense of nostalgia.

a Circle the right form. Check (✓) if both are correct.

Corinne and I (used to be) / would be very close, but recently we've grown apart.

1 When I came into the room, my aunt *sat* / *was sitting* with her back to me. When she turned around, I could see that her eyes were red, and I was sure that she *had been crying* / *had cried*.
2 Our grandmother *always used to have* / *would always have* a little surprise waiting for us when we visited.
3 My uncle *lived* / *used to live* on his own because his wife *died* / *had died* several years earlier.
4 When my brother was a child, *he didn't use to look* / *he wouldn't look* at all like my father, but the older he gets the more he looks like him.
5 When I was small, *I was always getting* / *I always used to get* into trouble at school and my parents *used to punish* / *would punish* me by not letting me play with my friends on the weekend.
6 We suddenly heard a tremendous crash, and we saw that a car *crashed* / *had crashed* into a tree, and gasoline *poured* / *was pouring* out of the car onto the street.

b Put the verbs in the right form, using a narrative tense or *would* / *used to*.

My earliest memory

When I was about four or five, my grandmother, who was Mexican, <u>was living</u> (live) in Los Angeles, and we children often ¹_____ (spend) weekends at her apartment. My grandfather ²_____ (die) a couple of years earlier, so I suppose she was in need of company. We loved going there, since my grandmother ³_____ (cook) special meals for us and ⁴_____ (take) us for beautiful walks along Venice Beach, which wasn't far at all. One occasion that I remember really well was when I ⁵_____ (invite) to stay with her on my own, without my brothers and sisters. On the first day, after lunch, my grandmother ⁶_____ (tell) me that she ⁷_____ (go) to take a nap, and that I should take a nap, too. I ⁸_____ (try) to sleep but I couldn't, so after a while I ⁹_____ (get) up and ¹⁰_____ (decide) to explore the apartment. Everything was very quiet so I was convinced that my grandmother ¹¹_____ (sleep). The room I most ¹²_____ (want) to explore was my grandfather's study, I imagine, exactly because I ¹³_____ (tell) not to go in there. I opened the door and went in, and was immediately attracted to his large old desk. I ¹⁴_____ (climb) onto the chair, and ¹⁵_____ (see) on the desk a green pen in a kind of stand, with a bottle of ink. I ¹⁶_____ (ask) my parents for a real pen for a long time, but they ¹⁷_____ (refuse), foreseeing the mess that I was almost bound to make with the ink. I picked up the pen and then tried to open the bottle of ink. At that moment, I ¹⁸_____ (hear) my grandmother's voice saying "Christina? Where are you? What are you doing?" To my horror I ¹⁹_____ (realize) that my grandmother ²⁰_____ (get up) out of bed and ²¹_____ (come) toward the study. Two seconds later she ²²_____ (open) the door. I will never forget the awful feeling of shame that she ²³_____ (catch) me doing something that she ²⁴_____ (forbid) me to do.

◀ p.19

3A get

1 I **got** an email from Marc today.
  If you're going to the post office, could you **get** me some stamps?
  When do you think we'll **get** to Beijing?
2 We'd better go home. It's **getting dark**.
  I seem to have **gotten very forgetful** recently.
  The traffic **gets worse** on the local roads every day.
  I don't think my mother will ever **get used to** living on her own.
3 We need to **get someone to fix** the central heating system — it's not working properly.
  Could you **get Jane to finish** the report? I'm too busy to do it this afternoon.
4 I'm going to **get my hair cut** next week.
  I need to **get my passport renewed** — it expires in a couple of months.
5 Did you know Dan **got fired** last week?
  My husband **got pulled** over for speeding again. That's the third time this year.

Get is one of the most common verbs in English and can be used in many different ways.

1 *Get* + noun / pronoun can mean "receive," "bring," "fetch," "obtain," "buy," or "catch," and with *to* + a place it means "arrive at / in."
2 We use *get* + adjective or comparative adjective to mean "become."
• Compare *be* + adjective and *get* + adjective.
  It's dark. It's getting dark.
  I'm used to the climate in Seattle now. I'm getting used to the climate in Seattle.
3 We can use *get* + object + infinitive to mean "make somebody do something" or "persuade somebody to do something."
4 In informal spoken English we sometimes use *get* (+ object + past participle) instead of *have* (+ object + past participle) to say that you ask or pay another person to do something for you. **See 1B *have*** on page 139.
5 We can use *get* (+ past participle) instead of *be* to make a passive structure. This is more informal than using *be*.

a Replace *get* with another verb so that the sentence has the same meaning.

> I **got** fined yesterday for returning an overdue book to the library. <u>was</u>

1 My father is **getting** increasingly forgetful in his old age. _____
2 Do you know anywhere near here where I can **get** a newspaper? _____
3 Could you try to **get** your brother to come tonight too? _____
4 We had to **get** the roof repaired because it was damaged in the storm. _____
5 I **got** an email out of the blue today from an old school friend. _____
6 I am going to school today to **get** my registration form. _____
7 Do you think they'll **get** here in time for lunch? _____
8 If you're going upstairs, could you **get** me my jacket, the one that's on my bed? _____
9 She **got** caught for cheating on the test. _____
10 How can I **get** you to change your mind? _____

b Complete the sentence with the right form of *get* and the word in parentheses. You may need to change the form of the verbs in parentheses.

> I <u>always get lost</u> (always / lose) when I'm driving. I think I'm going to start using my GPS.

1 I _____ just in time. It was about to expire. (my visa / renew)
2 My husband has only been in the UK for two months, and he just can't _____ on the left. He gets very confused at traffic circles. (used / drive)
3 Monica's fiancé _____ in a car crash. He was lucky to survive. (almost / kill)
4 I can _____ tomorrow night so we can go out. (my sister / babysit)
5 If you can't find your keys, we'll have to _____. (all the locks / change)
6 **A** You're two hours late! What happened?
  B My cell phone went dead and I didn't print out the directions, so I _____! (lost)
7 I went to the eye doctor yesterday to _____. (eyes / examine)
8 **A** What happened to your eye?
  B I _____ by a mosquito last night. (bite)

◀ p.27

3B discourse markers (2): adverbs and adverbial expressions

A I really like your shirt. Doesn't Harry have one just like it? **B** **Speaking of** Harry, did he get the job he applied for?	To change the direction of a conversation, but making a link with what has just been said.
So let's meet at five o'clock then. **By the way** / **Incidentally**, could you lend me some money until the weekend?	To introduce something you have just thought of, or to change the subject completely.
A Did you see the game last night? **B** No, I didn't. **Actually** / **In fact** / **As a matter of fact** I don't really like football.	To introduce additional surprising or unexpected information.
We didn't go away for the weekend because I had too much work. **In any case** / **Anyway** the weather was awful, so we didn't miss anything.	To introduce the idea that what you said before is less important than what you are going to say. To return to the main topic after a digression.
Yes, it was a bad accident. **At least** nobody was killed, though. Tom's coming to the meeting, or **at least** he said he was.	To introduce a positive point after some negative information. To make what you have just said less definite.
As I was saying, if Mark gets the job we'll have to reorganize the department.	To return to a previous subject, often after you have been interrupted.
On the whole, I think that women make better journalists than men.	To generalize.
I like both condos, but **all in all**, I think I prefer the one next to the cathedral.	To say that you are taking everything into consideration.
I think we should buy them. **After all**, we'll never find them anywhere cheaper than this.	To introduce a strong argument that the other person may not have taken into consideration.
I don't think I'll go to Nick's party. It will finish very late. **Besides**, I won't know many people there.	To add additional information or arguments.
Basically, my job involves computer skills and people skills.	To introduce the most important or fundamental point.
Obviously, you can't get a real idea of life in Japan unless you can speak the language.	To introduce a fact that is very clear to see or understand.
She's very selfish. **I mean**, she never thinks about other people at all.	To make things clearer or give more details.
A lot of people booed, and some people even left early. **In other words**, it was a complete disaster.	To say something again in another way.
Please try not to make a mess when you make the cake. **Otherwise** I'm going to have to clean the kitchen again.	To say what the result would be if something did not happen or if the situation were different.
That's all you need to know about the travel arrangements. **As far as** accommodations are **concerned**, **As regards** / **Regarding** accommodations, the options are living with a family or living in a dormitory.	To introduce a new topic or to announce a change of subject.
The government is going to help first-time buyers. **That is to say**, they are going to make mortgages more easily available.	To introduce an explanation or clarification of a point you have just made.
On (the) one hand, more young people today carry knives. **On (the) other hand**, the total number of violent crimes has dropped.	To balance contrasting facts or points. *On the other hand* is also used alone to introduce a contrasting fact or point.

a Circle the appropriate discourse markers in the dialogue.

A What a good movie! I really enjoyed it. Didn't you?
B (Actually) / Incidentally, I didn't like it very much.
A Why not?
B [1]*Basically* / *After all* I thought it was incredibly far-fetched. I couldn't believe in the characters at all, and the plot was totally implausible.
A I wouldn't call it far-fetched. [2]*At least* / *In any case* it wasn't supposed to be a true story.
B I know, but it was set in a very specific historical period. [3]*Otherwise* / *Obviously* you can't expect the dialogue to be totally authentic, [4]*I mean* / *on the other hand* nobody knows exactly how people spoke in the 17th century, but [5]*at least* / *anyway* the period details should be right. There was a clock in the king's palace, and they didn't have clocks until the eighteenth century! [6]*All in all* / *That is to say* I thought it was a pretty awful movie.
A We'll have to agree to disagree then. [7]*By the way* / *As a matter of fact*, do you know what time the last train leaves? I don't want to miss it. [8]*Otherwise* / *In any case* I'll have to get a taxi home.
B At 11:40. Don't worry, we have plenty of time. [9]*In fact* / *Besides*, I think we even have time to get something to eat. Do you feel like a quick pizza? There's a good Italian restaurant just around the corner.
A Yes, let's go. [10]*As I was saying* / *Speaking of* Italian food, I made a wonderful risotto with mushrooms last night…

b Complete the sentences with appropriate discourse markers. Sometimes more than one answer may be possible.

The food was delicious and the service was excellent. *All in all* the meal was a great success.

1 Jason is an excellent teacher, although _____ I think female teachers are usually better with four- and five-year-olds.
2 **A** Did you end up buying the shoes?
  B No, they were too expensive. And _____ I decided that I didn't really like them that much.
3 I really think you should apply for the manager position. _____, you have nothing to lose, and you might just get it, who knows?
4 **A** I just read a great book that Simon lent me.
  B _____ Simon, did you know he's moving to New York?
5 **A** How was your day?
  B Fine. I finished work a little earlier than usual. _____, did you remember to get a birthday present for your mom?
6 It was a very gray, overcast day, but _____ it didn't rain.
7 **A** Do your wife's parents live near you?
  B _____, they live in the apartment below us. It's not ideal but it does have some advantages.
8 They hired me as a kind of troubleshooter — _____ somebody who resolves problems whenever they occur.
9 _____ salary _____, you will be paid on the 30th or 31st of each month, with a bonus in December and in July.
10 You'd better hurry up with your homework. _____ you won't be able to watch TV tonight.

◄ *p.31*

4A speculation and deduction

modal verbs: *must* / *may* / *might* / *can't* / *should*

1 Dia **must be** very well off — she has an enormous house.
  You **must have seen** him — he was standing right in front of you!
2 They **can't be playing** very well — they're losing 3-0.
  You **can't / couldn't have spent** very long on this essay — you've only written 100 words.
3 I haven't seen the sales manager today. He **may / might / could be** off sick.
  The keys to the storage cabinet have disappeared. Do you think someone **may / might / could have taken** them?
  He **may / might not have heard** the message I left on his voice mail.
4 If I mail the letter today, it **should arrive** on Friday.
  I mailed the letter a week ago. It **should have arrived** by now.

1 As well as for obligation, we also use *must* + infinitive to say that we are almost sure something is true about the present, and *must have* + past participle to say that we are almost sure something was true or happened in the past.
2 We use *can't* and *can't / couldn't* + perfect infinitive (NOT *mustn't / mustn't have*) to say that we are almost sure that something isn't true in the present or didn't happen / wasn't true in the past.
3 We use *may / might / could* + infinitive and *may / might / could* + perfect infinitive to say that we think it's possible that something is true in the present or was true / happened in the past.
• Compare:
He might not have done it. (= Maybe he didn't do it.)
He couldn't have done it. (= It is impossible that he did it.)
4 Use *should* + infinitive (or *should have* + past participle) to describe a situation you expect to happen (or would expect to have happened in the past).

> ⚠ Compare the use of the infinitive and the continuous infinitive after these modals.
> *He **must work** really hard. He never gets home before 9:00 p.m.*
> = deduction about a habitual action
> *There's a light on in his office. He **must** still **be working**.* = deduction about an action in progress at the moment of speaking

adjectives and adverbs for speculation

1 He**'s bound / sure to** be here in a minute. He left an hour ago.
  She**'s sure to** know. She's an expert on the subject.
2 I think she**'s likely to** agree to our proposal — we've given her some very good reasons.
  The doctors say that at his age he**'s unlikely to** recover.
  I think **it's very likely that** the meeting will be over by 6:00.
  It's unlikely that the government will raise interest rates this year.
3 She**'ll definitely pass** the test. She's worked really hard.
  She **definitely won't pass** the test. She hasn't done any work at all.
  He**'ll probably be here** around 8:00. He usually leaves work at 7:30.
  He **probably won't be here** until about 8:15. He's stuck in a traffic jam.

1 *Bound* and *sure* are adjectives. We use *be bound* or *be sure* + infinitive to say that we think something is certain to be true or to happen.
2 *Likely / unlikely* are also adjectives (not adverbs). We can use subject + *be likely / unlikely* + infinitive, or *it is likely / unlikely* + *that* + clause.
3 *Definitely* and *probably* are adverbs. They go before a main verb and after the auxiliary (if there is one) in ⊞ sentences and before the auxiliary verb in ⊟ sentences.
• With *be* they go after the verb in ⊞ sentences and before it in ⊟ sentences, e.g., *He's probably Japanese. The painting definitely isn't genuine.*

> ⚠ *be likely to* and *will probably* are very similar in meaning, but *be likely to* is more formal. Compare:
> *The new coach is likely to be appointed today.*
> *The new coach will probably be appointed today.*

a Right (✓) or wrong (✗)? Correct the mistakes in the highlighted phrases.

  A When's Jim arriving?
  B I'm not sure, but he likely isn't to be here before 7:00. ✗ *he isn't likely to be here*
1 My glasses aren't in their usual place. Someone must move them. *have moved*
2 **A** Do you know where Ann is?
  B She should be in the library. That's where she said she was going. ✓
3 **A** What's that noise in the garage?
  B I think it can be the neighbor's cat. *may*
4 I'm sure Brazil will win tonight. They're unlikely to lose three times in a row. ✓
5 I don't think we should use that photo of Tina in the brochure. She won't definitely like it.
6 Julian is bound be late — he always is. *to*
7 No one's answering the phone at the store. They've probably gone home. ✓
8 I don't think Yasuko has gone to bed yet. I think she must still study. *be still studying*
9 It's very likely that the boss will retire in a year or two. ✓

b Rewrite the sentences using the **bold** word.

  Maybe he got lost. He has no sense of direction.
  MIGHT
  He *might have gotten lost*. He has no sense of direction.
1 I don't think he'll have time to stop by and see us. He's on a very tight schedule. **PROBABLY**
  He *probably won't have time*. He's on a very tight schedule.
2 I'm not sure she'll ever get over the break-up. **MAY**
  She *may never get over* the break-up.
3 They will probably have heard the news by now. **SHOULD**
  They *should have heard the news by* now.
4 I'm sure I didn't leave my credit card in the restaurant. I remember putting it in my wallet. **CAN'T**
  I *couldn't have left my credit card*. I remember putting it in my wallet.
5 I'm sure your sister will like the scarf. It's just her style. **BOUND**
  Your sister *is bound to like the scarf*. It's just her style.
6 The company director probably won't resign, despite the disastrous sales figures. **UNLIKELY**
  The company director *is unlikely to resign*, despite the disastrous sales figures.
7 I'm sure he was in love with her otherwise he wouldn't have married her. **MUST**
  He *must be* otherwise he wouldn't have married her.
8 Are you sure you locked the back door? **DEFINITELY**
  Did _____ the back door?
9 According to press reports, the couple will probably get divorced soon. **LIKELY**
  According to press reports, it's _____ soon.

◀ p.36

4B adding emphasis (1): inversion

1 **Not only is** my brother lazy, (but) he's also very selfish.
Not until you can behave like an adult **will we treat** you like an adult.
Never have I heard such a ridiculous argument.
No sooner had the football game **started than** it began to snow heavily.
2 **Not only did you forget** to shut the window, (but) you also forgot to lock the door!
Not until you become a parent yourself **do you understand** what it really means.
3 The train began to move. **Only then was I able to** relax.
Only when you leave home **do you realize** how expensive everything is.
Hardly had I sat down when the train began to move.
Rarely have I met a more irritating person.

In formal English, especially in writing, we sometimes change the normal word order to make the sentence more emphatic or dramatic.
1 This structure is common with negative adverbial expressions such as *Not only…, Not until…, Never…,* and *No sooner… than* (= a formal way of saying *as soon as*).
• When we use inversion after the above expressions, we change the order of the subject and (auxiliary) verb NOT ~~Not only my brother is lazy…~~ .
Compare:
My brother is not only lazy, but he's also very selfish.
(= normal word order)
Not only is my brother lazy, but he's also very selfish.
(= inversion to make the sentence more emphatic)
2 In the simple present and simple past tense, rather than simply inverting the subject and verb we use *do | does | did* + subject + main verb NOT ~~Not only forgot you to shut the window….~~
3 Inversion is also used after the expressions *Only then…, Only when…, Hardly | Scarcely… when,* and *Rarely…*

> ⚠ Inversion should only be used occasionally for dramatic effect. Overusing it will make your English sound unnatural.

◀ p.39

Rewrite the sentences to make them more emphatic.
    I had just sat down when the train left.
    No sooner *had I sat down than the train left*.

1 I didn't realize my mistake until years later.
    Not until *years later did I realise my mistake*

2 We had never seen such magnificent scenery.
    Never *had we seen such*.

3 They not only disliked her, but they also hated her family.
    Not only *did they dislike her, but*.

4 We only understood what he had really suffered when we read his autobiography.
    Only when *we had read his biog. did we understand*

5 We had just started to eat when we heard someone knocking at the door.
    Hardly *had we started to eat*.

6 I have rarely read such a badly written novel.
    Rarely *have a read*.

7 We did not put down our tools and rest until the sun set.
    Not until *the sunset did we put down*.

8 The hotel room was not only depressing, but it was cold as well.
    Not only *was the hotel room depressing but*.

9 They only lit the fire when it was unusually cold.
    Only when *it was unusually cold did the light the fire*.

10 Shortly after he had gone to sleep there was a knock on the door.
    No sooner *had he gone to sleep than there*.

11 I only realized the full scale of the disaster when I watched the six o'clock news.
    I watched the six o'clock news. **Only then** *did I realise*.

12 I had only just destroyed the evidence when the police arrived.
    Scarcely *had I destroy the evidence*.

13 He has never regretted the decision he made that day.
    Never *had he*.

14 I spoke to the manager and the problem was resolved.
    Only when *I had spoken to the manager was the problem resolved quickly*

5A distancing

seem / appear

1 **It seems / appears** (that) there is a direct relationship between your position in the family and your personality.
The new manager **seems / appears to be** very friendly.
Excuse me. **There seems to be** a mistake with the bill.
2 **It would seem / appear** (that) Mr. Hill had been using the company's assets to pay off his private debts.

1 We often use *seem* and *appear* to give information without stating that we definitely know it is true, and in this way distancing ourselves from the information.
We can use *It seems / appears* + *that* + clause, or subject + *seem / appear* + infinitive.
2 We use *It would seem / appear* + *that* + clause to distance us even further from the information, and to make it sound less sure. This is more formal than *It seems / appears…*

the passive with verbs of saying and reporting

1 **It is said that** using a washing machine saves people on average 47 minutes a day.
It has been announced by a White House spokesman **that** the President has been taken to the hospital.
2 The company director **is expected to resign** in the next few days.
The missing couple **is understood to have been living** in Panama for the last five years.
3 **There are thought to be** over a thousand species in danger of extinction.

Another way of distancing ourselves from the facts, especially in formal written English, is to use the passive form of verbs like *say, think,* etc. to introduce them.
We can use:
1 *It* + passive verb + *that* + clause.
• Verbs commonly used in this pattern are: *agree, announce, believe, expect, hope, report, say, suggest, think,* and *understand.*
2 subject + passive verb + *to* + infinitive.
• Verbs commonly used in this pattern are *believe, expect, report, say, think,* and *understand.*
3 *There* can also be used + passive verb + *to* + infinitive.
Compare:
It is said that there are more than five million people living in poverty in this country.
There are said to be more than five million people living in poverty in this country.

other distancing expressions: *apparently, according to, may / might*

1 **Apparently**, Maurice and Yvette have separated.
2 **According to** new research, the idea that we have to drink two liters of water a day is a myth.
3 Dinosaurs **may** have died out due to extremely rapid climate change.
There are rumors that the band, which broke up in the late 80s, **might** be planning to get back together and record a new album.

1 We can use *apparently* (usually either at the beginning or the end of a phrase) to mean that we have heard / read something, but that it may not be true. This is very common in informal conversation.
2 We can use *according to* to specify where information has come from. We use it to attribute opinions to somebody else NOT *According to me…*
3 Using *may / might* also suggests that something is a possibility, but not necessarily true.

---

a Complete the sentences with one word to distance the speaker from the information. Sometimes there is more than one possibility.

Apparently, Lisa and Dani are going to get married. Have you heard anything?

1 It _____ that the less children sleep, the more likely they are to behave badly.
2 It _____ appear that someone has been stealing personal items from the changing rooms.
3 Mark _____ to have aged a lot over the last year.
4 He may not look it, but he is _____ to be one of the wealthiest people in the country.
5 _____ to some sources, the latest research is seriously flawed.
6 Despite the fact that there will be an autopsy, his death _____ have been from natural causes.
7 _____ are thought to be several reasons why the species died out.
8 The missing couple is _____ to have had financial difficulties.
9 It is understood _____ the board member will be resigning in the near future.

b Rewrite the second sentence so that it means the same as the first.

People say that eating garlic prevents you from catching colds.
It is *said that eating garlic prevents you from catching colds.*

1 Apparently, people who work night shifts die younger.
It would _____.
2 It is possible that the prisoners escaped to France.
The prisoners may _____.
3 We expect that the Prime Minister will make a statement this afternoon.
The Prime Minister is _____.
4 The company has announced that the new drug will go on sale shortly.
It _____.
5 People believe that improvements in diet and lifestyle are responsible for the rise in life expectancy.
Improvements in diet and lifestyle _____
_____.
6 The manual says you have to charge the phone for at least 12 hours.
According _____.
7 It appears that the government is intending to lower interest rates.
The government _____.
8 People have suggested that the painting is a fake.
It _____.
9 It seems that there are more bicyclists around than there used to be.
There _____.

◀ p.45

5B unreal uses of past tenses

1 It's a difficult problem. I **wish** I **knew** the answer to it!
I **wish** I **hadn't spoken** to Jane like that — you know how
sensitive she is.
2 **If only** I **knew** the answer!
If only you **hadn't forgotten** the map, we'd be there by now.
3 **I'd rather you left** your dog outside — I'm allergic to animals.
Are you sure this is a good time to talk? **Would you rather
I called** back later?
4 Don't you think **it's time** you **found** a job? It's been six
months since you finished college!
It's time the government did something about
unemployment.

1 We use *wish* + simple past to talk about things we would like to
be different in the present / future (but which are impossible
or unlikely).
• We use *wish* + past perfect to talk about things that happened /
didn't happen in the past and that we now regret.
• We sometimes use *that* after *wish*, e.g., *I wish that I knew the answer.*
2 You can also use *If only...* instead of *wish* with the simple past
and past perfect. This can be used by itself (*If only I knew!*) or
with another clause.
• *If only* is more emphatic than *wish*.

> ⚠ When we want to talk about things we want to happen or
> stop happening because they annoy us, we use *wish* or *If only*
> + person / thing + *would* + infinitive, e.g., *I wish the bus would
> come! If only he wouldn't keep whistling when I'm working!*

3 We use *would rather* + subject + past tense to express
a preference.
• We can also use *would rather* + infinitive without *to* when there
is no change of subject, e.g., *I'd rather **not talk** about it.* However,
we cannot use this structure when the subject changes after
would rather, e.g., *I'd rather **you didn't talk** about it* NOT ~~I'd
rather you not talk about it.~~
4 We use the simple past after *It's time* + subject to say that
something has to be done now or in the near future.
• We can also use *It's time* + *to* + infinitive when we don't want to
specify the subject, e.g., *It's time to go now.*
• We sometimes use *high* before *time* for emphasis.

---

a Put the verbs in parentheses in the right form.

I wish I *hadn't lent* Gary that money now. Who knows
when he'll pay me back? (not lend)

1 It's time the government _____ that interest rates
are far too high. (realize)
2 My wife would rather we _____ closer to the
downtown area. (live)
3 I wish you _____ to stay a little longer — we're
having such a good time! (be able)
4 Would you rather we _____ the subject now?
(not discuss)
5 I think it's time the company _____ expecting us to
put in so much overtime for no extra pay. (stop)
6 If only I _____ a little more when I was earning a
regular salary, I wouldn't be so hard up now. (save)
7 I'd rather you _____ me in cash, if you don't mind.
(pay)
8 If only we _____ the name of the store, we could
Google it and see where it is. (know)
9 Do you wish you _____ to college or do you think
you made the right decision to leave school and start
working? (go)

b Rewrite the sentences using the **bold** word(s).

The children ought to go to bed. It's nearly nine o'clock.
TIME
It's time the children went to bed. It's nearly nine o'clock.

1 I'd prefer you not to run in here, if you don't mind.
RATHER
_____, if you don't mind.

2 I would like to be able to afford to travel more.
WISH
_____ travel more.

3 We shouldn't have painted the room blue — it looks
awful.
IF ONLY
_____ — it looks awful.

4 Don't you think you should start to look for a job?
TIME
Don't you think _____ for a job?

5 He should be less stingy! Then he'd enjoy life more.
IF ONLY
_____, he'd enjoy life
more.

6 Would you prefer us to come another day?
RATHER
_____ another day?

7 I should have bought the purple sweater and not the
beige one.
WISH
_____ the purple sweater
and not the beige one.

◀ p.51

6A verb + object + infinitive or gerund

verb + object + *to* + infinitive

> 1 We **expect the flight to arrive** at 7:50.
>   It **took me forever to get** there.
>   She **advised him not to travel** by train.
> 2 I **want you to call** the airline.
>   **I'd like you to send** me the bill.
> 3 I'm **waiting for my friend to arrive**.
>   We've **arranged for a taxi to come** at 6:30.

1 We often use the following verbs + object + *to* + infinitive: *ask, advise, allow, beg, cause, enable, encourage, expect, force, intend, invite, mean, order, persuade, remind, take (time), teach, tell, warn.*
- After *advise, persuade, remind, teach, tell,* and *warn* you can also use an object + *that* clause, e.g., *The airline advises that you carry your passport at all times.*
2 We also often use object + infinitive with *want, would like, would prefer.*
- After these verbs a *that* clause is impossible. NOT ~~I would hate that you think~~.
3 After some verbs, including *love, hate, arrange, ask, plan,* and *wait,* we put *for* immediately after the verb before the object + *to* + infinitive.

verb + object + base form

> Please **let me explain**!
> He **made me feel** really guilty.
> Can you **help me do** the dishes?

We can use object + base form after *let, make,* and *help.*

> ⚠ When *make sb do sth* is used in the passive, it is followed by the infinitive with *to,* e.g., *We were made to clean our rooms every morning.*

verb + object + gerund

> Please don't **keep me waiting**!
> I **dislike people telling** me what to do.
> I **don't mind you running** in the yard, but please don't run in the house.

Complete the second sentence so that it means the same as the first.

> "Be especially careful because of the snow and ice," the police told drivers.
>
> The police warned <u>drivers to be especially careful</u> because of the snow and ice.

1 I don't like it when people answer their cell phones in restaurants.
   I dislike people <u>answering their cell phones</u> _____ in restaurants.
2 I felt uncomfortable because of the situation at work.
   The situation at work made <u>me feel</u> <u>uncomfortable</u>
3 You are going to stay with an American family. We have made the arrangements.
   We have arranged <u>for you to stay</u> with an American family.
4 I don't have a problem if Jane comes, but I'd prefer that her boyfriend didn't.
   I don't mind <u>Jane coming</u>, but I'd prefer that her boyfriend didn't.
5 Ana needs someone to water her plants. She'll probably ask Sandra.
   Ana asked _____ _____ _____ her plants.
6 You paid for everything, which wasn't what I expected.
   I didn't expect _____ _____ _____ _____ everything.
7 She wants her children to get in the car now.
   She ordered _____ _____ _____ _____ in the car.
8 If you get this job, you will have to travel a lot.
   This job will involve _____ _____ _____ _____.
9 I told Hannah not to forget to do the dishes.
   I reminded _____ _____ _____ the dishes.
10 Did you really use to be shy? I can't imagine it!
   I can't imagine _____ _____ shy!
11 We were able to buy a bigger condo thanks to the money my uncle left me.
   The money my uncle left me enabled _____ _____ _____ a bigger condo.
12 The guards wouldn't let us cross the border.
   The guards prevented _____ _____ _____ the border.
13 I could call back later if you're busy now.
   Would you prefer _____ _____ _____ _____ later?
14 The car might break down on vacation. We don't want to take the risk.
   We don't want to risk _____ _____ _____ _____ while we're on vacation.

◀ p.55

6B conditional sentences

real and unreal

> 1 They **won't get** a table unless they**'ve** already **made a reservation**.
> **Can** I **borrow** your dictionary for a minute if you**'re not using** it?
> If it **stops** raining, I**'m going to** walk into town.
> 2 How **would** you **know** if he **wasn't telling** the truth?
> If we **had** a little more time here, we **could go** on an all-day river trip.
> 3 I **would have picked** you up if **I had known** what time your flight arrived.
> If I**'d been looking** where I was going, I **would've seen** the hole in the road.

1 Type 1 conditional sentences are used to talk about a possible present or future situation and its result.
You can use any present tense in the *if* clause and any form of the future in the other clause.
2 Type 2 conditional sentences are used to talk about hypothetical or improbable situations in the present or future.
You can use the past tense (simple or continuous) in the *if* clause and *would* + infinitive (or *could* / *might*) in the other clause.
3 Type 3 conditional sentences are used to talk about a hypothetical situation in the past.
You can use the past perfect (simple or continuous) in the *if* clause and *would have* + past participle (or *could* / *might have*) in the other clause.

mixed conditionals

> I **wouldn't be** in this mess if I **had listened** to your advice.
> Jane **would have left** Mike by now if she **didn't** still **love** him.

If we want to refer to the present and the past in the same sentence, we can mix tenses from two different types of conditional, e.g.:
I wouldn't be in this mess (type 2) *if I had listened to your advice* (type 3).
Jane would have left Mike by now (type 3) *if she didn't still love him* (type 2).

alternatives to *if* in conditional sentences

> 1 I'll tell you what happened **as long as** / **so long as** you promise not to tell anyone else.
> **Provided** / **Providing (that)** the bank lends us all the money we need, we're going to buy that condo we liked.
> They agreed to lend us the car **on the condition (that)** we returned it by the weekend.
> 2 I'm going to sell the car **whether** you agree with me **or not**.
> 3 **Even if** I get the job, I'm going to continue living with my parents for a while.
> 4 **Suppose** you lost your job, what would you do?
> 5 **Had I known** that you were coming, I would have bought some coffee.

a Right (✓) or wrong (✗)? Correct the mistakes in the highlighted phrases.

> If you hadn't been here last night, I don't know what I would do. *what I would have done*

1 They wouldn't have made you marketing manager if they didn't think you were right for the job.
2 The government would accept more refugees if the camp isn't so crowded.
3 If you've done all your homework, you can go out this evening.
4 We wouldn't be living in Singapore now if my company hadn't been taken over by a multinational.
5 Hannah would be on the varsity team if she didn't get injured last month.
6 If you've ever been to New York, you will know exactly what I'm talking about.
7 They would get divorced long if they didn't have young children.
8 If the storm wasn't at night, more people would have died.
9 If their flight hasn't been delayed, they will have arrived by now.

b Complete the sentences with *one* word. Don't use *if*.

> *Suppose* we missed the last train, how would we get home?

1 My father has agreed to lend me the money _____ I pay it back by the end of the year.
2 _____ if I had played my best, I still wouldn't have beaten him.
3 I'll tell you exactly what happened as _____ as you promise not to tell anyone.
4 _____ the rebels not surrendered, there would have been a lot more casualties.
5 The company will only hire me on the _____ that I sign a two-year contract.
6 We've decided we're going to go ahead with the event _____ we sell all the tickets or not.
7 I'm convinced Amy won't get back together with her boyfriend, _____ if he apologizes.
8 You can go to the party _____ long as you are home by midnight at the latest.
9 _____ we do buy a dog, who's going to take it for walks?
10 I'm going to make a doctor's appointment for you _____ you like it or not.
11 _____ the plane not caught fire, there would have been more survivors.

◀ p.59

7A permission, obligation, and necessity

can, must, should, ought to, had better

> 1 I **couldn't** take any photos in the gallery, so I bought some postcards of the paintings.
> Passengers on the bus **must not** distract the driver.
> We **should / ought to** take the highway home — it's much quicker.
> 2 We **should have** taken the highway home — it would have been quicker.
> 3 You**'d better** send the packages today or they won't get there in time.

1 The most common modal verbs for talking about permission and obligation are *can / could*, *must*, and *should / ought to*. *Must* is the most formal and often occurs on public signs or notices having to do with laws, rules, etc.
2 We can use *should have* + past participle to talk about past events which did not happen and which we regret.
3 *Had better* is stronger and more urgent than *should / ought to* and is often used to give strong advice or a warning. It normally refers to the immediate future.
• The negative is *had better not* NOT ~~*hadn't better*~~.

have to / have got to

> 1 All passengers **will have to** fill in an immigration form on arrival.
> You **don't have to** tip here unless you think the service was especially good.
> 2 I**'ve got to** buy a birthday present for my brother.

1 We also use *have to* to express obligations. It can be used in any tense.
2 We can also use *have got to* to express obligation. It is less formal than *have to* and mostly used in spoken English.

need

> 1 You usually **need to** check in at least two hours before a flight leaves.
> I **don't need to** take a jacket. It's going to be hot today.
> 2 We **didn't need to make** a reservation. The restaurant is empty!
> 3 We had plenty of gas so we **didn't need** to stop, which saved time.

1 We use *need / don't need* + *to* + infinitive to say that something is necessary / unnecessary. You can use these forms for habitual, general, and specific necessity.
2 When something was not necessary, but you did it, you can use *didn't need to* + infinitive.
3 When something was not necessary, so you did <u>not</u> do it, you also use *didn't need to*.

be able to, be allowed to, be permitted to, be supposed to

> 1 Starting tomorrow we **won't be able to** park on this street.
> You**'re not allowed to** smoke in any public buildings in our country.
> 2 It **is not permitted to** use a cell phone while taking a test.
> 3 We **are supposed to** check in at 3:30. What's the time now?
> You **aren't supposed to** park here — it's a hospital entrance.

1 We often use *be able to* or *be allowed to* + infinitive to talk about what is possible or permitted instead of *can*, particularly when we want to use a form which *can* does not have.
2 *be permitted to* + infinitive is used in formal situations, e.g., notices and announcements, to say what can / can't be done according to the law or to rules and regulations.
3 We can also use *be supposed to* + infinitive to say what people should or shouldn't do, often because of rules. There is often a suggestion that the rules are not necessarily obeyed, e.g. *Students are not supposed to have guests after 12:00, but everyone does.*

---

a Complete the second sentence so that it means the same as the first.

> We couldn't go out at night when we were at boarding school.
> We weren't *allowed to go out at night when we were at boarding school*.

1 Officially you can't park here — but everyone does.
You aren't _____ here.

2 I regret losing my temper last night.
I shouldn't _____ last night.

3 You can't take flash photographs in this museum.
Flash photography is _____ in this museum.

4 Wearing a seat belt in the back seat of the car is compulsory.
You _____ in the back seat of the car.

5 Swimming in the lake is strictly prohibited.
You aren't _____ in the lake.

6 Wearing a tie is optional in this restaurant.
You don't _____ in this restaurant.

7 The best thing to do would be to seek legal advice.
You really _____ legal advice.

8 I need to finish the sales report by Friday.
I've _____ by Friday.

9 You don't have to bring your car — we can go in mine.
You _____ — we can go in mine.

b Complete the sentences with **three** words.

> If you don't finish your homework, you won't be *able to watch* TV.

1 You don't _____ to go into the art gallery. Entrance is free.
2 You'd _____ late — you know what Jane is like about punctuality!
3 You _____ you didn't like the pasta. You know how sensitive he is about his cooking.
4 It was a difficult trip because we _____ trains three times.
5 A lot of people think that governments _____ more to protect young people's health.
6 You aren't _____ your cell phone while you are driving.
7 We didn't _____ sweaters after all — it's really warm!
8 Am I _____ a suit to the wedding or is it casual?

◀ p.65

7B verbs of the senses

hear, see, smell, feel, taste

I **can hear** a noise downstairs.
Can you see the blue circle at the top of the painting?
I **can smell** something burning. Are you sure you turned the stove off?
I **can feel** a draft. Is there a window open?
I **can't taste** the garlic in the soup.

- The five basic verbs of the senses, *hear, see, smell, feel,* and *taste* are stative (non action) verbs. We normally use *can* with these verbs to refer to something happening at the moment.
- We don't usually use verbs of the senses in the continuous form NOT ~~I am hearing a noise. I'm feeling a pain behind my eye.~~
- *hear* and *see* can also be dynamic verbs and used in the continuous form, but with a different meaning:
I've been hearing good things about you recently. (= I have been receiving information.)
I'm seeing James tonight. (= I have arranged to meet him).

see / hear + infinitive or gerund

1 I **heard** the girl **play** a piece by Chopin.
  I **saw** the man **hit** his dog.
2 I **heard** the girl **playing** a piece by Chopin.
  I **saw** the man **hitting** his dog.

- We often use *see / hear* + object + verb in the infinitive or gerund. The meaning is slightly different:
1 *see / hear* + object + verb in infinitive = you saw or heard the whole action.
2 *see / hear* + object + verb in gerund = you saw / heard an action in progress or a repeated action.
- The same distinction also applies to verbs after *watch* and *notice*.

look, feel, smell, sound, taste + adjective / noun

1 You **look** tired. That **smells** delicious. This music **sounds** awful.
  These shoes **feel** uncomfortable. The soup **tastes** a little salty.
2 You **look like** your mother. It **sounds like** thunder. This **tastes like** tea, not coffee.
3 She looked **as if / as though** she had been crying.
4 This smells / tastes **of** garlic. This smells / tastes **like** garlic.

When we talk about the impression something or someone gives us through the senses, we use *look, feel, smell, sound,* and *taste.*
- After these verbs we can use
1 an adjective.
2 *like* + a noun.
3 *as if / as though* + a clause.
4 Compare *smell / taste of* and *smell / taste like.*
   It tastes / smells of garlic (= it has the taste / smell of garlic).
   *It tastes / smells **like** garlic* (= it's taste / smell is similar to garlic, but it probably isn't garlic).

seem

1 You **seem** worried. Is something wrong?
2 You **seem to be** a little down today. Are you OK?
   The waiter **seems to have made** a mistake with the bill.
3 It **seemed like** a good idea at the time, but in fact it wasn't.
   It **seems as if / as though** every time I wash the car it rains.

- We use *seem* when something / somebody gives us an impression of being or doing something through a combination of the senses and what we know, but not purely through just one sense, e.g., the visual sense. Compare *seem* and *look:*
You look worried. (= I get this impression from your face.)
You seem worried. (= I get this impression from the way you are behaving in general, e.g., voice, actions, etc.)
- After *seem* we can use
1 an adjective.
2 an infinitive (simple or perfect or continuous).
3 *like* + noun or *as if / as though* + a verb phrase.
- *seem* is not used in the continuous form.

---

a Right (✓) or wrong (✗)? Correct the mistakes in the highlighted phrases.

> I'm smelling something funny in here. What on earth is it? ✗ *I can smell something funny*

1 Kerry says she hasn't been feeling very well recently — do you know what's the matter with her?
2 We could hardly sleep at all, as we could hear the wind howling through the trees all night.
3 I was very close to where it happened. I actually heard the bomb exploding.
4 Do you know what this piece is? It sounds of Beethoven's 7th, but I'm not quite sure.
5 I think we should send the coffee back. It tastes like mud.
6 They said this bag was leather, but it's feeling more like plastic.
7 You and Raquel seemed to be getting along very well last night. What did you think of her?

b Circle the right form. Check (✓) if both are possible.

> The salesperson *looks* /(*seems*) to have forgotten about us.

1 He *looked | seemed* very angry about something.
2 It *looks | seems* as if children today are only interested in playing with gadgets.
3 It doesn't *look | seem* possible that ten years have passed since we last met.
4 Jane *is looking | is seeming* very tired, don't you think?
5 You *look | seem* much more like your father than your mother.

c Complete the sentences with one word.

> The clouds are very black. It looks *as* if it's going to rain.

1 This tastes a little _____ a soup my mother used to make. What's in it?
2 I haven't met the boss yet. I've only spoken to him on the phone. He _____ very nice, though.
3 She must have gone out because I heard the front door _____ about five minutes ago.
4 The engine sounds as _____ there's something wrong with it. I think we should stop at the next service station.
5 My mother's favorite perfume is one that smells _____ roses. Apparently it's made from thousands of petals.
6 We stopped for a minute and watched the men _____ on the edge of the pier, but since they didn't seem to be catching anything, we walked on by.
7 Would you mind speaking up a little? I _____ hear you very well.

◀ p.69

8A gerunds and infinitives

complex gerunds and infinitives

> 1 She loves **being told** how pretty she is.
> I'm tired of **being lied to**. I want the truth.
> It's very difficult **to get promoted** in this company.
> My car needs **to be serviced**.
> 2 He thanked them for **having helped** him.
> **Having studied** one language before makes it easier to learn another.
> How wonderful **to have finished** all our tests!
> By the time I'm 30, I hope **to have started** a family.
> 3 I would like **to have seen** your face when they told you you won the competition!
> We would rather **have stayed** in a more central hotel, but they were all full.
> 4 I'd like **to be lying** on the beach right now.
> She seems **to be coughing** a lot — do you think she's OK?

1 We use a passive gerund (*being done*) or a passive infinitive (*to be done*) to describe actions done to the subject.
2 We use a perfect gerund (*having done*) or a perfect infinitive (*to have done*) to emphasize that an action is completed or in the past.
• There is often no difference between using a simple gerund or infinitive and a perfect gerund or infinitive, e.g.,
He denied stealing | having stolen the money.
It was our fault. It was foolish not to lock | not to have locked the car.
3 We use the perfect infinitive after *would like, would love, would hate, would prefer*, and *would rather* to talk about an earlier action. Compare:
I would like to visit Bali. (= when I go to Indonesia in the future.)
I would like to have visited Bali. (= I was in Indonesia, but I didn't visit it.)
4 We use a continuous infinitive (*to be* + verb + *-ing*) to say that an action / event is in progress around the time we are talking about.

other uses of gerunds and infinitives

> 1 **It's no use worrying.** There's nothing you can do.
> **Is there any point (in) asking** him? He never has anything useful to say.
> **It's no good talking** to my dad because he doesn't listen to me.
> 2 We had **an agreement to share** the costs.
> Our **plan** is **to leave** on Saturday.
> 3 You can't visit the Metropolitan Museum of Art in a day — there's **too much to see**.
> There wasn't **enough** snow for us **to ski**.
> 4 Is there **anything to eat**? There's **nowhere to go** at night.
> 5 I don't know **where to go** or **what to do**.
> 6 He's the **youngest** player ever **to play** for Peru.

1 We use the gerund after certain expressions with *it* or *there*, e.g., *It's no use, There's no point, It's not worth*, etc.
We use the infinitive with *to*:
2 after nouns formed from verbs that take the infinitive, e.g., *agree, plan, hope*, etc.
3 after expressions with quantifiers, e.g., *enough, too much, a lot, plenty of*, etc.
• When we want to refer to the subject of the infinitive verb we use *for* + person or object pronoun before the infinitive. This can be used before any infinitive structure, e.g., after adjectives:
*It's very difficult **for me to decide**.*
4 after *something, anywhere*, etc.
5 after question words (except *why*).
6 after superlatives and *first, second, last*, etc., e.g., *Who was the first person to walk on the moon?*

---

a Put the verbs in parentheses in the correct form of the gerund or infinitive.

> I hate *being told* (tell) what to do. I prefer to make my own decisions.

1 I was really smart _____ (follow) my mother's advice. She was exactly right.
2 I'd love _____ (be) there when you told him you were leaving.
3 If I had a serious disease, I would prefer _____ (tell) the truth.
4 It's no use _____ (run). The train has left by now.
5 Mark seems _____ (work) too hard these days. He looks very tired.
6 By the time I'm 55, I expect _____ (save) enough to be able to just work part-time.
7 The man denied _____ (commit) the crime.
8 There will be plenty of time to get something _____ (eat) at the airport.
9 It's no good _____ (call) him because he didn't take his cell phone with him.
10 Who was the second man _____ (walk) on the moon?
11 There wasn't enough room for us _____ (sit down).

b Rewrite the sentences with the **bold** word.

> Don't get angry. That won't help. **POINT**
> *There's no point getting* angry.

1 We don't have many eggs so we can't make an omelet. **ENOUGH**
We _____
make an omelet.

2 I hate it when people wake me up from a sound sleep. **WOKEN**
I _____
from a sound sleep.

3 Are you sorry you didn't have more children? **REGRET**
_____
more children?

4 It's amazing what she's managed to achieve considering she didn't finish school. **WITHOUT**
It's amazing what she's managed to achieve _____.

5 I really wish I'd been able to go to your birthday party. **LOVE**
I _____ to
your birthday party.

6 The children look as if they're having a good time, don't you think? **SEEM**
_____,
don't you think?

7 We're not planning to redecorate the kitchen until we've finished the rest of the house. **PLAN**
Our _____
until we've finished the rest of the house.

◄ p.75

8B expressing future plans and arrangements

present and future forms

1 **I'm seeing** Sarah tomorrow. We**'re having** lunch together.
2 **I'm going to** get my hair cut tomorrow.
   She**'s going to** get the last train home.
3 **I'm meeting** Cathy this evening. **I'm going to** tell her that it's all over.
4 **I'll be going** to the supermarket later — do you want anything?
   Will we **be having** dinner at the usual time? I'm going to see a movie, and it starts at 8:00.
5 The train **leaves** in five minutes. Our classes **start** next Tuesday.

1 The present continuous is the most common way to talk about arrangements, e.g., fixed plans for the future, when the time and place have been decided.
2 *be going to* is the most common way to express future plans and intentions, and to imply that a decision has been made.
3 In most cases you can use either *going to* or the present continuous, but there is a subtle change of emphasis. The present continuous emphasizes that a time and place to do something has been decided; *going to* emphasizes the intention. Compare:
   I'm meeting Cathy. (= We've arranged to meet.)
   I'm going to meet Cathy. (= It's my intention, but arrangements may or may not have been made.)
   We do not use the present continuous when it is clear that something is just an intention, not something that has been arranged NOT ~~I'm telling her that it's all over.~~
4 The future continuous can often be used instead of the present continuous to refer to future arrangements.
• We sometimes use it to emphasize that we are talking about something that will happen anyway rather than something we have arranged. Compare:
   I'm seeing Sarah tomorrow. (= I have arranged it.)
   I'll be seeing Sarah at the party tomorrow. (= It will happen anyway, but I didn't arrange it.)
• It is often used to make polite requests for information about arrangements, e.g., *Will you be meeting us at the airport?*
5 We can also use the simple present to talk about future events which are scheduled or part of a regular routine.

other ways of expressing future arrangements

1 My sister **is due to** arrive at 7:30. Can you meet her at the station?
2 My sister **is about to** have a baby, so I need to keep my cell phone turned on.
   It is believed that the mayor **is at the point of** resigning.
3 It has been announced that the President **is to visit** Brazil next month.

1 *be due to* + infinitive can be used to say that something is arranged or expected.
• We also use *due* on its own to mean "expected," e.g., *The next train is due in five minutes.*
2 We use *be about to* + infinitive to say that something is going to happen very soon.
• We can also use *be on the point of* + gerund with a similar meaning, but this is slightly more formal and implies something is more imminent.
3 We can use *be + to + infinitive* in a formal style to talk about official plans and arrangements.

a Circle the right form. Check (✓) if both are possible.
   I see | (*I'm seeing*) some friends after class tonight.
1 The train *is going to leave soon* | *is about to leave.*
2 Don't call me between 5:00 and 6:00 because *I'll be getting* | *I'll get* a massage.
3 **A** What are you going to do this evening?
   B I'm not sure. I'm probably *going to watch* | *watching* the game.
4 When are you *going to pay me* | *paying me* back the money I lent you?
5 My dad *is retiring* | *will be retiring* at the end of this year.
6 My flight *is due to arrive* | *arrives* at 6:00.
7 You'll easily recognize me. *I'll be wearing* | *I wear* a white suit.
8 The President *is to open* | *is going to open* the new gallery on Saturday.
9 *I'll be seeing* | *I'm going to see* John at work tomorrow. I can give him your message then.

b Look at the sentences you have checked. Is there any difference in meaning or register between the two forms?

c Rewrite the sentences with the **bold** word.
   I'm meeting Myriam tonight.
   GOING
   I'm *going to meet* Myriam tonight.

1 We're going to go out in a minute. Could you call me back later?
   ABOUT
   _____. Could you call me back later?

2 Our manager is going to be promoted in the next few months.
   DUE
   _____ in the next few months.

3 Are you going to the cafeteria at lunchtime? If so, could you get me a sandwich?
   WILL
   _____? If so, could you get me a sandwich?

4 The Board of Directors are about to sign a new agreement.
   POINT
   _____ a new agreement.

5 James will be at the meeting so I'll see him there.
   SEEING
   _____ at the meeting.

◀ p.80

9A ellipsis and substitution

ellipsis: leaving out subjects and auxiliaries

1 He got up **and (he) took** a shower.
   She came to the meeting **but (she) didn't say** anything.
   We should call him **or (we should) send** him an email.
   We usually have dinner at 10:00, and **then (we) watch** TV.
2 They locked the door and windows **before they left**.
   Why don't we look at the photos **after we finish** dinner.
   He's stressed **because he has** too much work.
   She was horrified **when she saw** the mess he had left.
   I met Sam **while I was working** in Italy.

1 After *and*, *but*, and *or* we often leave out a repeated subject or a repeated subject and auxiliary verb, especially when the clauses are short.
• After *then* we can also leave out a repeated subject pronoun.
2 You cannot leave out the subject pronoun after *before*, *after*, *because*, *when*, and *while*.

ellipsis: leaving out verb phrases or adjectives

1 Laura has never been to the US, but her sister **has**.
   Gary thinks he's right, but he **isn't**.
   I didn't like the movie, but Mike **did**.
   They said I would love the movie, but I don't think I **would**.
2 I thought I **would be able to** come tonight, but in fact I **can't**.
   I know you never **learned** to drive, but I really think you **should have**.
   A You **must** see his latest movie!
   B I already **have**.
3 I haven't been to Egypt, but **I'd love to**.
   The students cheated on the exam, even though I **told** them **not to**.

1 We often leave out a repeated verb phrase or adjective, and just repeat the auxiliary or modal verb, or the verb *be*, e.g.: *Laura has never been to the US, but her sister has been there; Gary thinks he's right, but he isn't right*.
• If the verb we don't want to repeat is in the present or simple past, we substitute the verb with *do | does | did*.
2 We can use a different auxiliary or modal verb from that used in the first part of the sentence.
3 We can also leave out a repeated verb phrase after the infinitive with *to*. This is called a reduced infinitive, e.g., *I haven't been to Egypt, but I'd love to (go)*.

substitution: *so* and *not*

1 I'll have finished the work by Friday, or at least I **hope so**.
   A Will you be working on Saturday?
   B I **suppose so**, unless we get everything done tomorrow.
   Mark loves animals, and his sister **even more so**.
2 **A** Do you think it'll rain tonight?
   B I **hope not**.
   A She didn't pass the test, did she?
   B No, I'm afraid not.
   The children may be back, but I **don't think so**.
   I know she liked the present, even though she **didn't say so**.

1 We often use *so* instead of repeating a whole ⊞ clause after verbs of thinking (*assume, believe, expect, guess, hope, imagine, presume, suppose, think*) and also after *be afraid, appear | seem*, and *say*.
2 With negative clauses we use ⊞ verb + *not* (e.g., *I hope not*) with *be afraid, assume, guess, hope, presume*, and *suspect*.
• We usually use ⊟ verb + *so* (e.g., *I don't think so*) with *believe, expect, imagine*, and *think*.

---

a Cross out the words / phrases which could be left out.

   They look happy, but they aren't really ~~happy~~.

1 Everyone else loved the hotel we stayed in, but I didn't like it.
2 Nobody expects us to win, but you never know, we might win.
3 I didn't take the job in the end, but now I think that I should have taken it.
4 I got into the car and I turned the radio on.
5 I'd love to come over for dinner, but I'm afraid I can't come over for dinner.
6 We don't go to the theater very often now, but we used to go before we had children.
7 I won't be able to go to the exhibition, but my wife will be able to go.

b Complete the sentences with a modal or an auxiliary verb in the right form.

   I'd like to help you this week, but I *can't*.

1 I'm not vegetarian, but my wife _____.
2 I would love to fly a plane, but I know that I never _____.
3 Nobody believes me when I say that I'm going to resign, but I _____.
4 We thought that Karen would get the job, but she _____.
5 In the end they didn't come, even though they had promised that they _____.
6 If you haven't seen the movie yet, you _____. It's absolutely fantastic!
7 If I could help you, I would, but I'm afraid I _____.
8 I don't speak Arabic, but my friend _____.

c Write the responses using the right form of the verb in parentheses and a reduced infinitive or adding *so* or *not*.

   A Would you like to come over for dinner?
   B I'd love to. (love)

1 **A** The weather forecast said it would snow this weekend.
   B I _____. I was planning to do some gardening. (hope)
2 **A** Do you run?
   B I _____, but I gave it up recently. (use)
3 **A** If you think she's coming down with the flu, you shouldn't send her to school tomorrow.
   B I _____. She might infect the other children. (suppose)
4 **A** Have you spoken to Martin yet?
   B No, but I _____ after the meeting. (try)
5 **A** Do you think we should leave early to avoid the traffic?
   B I _____, though I'm really enjoying myself. (guess)
6 **A** Why are you going to try skydiving?
   B I don't know. I _____. (always / want)

◀ p.85

9B nouns: compound and possessive forms

apostrophe s

> 1 I borrowed my **father's** car.
> I accidentally stepped on the **cat's** tail.
> The **company's** main office is in New York.
> The **government's** decision to raise taxes has not been well received.
> *Sarong* is one of **Bali's** most famous restaurants.
> 2 It's **Chris's** book.
> It's my **friends'** wedding.
> That's the **children's** room.
> The blonde girl is **Alex** and **Maria's** daughter.
> 3 We had dinner at **Tom's** last night.

Possessive forms express the idea of "having" (in a very general sense) which exists between two nouns.

1 We normally use a possessive (+ *'s*) when something belongs to a particular person or thing, e.g., a person, an animal, an organization, a group of people, or a place.
• With places we can also say, e.g., Sarong *is one of the most famous restaurants in Bali.*
2 If a name (or singular noun) finishes in *s*, we either add *'s, e.g., Chris's book,* or put an apostrophe at the end of the word, e.g., *Chris' book.* With plural nouns we put the apostrophe after the *s*, e.g., *friends'*. With irregular plurals which don't end in *s* (*people, children, men,* etc.) we add *'s*.
• If there are two people, we add the *'s* to the second name.
3 When *'s* refers to "the house of" or "the store of," we often omit the word *house* or *store*.

using *of* (instead of apostrophe *s*)

> 1 Can you remember the name **of** the movie?
> My brother lives at the end **of** the street.
> The problems **of** old age are many and varied.
> 2 Helen is the sister **of** my cousin in Rome I told you about.
> 3 Jim is a friend **of** my brother's.

1 We normally use an *of* phrase, not *'s*, with things or abstract nouns, especially when one thing is part of another.
2 We use *of* to express possession with a long phrase, e.g., NOT ~~my cousin in Rome I told you about's sister.~~
3 With *friend*, we often say *a friend of* + name / noun + *'s*.

compound nouns

> 1 I need the **can opener**. Do you know where it is?
> I bought a huge **flowerpot** in a **garden center** near my house.
> My brother is a **company director** and my sister is a **history teacher**.
> I opened the **car door**, got in, and put on my **seat belt**.
> 2 There was a **milk bottle** on the table and two empty **soda cans**.

1 We use compound nouns, not possessive forms, to refer to people or things in terms of what they are for, what they are made of, what work they do, or what kind they are. The second noun is the main thing or person, and can be singular or plural. The first noun gives more information about the second noun. It is usually singular, unless it has no singular form, e.g., *jeans store*.
can opener = an opener for cans, *history teacher* = a teacher of history

> ⚠ Compound nouns are usually two separate words, but they are occasionally joined together as one word, e.g., *sunglasses, bathroom* or hyphenated, e.g., *house-hunter, fortune-teller*.

2 With containers, a compound noun (*a milk bottle*) focuses on the container (usually empty), whereas the container + a possessive noun (*a bottle of milk*) focuses on the contents (the container is usually full).
• Other common examples are *a milk carton | a glass of juice, a jam jar | a jar of jam, a tuna can | a can of tuna, a matchbox | a box of matches,* etc.

---

a Circle the right phrase. Check (✓) if both are possible.

> Should I make (chicken soup) | *soup of chicken* for dinner tonight?

1 I enjoy spending time with *my friend's children | my friends' children*.
2 Didn't I meet you *at Jenny's | at Jenny's house* one night?
3 The hero dies at *the end of the movie | the movie's end.*
4 She's *the wife of my friend who lives in Brazil | my friend who lives in Brazil's wife.*
5 I want to introduce you to Jake. He's *a colleague of my sister's | a my sister's colleague.*
6 When you go to the supermarket, can you buy me *a milk bottle | a bottle of milk?*
7 The *photo of the house | house's photo* made me want to buy it.
8 I'm looking for a *dogs collar | dog collar* that would fit a large rottweiler.
9 We bought a beautiful *table of glass | glass table* for the living room.
10 Machu Picchu is *Peru's most popular tourist attraction | the most popular tourist attraction in Peru.*
11 There's *a glass of juice | a juice glass* on the table. Did you leave it there?

b What difference, if any, is there between the two phrases in the sentence(s) you have checked?

c Combine a word from each list to make compound or possessive nouns to fill in the blanks, adding *'s* or *'* where necessary.

Alice and Yen   bottle   cats   ~~children~~   dessert
garage   government   marketing   ocean   female

~~bedroom~~   bowls   door   intuition   manager
menu   opener   program   view   wedding

> I always leave the light on in the *children's bedroom* — my youngest child is a little afraid of the dark.

1 I can't find the _____. It's usually in this drawer, but it's not there now.
2 It's _____ next week and I don't have anything to wear yet.
3 I'm in the mood for something sweet. Could I see the _____, please?
4 When I asked Claire how she knew I had recently broken up with my girlfriend, she said it was just her _____.
5 Can I introduce you to Jenny Kim, our _____? She's been with our company for six years.
6 Don't forget to lock the _____ when you go out.
7 We would like a room with a (n) _____, if that's possible.
8 Fraud and abuse has been discovered in the _____ providing relief funds to storm victims.
9 Make sure you fill the _____ with water every day.

◄ *p.90*

10A adding emphasis (2): cleft sentences

When we want to focus attention on or emphasize one part of a sentence, we can do this by adding certain words or phrases to the beginning of the sentence. This is sometimes called a "cleft sentence."

More emphatic sentence

1 beginning with *What* or *All*

I need a coffee.	**What I need is** a coffee.
I don't like the weather here.	**What I don't like here is** the weather.
I just want to travel.	**All I want is** to travel.
I only touched it!	**All I did was** touch it.

2 beginning with *What happens is…* | *What happened was…*

You take a test and then you have an interview.	**What happens is** (that) you take a test and then you have an interview.
We left our passports at home.	**What happened was** (that) we left our passports at home.

3 beginning with *The person who…, The place where…, The first | last time…, The reason why…,* etc.

I spoke to the manager.	**The person (who / that) I spoke to was** the manager.
We stayed in a five-star hotel.	**The place where we stayed was** a five-star hotel.
I last saw him on Saturday.	**The last time I saw him was** on Saturday.
I bought it because it was cheap.	**The reason (why / that) I bought it was** that / because it was cheap.

4 beginning with *It*

A boy in my class won the prize.	**It was a boy in my class who** won the prize.
We had the meeting last Friday.	**It was last Friday when** we had the meeting.
They charged us extra for the bread.	**It was the bread (that)** they charged us extra for.

1 We can make some kinds of sentences more emphatic by beginning with *What* (= the thing) or *All* (= the only thing) + clause + *be*, and then the part of the sentence we want to emphasize.
2 To emphasize an event or sequence of events, we can begin with *What happens is (that)…What happened was (that)…*
3 We can also make part of a sentence more emphatic by beginning with an expression like *The person who…, The place where…, The first | last time that…, The reason why…,* etc. + clause + *be*, with the emphasized part of the sentence at the end.
4 We can also use *It is | was* + the emphasized part of the sentence + a relative clause.

> ⚠ If the emphasized part is a pronoun, we normally use the object pronoun after *It is | was*, e.g., *It was me who paid the bill.* NOT *It was I who paid the bill.*

a Complete the sentences with one word.

The *last* time I saw my brother was at his 40th birthday party.

1 _____ was my father who told me not to marry him.
2 _____ I hate about Sundays is knowing you have to work the next day.
3 The _____ why I want you to come early is so that we can have some time on our own before the others arrive.
4 After you've sent in your resume, what _____ next is that you get called for an interview.
5 It's not my fault you can't find them! I did was organize your desk a little.
6 The _____ where we're going to have lunch is a kind of artist's cafe near the theater.
7 _____ happened was that I lost the piece of paper with my flight details on it.
8 It was _____ who told Angela about the party. I'm terribly sorry. I didn't know you hadn't invited her.

b Rewrite the sentences with the **bold** word.

I only need a small piece of paper. **ALL**
All I need is a small piece of paper.

1 She left her husband because he cheated on her. **REASON**
_____ he cheated on her.

2 We stopped in an absolutely beautiful place for lunch. **PLACE**
_____ was absolutely beautiful.

3 We got stuck in an enormous traffic jam. **HAPPENED**
_____ we got stuck in an enormous traffic jam.

4 They didn't apologize for arriving late, which really annoyed me. **WHAT**
_____ they didn't apologize for arriving late.

5 A girl from my town won the silver medal. **IT**
_____ won the silver medal.

6 I only said that I didn't like her dress. **ALL**
_____ that I didn't like her dress.

7 I like my Aunt Emily best of all my relatives. **PERSON**
_____ is my Aunt Emily.

8 You pick up your tickets at the box office. **HAPPENS**
_____ you pick up your tickets at the box office.

9 Right now you need to sit down and put your feet up. **WHAT**
_____ to sit down and put your feet up.

10 I first met Serena at a conference in Taiwan. **TIME**
_____ at a conference in Taiwan.

◀ p.95

10B comparison

modifiers with *as…as…*

> My sister's **almost as tall** as me / **almost as tall as** I am.
> She's **just as bossy** now as when she was a child.
> Their house is **nearly as big as** yours.
> His latest movie isn't **half as good** as his previous one.
> Our new apartment is **twice as big as** our old one.
> The vacation cost **three times as much as** I'd expected.

We often use the modifiers *almost*, *just*, and *nearly*, and *half*, *twice*, *three times*, etc. with *as…as…*
- After *as…as…* we can either use a subject pronoun + auxiliary verb, or an object pronoun, e.g., *She drives as fast as I do* OR *She drives as fast as me*.

> ⚠ Twice can only be used before *as…as…* NOT ~~Our new apartment is twice bigger than our old one.~~
> However *three times*, *four times*, etc. can be used with *as… as…* or with a comparative adjective or adverb, e.g., *The vacation cost three times more than I'd expected.*

modifiers with comparative adjectives or adverbs

> 1 The play was much better than I'd expected.
> He's driving a lot more carefully since he got points on his license.
> The Hawaiian coffee is far more expensive than the Colombian one.
> 2 She earns much more money than I do.
> Women today have many more opportunities than they used to.
> 3 She's a little better than she was yesterday.
> The later train is slightly cheaper than the earlier one.
> Could you two talk a bit more quietly, please? I'm trying to concentrate.
> 4 **A** Would you like some more coffee? **B** Just a little more, please.
> We only have a few more minutes before the show starts.
> 5 The taxi driver drove faster and faster.
> It's getting more and more difficult to make ends meet nowadays.

1 We use *much*, *a lot*, or *far* + comparative adjective or adverb for a big difference.
2 When we use *more* + noun for big differences, we use *much / far / a lot more* + an uncountable noun and *many / far / a lot more* + a plural countable noun.
3 We use *slightly* or *a little* + comparative adjective or adverb for a small difference.
4 When we use *more* + noun for small differences, we use *a little / slightly / a little bit more* + an uncountable noun and *a few* or *slightly* + a plural countable noun.
5 We sometimes repeat a comparative adjective or adverb for emphasis. When the comparative is formed with *more*, the adjective / adverb is only used after the second *more* (NOT ~~It's getting more difficult and more difficult~~).

modifiers with superlatives

> It was **by far the nicest** of all the hotels we stayed at.
> That was **easily the best** fish I've had in a long time.
> I'm **almost the oldest** in my class.

- We often use *by far / easily*, and *nearly / almost* to modify superlative adjectives or adverbs.

the…the… + comparatives

> **The more dangerous** a sport (is), **the more exciting** it is to watch.
> **The bigger** the car (is), **the more expensive** it is to run.
> **The faster** I speak in English, **the more mistakes** I make.
> **A** When do you want me to do it? **B** **The sooner the better**.

We can use comparatives with *the…the…* to say that things change or vary together.
- When the verb in the first part is be, it can be left out, e.g., *The more dangerous a sport (is), the more some people seem to be attracted to it.*
- We often use more + noun in this structure, e.g., *The more coffee you drink, the less well you sleep.*
- When the second comparative is *better*, a reduced structure can be used, e.g., *the bigger the better*, etc. and also in set phrases like *the more the merrier*.

---

a Add one word to make the sentence correct.

> My new broadband server is twice as fast the old one. *twice as fast as*

1 Our team is terrible — the more important the game, worse we play.
2 That was far the best meal I have ever had in any restaurant.
3 He's just good a player as he used to be.
4 Yoga is lot easier than I expected it to be.
5 This morning I was almost late for work as I was yesterday.
6 Generally speaking, the earlier you book the flight, the cheaper is.
7 Fortunately, our new boss is far laid-back about punctuality than our previous one.
8 Dan's slice is little bigger than mine — that's not fair!
9 He's easily most talented player to play on our team in the past five years.

b Circle the right word or phrase. Check (✓) if both are possible.

> That hotel is *much more expensive / far more expensive* than ours. ✓

1 There are twice as many cars on the road *than / as* there used to be.
2 I think our kitchen is *slightly bigger / a little bigger* than yours.
3 I think her new movie was *by far / by much* her best one.
4 **A** When do you need it by?
   B *The sooner better / The sooner the better*.
5 Their condo cost *twice as much as / twice more than* ours.
6 The harder I try, *the worse I do / I do worse*.
7 It's getting *easier and easier / every time easier* to do all your shopping online.
8 We need *a few more / a little more* days to train for the fun run.
9 There were *many more / much more* people in the Pilates class than we had expected.

◀ p.100

Work

1 ADJECTIVES DESCRIBING A JOB

Match sentences 1–6 with A–F.

1 My job is very **challenging**.
2 I'm a cashier in a supermarket. I really enjoy my job, but it can be a little **monotonous / repetitive**.
3 I'm an elementary school teacher. I think working with young children is very **rewarding**.
4 I work in a small graphic design company, and I think my job is really **motivating**.
5 Being a surgeon is very **demanding**.
6 I work at an accounting firm. My job is incredibly **tedious**.

[6] A Everything takes a long time and it's boring.
[2] B I have to do exactly the same thing every day.
[3] C It makes me happy because I think it's useful and important.
[1] D It tests my abilities in a way that keeps me interested.
[5] E It's very high pressure, requires a lot of skill, and you have to work long hours.
[4] F The kind of work I do and the people I work with make me want to work harder / do better.

2 NOUNS THAT ARE OFTEN CONFUSED

Complete the noun column with the best word from each group. Sometimes you need to use a word twice.

Noun

career / position / profession
1 My sister has applied for the ▨ of head of human resources at a multinational company based in Seoul. — *position*
2 Nursing is a rewarding ▨, but one that is not usually very highly paid. — *career*
3 It's difficult for a woman to have a successful ▨ and bring up young children at the same time. — *profession*

wage / salary / bonus / perks
4 The ▨ (*informal* **The money**) isn't fantastic — about 20,000 dollars a year — but the work is rewarding. — *salary*
5 I'm a waiter and I get paid every Friday. The hourly ▨ isn't very high but I can earn a lot from tips if I do my job well. — *wage*
6 The company made a huge profit this year and so all the employees were given a ▨. — *bonus*
7 One of the ▨ (*formal* **benefits**) of this job is that I get free health insurance. — *perks*

staff / employer / employees
8 The company has a ▨ of nearly 600 ▨. — *employees, staff*
9 I wouldn't describe the factory owner as a very generous ▨. — *employer*
10 It's a great hotel and the ▨ is very friendly. — *employees*

skills / training / qualifications
11 All the managers were sent on a three-week ▨ course. — *training*
12 He left school without any ▨ at all. He failed all his tests. — *qualifications*
13 There are certain ▨ you need to be a web designer. For example, you need to be able to use words effectively. — *skills*

3 COLLOCATIONS

Complete the phrases with the missing words.

1 I'm a manager. **I'm in ch_____** of the sales department. I have to d_____ **with** some very difficult clients. **I'm also res_____** for publicity. **I'm o_____** work at the moment. I'm on maternity leave.

2 I'm part of a t_____. I always work with other people. **I have** the opp_____ to travel, which is something I appreciate. **I have good opportunities for** ad_____ in this job. I think I can go far. I'm hoping to **get pr_____** to senior manager next year.

3 I'm hoping to **get a r_____**. I think my salary is very low. It's a temp_____ **job** — I'm only **on a short-t_____** contract, so **I have no job sec_____**.

4 I was f_____ **from** my last job. My boss didn't like the way I worked. Now **I'm self-employed. I r_____ my own** business and I'm much happier. I only **work p_____-t_____**, from 10:00 to 2:00, and in the afternoon I'm taking a continuing education course.

5 I was laid o_____. There were too many workers and the company was losing money. **I've been o_____ of work** for three months now, and my **job p_____** aren't great. I've been **doing** some vol_____ **work** at the local community center. **It's** un_____, but at least **I'm** getting some more **work** exp_____.

Can you remember the words on this page?
Test yourself or a partner.   ◀ *p.7*

Family

1 21ST CENTURY FAMILIES IN THE US

Read the information about 21st century families in the US. What do the **bold** expressions mean?
With a partner, say if the same is true in your country.

The **nuclear family** is no longer the norm. Because of divorce and people remarrying, many children live with **stepparents** and have **half-brothers** or **half-sisters**, or **stepbrothers** and **stepsisters**.

Members of **extended families** no longer live close to each other in the same town, but are very often **spread out** around the country or even abroad, so many people rarely see their **relatives**.

One in four families is a **single-parent** family. According to a recent survey, over 80 percent of single parents are women. As a result many children **grow up** today without a **father figure**.

Due to the fact that people are living longer, many more children have **great-grandparents**, or even **great-great-grandparents**.

2 DESCRIBING FAMILIES

Circle the right word or expression from the pair on the right. Check (✓) the sentences where both options are possible.

1 He ___ his mother. They have exactly the same sense of humor.   **takes after** / looks like
2 Jack is a ___ relative. He's my father's second cousin.   far / **distant**
3 She's ___ child. She has no brothers or sisters.   a single / **an only**
4 My sister and I are very much ___. We're both cheerful and hard-working.   **alike** / like
5 They are a very ___ family. They enjoy spending time together.   **close** / near
6 After their parents died, the ___ rarely met.   **brothers and sisters** / **siblings**
7 His mother died when he was young. He was ___ by his father.   educated / **brought up**
8 My father was a farmer, so I ___ in the country, surrounded by animals.   grew / **grew up**
9 My niece has ___ a lot recently. She's now almost as tall as I am.   grown / **grown up**
10 I have a very good ___ with my cousins. We see a lot of each other.   relation / **relationship**
11 It's going to be a small wedding. Only a few friends and ___ have been invited. **relations** / **relatives**
12 My ___ originally came from Peru.   **ancestors** / descendants

3 FAMILY IDIOMS

Match the idioms 1–8 with their meanings A–H.

1 My sister is **the black sheep** of the family.   F   A having very different opinions on the matter
2 My father doesn't **see eye to eye** with my brother about politics.   A   B making the decisions and telling the other spouse what to do
3 My aunt and I are **not on speaking terms**.   C   C not talking to each other
4 We usually have a family **get-together** on New Year's Day.   H   D Something happened in the past that they would prefer to keep secret.
5 My sister-in-law **wears the pants** in that family!   B   E You are related to each other.
6 Red hair **runs in the family**.   G   F different from the rest of the family who don't approve of the person
7 Most families **have a skeleton in the closet**.   D   G several people in the family have it
8 He's your brother! How can you say that about your **own flesh and blood**?   E   H We all meet at someone's house for a meal.

Can you remember the words on this page? Test yourself or a partner.

◄ p.11

Get

1 EXPRESSIONS WITH *GET*

a Complete the sentences with an expression from the list.

get even	get a hold of	get in trouble	get out of the way	get rid of
get the chance	get the impression	get the joke	get to know	get back at

1 I _____ you're a little annoyed with me. Have I done something wrong?
2 When Alice found out her sister broke her laptop, she decided to _____ and break her sister's cell phone.
3 Since we stopped working together we hardly ever _____ to see each other.
4 I didn't laugh because I didn't _____.
5 When you _____ him, I think you'll really like him.
6 I need to speak to Marina urgently, but I just can't _____ her.
7 I want to _____ that awful painting, but I can't because it was a wedding present from my mother-in-law.
8 I'm going to _____ my brother for telling my parents I got home late. Next time he asks to borrow my bike, I won't lend it to him.
9 He's going to _____ with his wife if she finds out that he's been emailing his ex-girlfriend.
10 I tried to walk past him, but he wouldn't _____. He just stood there, blocking my way.

b With a partner, say what you think the expressions mean.

"Well, I've managed to get rid of the annoying double vision effect on your TV."

2 IDIOMS WITH *GET*

a Match the sentence halves.

1 **Get real**!
2 **Get a life**!
3 I'm **not getting anywhere** with this crossword.
4 She really **gets on my nerves**.
5 She really needs to **get her act together**.
6 They get **along** really well
7 When I bought this computer, I **got the short end of the stick**.
8 My boyfriend just never **gets the message**.
9 She always **gets her own way**.

A It's just too difficult for me.
B They seem to have exactly the same tastes and interests.
C Her test is in two weeks and she hasn't even started studying.
D I paid over $2,000 for it, but it isn't even worth $200.
E Everything about her irritates me, her voice, her smile — everything
F He just does whatever she tells him to.
G I keep dropping hints about his awful cooking but he pays no attention.
H There's no way you can afford that car!
I You're 40 and you're still living with your parents!

b With a partner, say what you think the idioms mean.

3 PHRASAL VERBS WITH *GET*

Match the phrasal verbs with their meanings.

1 Do you want to try to **get together** for dinner next weekend?
2 I hope my brother **gets over** his breakup soon. He's very depressed.
3 I've tried to talk about it, but I just can't **get through to** him.
4 How did you **get into** journalism?
5 The best way to **get around** the city is by taxi — they're very cheap here.
6 She's cheated on tests several times, but she always **gets away with** it.
7 My wife is out of work, so we'll just have to **get by** on less money.
8 She **gets ahead** by taking credit for other people's work.
9 This terrible weather is really **getting** me **down**.
10 I want to **get out of** going to Ann's party. Can you think of a good excuse?
11 Thanks for your email. I'll **get back to** you as soon as possible.

A recover from
B start a career or profession
C move from place to place
D make someone understand
E manage with what you have
F advance in work or society
G depress
H write or speak to sb again later
I avoid a responsibility or obligation
J meet socially
K do something wrong without getting caught or punished

Can you remember the expressions on this page? Test yourself or a partner.

Sounds and the human voice

1 SOUNDS

a (**2** **16**)) All the words in the list can be both nouns and regular verbs, and they describe sounds. Many of the words are onomatopoeic, (i.e., they sound like the sound they describe). Listen to the sounds and the words.

bang	buzz	click	crash	creak	crunch	drip	hiss
honk	hum	rattle	roar	screech	slam	slurp	sniff
snore	splash	tap	tick	wh<u>i</u>stle			

b Now complete the **Sounds** column with a word from the list.

Sounds

1 This clock has a very loud ▢. *tick*
2 Don't ▢! Get a tissue and blow your nose. *sniff*
3 To download the new software just ▢ on the "download" icon. *than click.*
4 There was a ▢ as he jumped into the swimming pool. *splash*
5 Did you hear that ▢? It sounded like a gun. *bang*
6 I heard a floorboard ▢ and I knew somebody had come into the room. *creak*
7 I lay there hearing the ▢ of a fly, but I couldn't see it anywhere. *buzz*
8 I hate people who ▢ at me when I slow down at a yellow light. *honk.*
9 When I'm nervous I often ▢ my fingers on the table. *tap*
10 Don't ▢ your soup! Eat it quietly. *slurp*
11 The snake reared its head and gave an angry ▢. *hiss.*
12 Please turn the faucet off properly otherwise it'll ▢. *drip*
13 We could hear the ▢ of the crowd in the baseball stadium from our hotel. *roar*
14 Some of the players went on playing because they hadn't heard the ▢. *whistle*
15 I don't remember the words of the song, but I can ▢ the tune. *hum*
16 Please don't ▢ the door. Close it gently. *slam*
17 I heard the ▢ of their feet walking through the crisp snow. *creak*
18 I can't share a room with you if you ▢ — I won't be able to sleep. *snore*
19 Every time a bus or truck goes by, the windows ▢. *crunch*
20 I heard the ▢ of brakes as the driver tried to stop and then a loud ▢. *screech, crash.*

2 THE HUMAN VOICE

a Match the verbs and definitions.

giggle	groan	<u>mum</u>ble	scream	sigh
sob	<u>stut</u>ter	<u>whis</u>per	yell	

1 *scream* ▢ to make a loud, high cry because you are hurt, frightened, or excited
2 *yell* (*at sb*) to shout loudly, e.g., because you are angry
3 *giggle* (*at sth*) to laugh in a silly way
4 *whisper* (*to sb*) to speak very quietly so that other people can't hear what you are saying
5 *mumble* to speak or say sth in a quiet voice in a way that is not clear
6 *groan* to make a long deep sound because you are in pain or annoyed
7 *stutter* to speak with difficulty, often repeating sounds or words
8 ▢ to cry noisily, taking sudden sharp breaths *sob*
9 *sigh* to take in and then let out a long deep breath that can be heard, e.g., to show that you are disappointed *example given*

b Answer the questions using one of the verbs above.

What do people do…?
• when they are nervous
• when they are terrified
• when they lose their temper
• when they are not supposed to be making any noise
• when they speak without opening their mouth enough
• when they are relieved
• when they are disappointed
• when they are deeply saddened

Can you remember the words on this page? Test yourself or a partner.

◀ p.34

Time

1 VERBS WITH *TIME*

Complete the sentences with the right verb from the list.

give   have   kill   make up for   run out of   save   spare   spend   take up   waste   take (x2)

1 I ___spend___ **a lot of time** playing games on my computer instead of studying.
2 If you take the highway, you'll ___save___ time — it's much quicker than the local roads.
3 I had three hours to wait for my flight, so I sat there doing *sudoku* puzzles to ___kill___ time.
4 There's no hurry, so ___take___ **your time**.
5 When my mother was young she never had the chance to travel. Now she's retired and wants to ___make up___ **lost time** — she has booked a trip around the world.
6 The novel is 700 pages long and I'm a slow reader. It's going to ___take___ **me a long time** to finish it.
7 I'd better go home now. If I'm late again, my dad will ___give___ **me a hard time**.
8 I would like to go camping with my friends this weekend, but my final tests are next week, so I can't ___spare___ **the time**.
9 My children ___take up___ **all my time** — I never seem to get to read a book or watch a movie!
10 New York's such a fantastic city! You're going to ___have___ **the time of your life** there.
11 Let's not spend too long at the museum or we'll ___waste___ time. We have to get the train back at 10:30 and there are lots of other things I want to see. *waste / run out of time*

2 PREPOSITIONAL PHRASES WITH *TIME*

Complete the prepositions column with a preposition from the list.

at (x2)   before   by   for   from   in   off   on   to

1 I'm really punctual, so I hate it when other people aren't ▢ time.
2 I've never heard of that singer. He must have been ▢ my time.
3 ▢ the time we got to our hotel, it was nearly midnight.
4 I missed the birth of my first child. I was on a plane ▢ the time.
5 He's been working too hard recently. He needs some time ▢.
6 If we don't take a taxi, we won't get to the airport ▢ time ▢ the flight.
7 I don't eat out very often, but I do get takeout ▢ time ▢ time.
8 He suffers from back pain, and it makes him a little irritable ▢ times.

Prepositions
on
before
By
at
off
in   for
from   to
at

3 EXPRESSIONS WITH *TIME*

Match sentences 1–10 with A–J.

1 The referee's looking at his watch.	A But in the end I got to the airport **with time to spare**.
2 He hardly spoke to me at lunch.	B He spent **the whole time** talking on his cell phone.
3 I'm really looking forward to my vacation.	C **Time's up.** The test is over.
4 I'm sorry, I can't help you this week.	D **I'm** a little **short on time**.
5 I can't afford a new computer.	E **I've got time on my hands** since I retired.
6 She's sure to find a job eventually.	F I'll have to make do with this one **for the time being**.
7 I think I need to take up a hobby.	G It's only **a question of time**.
8 Stop writing, please.	H It must have been taken **a long time ago**.
9 I really thought I was going to be late.	I **There isn't much time left**.
10 You look very young in that photo.	J **This time next week** I'll be lying on the beach.

Answers marked: 1 = I, 2 = B, 3 = J, 4 = D, 5 = F

Can you remember the expressions on this page? Test yourself or a partner.

◀ p.47

Money

1 NOUNS FOR MONEY OR PAYMENTS

Match the words and definitions.

budget	charge	down payment
donation	fare	fees	fine	grant
installment	loan	lump sum
overdraft	savings	will

1 __budget__ the money that is available to a person or organization

2 _____ a sum of money that is given by the government or another organization to be used for a particular purpose, e.g., education

3 _____ money that a bank lends and somebody borrows

4 _____ an amount of money you pay for professional advice or services, e.g., to a lawyer or architect

5 _____ the money you pay to travel by bus, plane, taxi, etc.

6 _____ the amount of money sb asks for goods and services, etc.

7 _____ money that you keep in the bank and don't spend

8 _____ money that you give to an organization such as a charity in order to help them

9 _____ a sum of money that must be paid as punishment for breaking a law or a rule

10 _____ one of a number of payments that are paid regularly until sth has been paid for

11 _____ a sum of money that is given as the first part of a larger payment

12 _____ a legal document that says what is to happen to sb's money and property after they die

13 _____ the amount of money that you owe to a bank when you have spent more than is in your bank account

14 _____ an amount of money that is paid at one time and not on separate occasions

2 MONEY IN TODAY'S SOCIETY

a With a partner, say what you think the **bold** phrases mean.

1 We live in **a consumer society**, which is dominated by spending money and buying material possessions.

2 The **standard of living** has risen a lot over the last ten years.

3 People's **income** has gone up, but **inflation** is high, so the **cost of living** has also risen.

4 House prices are rising, and many young people **can't afford** to buy a home.

5 People who have mortgages or loans have to pay high **interest rates**.

6 A lot of people are **in debt** /dɛt/, and have problems paying their **mortgages** /ˈmɔrɡɪdʒɪz/.

7 Some people make money by buying and selling **shares of stock** on the **stock market**.

8 Our **currency** is unstable and **exchange rates** fluctuate a lot.

b Which aspects of the sentences above are true in your country?

3 ADJECTIVES RELATED TO MONEY

Look at the *Oxford Learner's Thesaurus* entries for *rich* and *poor*.
Match the synonyms to their definitions.

rich *adj.* **rich, affluent, loaded, wealthy, well-off**
1 _____ / _____ having a lot of money, property, or valuable possessions
2 _____ (*rather formal*) rich and with a good standard of living. *The ~ Western countries are better equipped to face the problems of global warming.*
3 _____ (often used in negative sentences) rich: *His parents are not very ~ .*
4 _____ [not before noun] (*very informal*) very rich: *Let her pay. She's ~ .*
poor *adj.* **poor, broke, hard up, penniless**
1 _____ having very little money; not having enough money for basic needs
2 _____ (*literary*) having no money, very poor: *She arrived in 1978 as a virtually ~ refugee.*
3 _____ (*informal*) having very little money, especially for a short period of time: *After he lost his job he was so ~ he couldn't afford to eat out at all.*
4 _____ [not before noun] (*informal*) having no money: *I'm always ~ by the end of the month.*

4 IDIOMS RELATED TO MONEY

a Match sentences 1–8 with A–H.

1 Maria has a ten-bedroom house.
2 Jack's broke again.
3 The dinner special is only $6.99.
4 Her income doesn't cover her expenses.
5 Our company lost money this year.
6 Do you think Mark will lend me the money?
7 Dan has bought two sports cars.
8 They have a luxurious lifestyle which they can't really afford.

A He has more **money than sense**.
B No way. He's really **tight-fisted**.
C We're **in the red** (*opp* **in the black**).
D It must have **cost a fortune**.
E That sounds like **a good deal**.
F I'm not surprised. He **spends money like water**.
G They're **living beyond their means**.
H She **can't make ends meet**.

b With a partner say what you think the **bold** idioms mean.

Can you remember the words and expressions on this page?
Test yourself or a partner.

◀ p.49

Place and movement

a Complete the column on the right with one of the words. Sometimes there is more than one possibility.

1 above / over
  a She lives in an apartment ☐ a store.   _____
  b In a few minutes we'll be flying ☐ Ho Chi Minh City.   _____
  c The plane flew ☐ the clouds.   _____

2 below / under
  a We kept an eye open for speed cameras as we drove ☐ the bridge.   _____
  b She lives on the floor ☐ us.   _____
  c There's a wastepaper basket ☐ the table.   _____

> ⚠ **beneath** (*formal*) = below, e.g., *He considered such jobs beneath him.*

3 off / away
  a I fell ☐ my bike and cut my knee.   _____
  b She walked ☐ from me and didn't look back.   _____
  c The thief ran ☐ with her camera.   _____

4 in / inside / into
  a We decided to eat ☐ because it was cold on the terrace.   _____
  b He poured some juice ☐ his glass and drank it.   _____
  c Please keep this document ☐ a safe place.   _____

5 on / on top / on top of / onto
  a Don't leave the towel ☐ the floor. Pick it up.   _____
  b I'm going to put your books ☐ the shelf so they're not in the way.   _____
  c The toddler climbed ☐ the chair and then stood up.   _____
  d It's a chocolate cake with cream ☐.   _____

> ⚠ **upon** (*formal*) = on, e.g., *The child sat upon his father's knee.*

6 outside / out / out of
  a Take your hands ☐ your pockets.   _____
  b Let's meet ☐ the movie theater.   _____
  c He took his wallet ☐ and gave the driver a twenty-dollar bill.   _____

7 across / through
  a We walked ☐ a very dense forest until we came out into a clearing.   _____
  b He was walking ☐ the road on a crosswalk when he was hit by a car.   _____
  c We can go ☐ the park to get to Kate's house. It's a shortcut.   _____

8 along / past / around
  a He walked ☐ the corridor until he reached the door.   _____
  b If you go ☐ the supermarket, the church is on your left.   _____
  c She drove ☐ the traffic circle twice because she wasn't sure which exit to take.   _____

9 to / toward
  a Jane has gone ☐ the hair salon.   _____
  b If you walk ☐ the beach, you'll see the hair salon on the right after about 100 feet.   _____

10 in / at
  a I called David at home, but they told me he was ☐ the cafe.   _____
  b There are some sofas and armchairs ☐ the cafe, so we can relax and read the newspaper.   _____
  c Turn left ☐ the lights, and you'll see it on your right.   _____

b Test yourself with the words on the page by covering the right-hand column and trying to remember the missing words in the sentences.

◀ *p.71*

Travel and tourism

1 NOUNS AND NOUN PHRASES

a Complete the missing words. What do you think they mean?

Weekend
g_____
— three days in
Mexico City
$487.

Eight-day **p**_____ **tour** to
CHINA
including flights, hotels (breakfast included) and sightseeing.

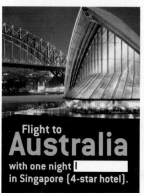

Flight to
Australia
with one night l_____
in Singapore (4-star hotel).

4
Day t_____ **to**
Niagara
Falls
— bus leaves at
9:00 a.m., return
approx. 6:30 p.m.

Grand Central Terminal
— **guided t**_____
Every day at 12:30 p.m.
The tour lasts 75 minutes.

Visit **Thingvellir**
National Park,
located 31 miles east of
Reykjavik, this is one of Iceland's
most spectacular landscapes
and the **s**_____ of the
ancient Icelandic parliament.

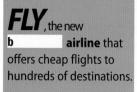

FLY, the new
b_____ **airline** that
offers cheap flights to
hundreds of destinations.

8
Cheap **r**_____-**trip**
flights to California and
the Far East.
CALIFORNIA
from $1,577
JAPAN from $1,173

b Complete each definition with the correct word.

_____ [c] an act of traveling from one place to another, and usually back again: *a business ~ , a school ~ to Ecuador, Tomorrow there will be a boat ~ to the island. They had to make several ~ to bring all the equipment over.*

_____ [c] an act of traveling from one place to another, especially when they are a long distance apart: *It was a long and difficult ~ across the mountains. They continued their ~ on foot.*

_____ [u] the activity of going to different places for business or pleasure, especially over long distances: *Her interests include music and foreign ~. Continued fighting makes ~ in the area dangerous. air / train / space ~. ~ insurance / ~ documents / ~ guide.*

adapted from the Oxford Learner's Thesaurus

2 VERB PHRASES

Complete the collocations with the right verb.

cancel extend go go on postpone / put off
start off / start out take out

1 _____ travel insurance
2 _____ on a journey / early
3 _____ a trip / a visit (= finish later than planned)
4 _____ camping / backpacking / sightseeing
5 _____ an outing / a trip / vacation / a safari / a cruise
6 _____ a trip / a visit (= reschedule it for a later time)
7 _____ a trip / a flight / a visit (= decide not to go)

3 ADJECTIVES AND PHRASES TO DESCRIBE PLACES

Match the adjectives and definitions.

breathtaking dull lively off the beaten track
overcrowded overrated picturesque spoiled touristy

1 _____ with a better reputation than it really deserves
2 _____ boring
3 _____ designed to attract a lot of tourists
4 _____ changed for the worse
5 _____ full of life and energy
6 _____ far away from other people, houses, etc.
7 _____ with too many people or things in it
8 _____ very impressive or surprising, spectacular
9 _____ pretty, especially in a way that looks old-fashioned

Can you remember the words on this page? Test yourself or a partner.

◀ p.79

1 ANIMALS, BIRDS, AND INSECTS

a Match the words and pictures.

wings [1] [2] [3]
a shell
paws
a beak
horns [4] [5] [6]
a tail
claws
fur
fins [7] [8] [9]

b Can you name an animal or insect which can…?

a bite _____
b sting _____
c scratch _____
d kick _____
e spit _____

2 ISSUES RELATING TO ANIMALS

a Look at the **bold** words and phrases with a partner and say what they mean.

In your country are there…?

1 any organizations that **protect** animals and their **environment**, or **animal charities**
2 **animal rights activists**, who organize protests against the use of animals for entertainment, product testing or in medical research
3 national or regional celebrations where animals are **treated cruelly**
4 national parks or conservation areas where animals **live in the wild**
5 **endangered species** /ˈspiːʃiz/
6 animals that are **hunted for sport**
7 animals that are being **bred in captivity** in order to reintroduce them into the wild
8 animals that are kept or transported in inhumane conditions, e.g. **veal calves**

b Answer the questions. Give examples.

3 ANIMAL IDIOMS

a Read the sentences and try to guess the meaning of the **bold** idioms. Then match them to definitions A–O.

1 I **worked like a dog** on this project, so I hope I'm going to get the credit for it.
2 I told him what I thought of him but it's **like water off a duck's back** for him.
3 He was **like a fish out of water** when he left his small town and went to live in Los Angeles.
4 You *think* you've passed the test, but **don't count your chickens (before they hatch)**.
5 I decided to **take the bull by the horns** and went to see my boss.
6 When they divorced, Nick's wife got **the lion's share** of everything they owned.
7 Jim Phelps was a **dark horse** in the mayoral election, but he ended up winning
8 I'm **in the doghouse** because I forgot our wedding anniversary.
9 He **made a** real **pig of himself** at the dinner. He had second helpings of everything.
10 When my car broke down at the end of such an awful day, it was really **the last straw** (that breaks the camel's back).
11 The company says they're not going to lay anyone off with the restructuring, but **I smell a rat**.
12 If we have the meeting in Salt Lake City, we can go and visit my mother at the same time and **kill two birds with one stone**.
13 My boss can seem kind of aggressive, but in fact **her bark is worse than her bite**.
14 After playing so badly he walked off **with his tail between his legs**.
15 I wouldn't bring up the subject again if I were you. I'd **let sleeping dogs lie**

A face a difficult situation directly and with courage
B work very hard
C not mention something that happened in the past to avoid arguments or problems
D criticism doesn't affect him
E manage to achieve two things by doing one action
F a little-known participant in a competition who surprises everyone by winning
G the largest or best part
H not be <u>too</u> confident that something will be successful
I eat and drink too much, be very greedy
J the last in a series of bad events that makes you unable to accept the situation any longer
K feeling ashamed, embarrassed, or unhappy because you have been defeated or punished
L somebody (usually your partner) is annoyed with you about something
M sb whose words are worse than their actions
N think that sth is wrong or that sb is trying to deceive you
O feel uncomfortable or awkward in unfamiliar surroundings

b Do you have the same or similar idioms in your language?

Can you remember the words and phrases on this page? Test yourself or a partner.

◀ p.86

Preparing food

Match the words and the pictures.

- heat (sth in the microwave)
- beat (eggs)
- stir (a sauce)
- mix (the ingredients)
- drain (the pasta)
- pour
- simmer
- a saucepan /ˈsɔspæn/
- a frying pan
- a cutting board
- a baking pan
- an oven

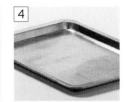

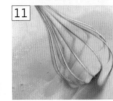

- baked figs
- poached eggs
- melted chocolate
- steamed mussels
- mashed potatoes
- roast lamb
- stuffed peppers
- scrambled eggs
- grated cheese
- chopped onions
- peeled shrimp
- whipped cream
- sliced bread
- pressed sandwich
- ground beef
- pork ribs
- turkey breast
- shellfish
- herbs
- spices

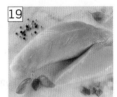

Can you remember the words and phrases on this page? Test yourself or a partner.

◀ p.88

English sounds

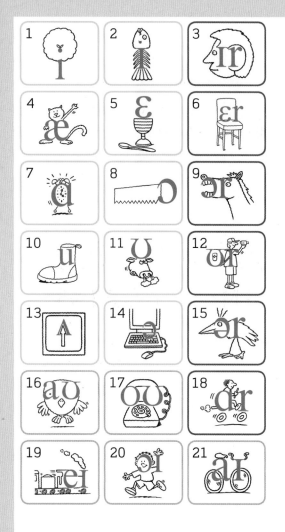

1 tree /tri/	12 tourist /ˈtʊrɪst/
2 fish /fɪʃ/	13 up /ʌp/
3 ear /ɪr/	14 computer /kəmˈpyutər/
4 cat /kæt/	15 bird /bərd/
5 egg /ɛg/	16 owl /aʊl/
6 chair /tʃɛr/	17 phone /foʊn/
7 clock /klɑk/	18 car /kɑr/
8 saw /sɔ/	19 train /treɪn/
9 horse /hɔrs/	20 boy /bɔɪ/
10 boot /but/	21 bike /baɪk/
11 bull /bʊl/	

22 parrot /ˈpærət/	34 thumb /θʌm/
23 bag /bæg/	35 mother /ˈmʌðər/
24 keys /kiz/	36 chess /tʃɛs/
25 girl /gərl/	37 jazz /dʒæz/
26 flower /ˈflaʊər/	38 leg /lɛg/
27 vase /veɪs/	39 right /raɪt/
28 tie /taɪ/	40 witch /wɪtʃ/
29 dog /dɔg/	41 yacht /yɑt/
30 snake /sneɪk/	42 monkey /ˈmʌnki/
31 zebra /ˈzibrə/	43 nose /noʊz/
32 shower /ˈʃaʊər/	44 singer /ˈsɪŋər/
33 television /ˈtɛləvɪʒn/	45 house /haʊs/

○ vowels ○ vowels followed by /r/ ○ diphthongs ○ voiced consonants ○ unvoiced consonants